TIPS • TECHNIQUES • FIELDCRAFT

A FOXER'S YEAR

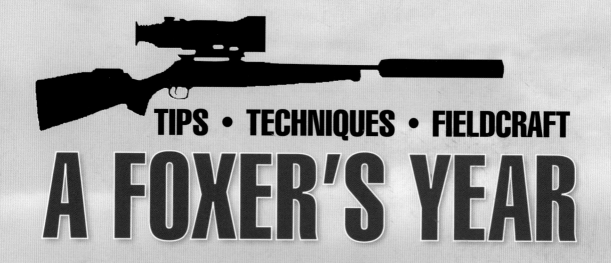

TIPS • TECHNIQUES • FIELDCRAFT
A FOXER'S YEAR

Patrick Hook

Quiller

Copyright © 2013 Patrick Hook

First published in the UK in 2013
by Quiller, an imprint of Quiller Publishing Ltd

British Library Cataloguing-in-Publication Data
A catalogue record for this book
is available from the British Library

ISBN 978 1 84689 186 1

Packaged and designed by Forty Editorial Services Ltd

Printed in China

Quiller

An imprint of Quiller Publishing Ltd

Wykey House, Wykey, Shrewsbury, SY4 1JA
Tel: 01939 261616 Fax: 01939 261606
E-mail: info@quillerbooks.com
Website: www.countrybooksdirect.com

Acknowledgements

I would like to thank everyone who has contributed to the compilation of this book; my especial thanks go to Robert Bucknell for so kindly agreeing to write the foreword.

I would also like to thank everyone who has helped me with the activities described within it. This does, of course, include all the landowners who have been kind enough to allow me access to their grounds.

Particular mention must go to my wife, Claire, who has had the patience of a saint, putting up with me forever disappearing into the night on yet another foxing mission!

Abbreviations

BT	ballistic tip
DEFRA	Department of Environment, Food and Rural Affairs
FERA	Food and Environment Research Agency
GenIII	generation 3 NV equipment (see page 12)
gm	gramme
gr	grain
IR	infrared
NV	night vision (see page 23)
PPU	Privi Partizan, Serbian ammo manufacturer
SP	soft point
TI	thermal imaging (see pages 21–2)
Win	Winchester Ammunition, US manufacturer
yd	yard

Note

In two-part stories (eg page 96) figures in brackets in boxes relate to the second story.

CONTENTS

FOREWORD

BY ROBERT BUCKNELL

Here is the art and practice of foxing by Dr. Patrick Hook – Paddy to his friends – it is a testament to his dedication to not only the hunting, but also the understanding of one of the top predators in our country.

Whilst trying to protect farmed stock and vulnerable wildlife from the depredations of this versatile and highly intelligent animal, Paddy has cataloged "A Foxer's Year". His field observations and comments are a valuable addition to our fox knowledge as he views his Devon world through hunter's eyes. This is often at very short range in the small livestock fields and thick hedges of the red-soiled county.

Each month is highlighted as to what is happening on the farm or in the covert alongside the annual cycle of the fox. He has worked his way though a number of technical solutions until he has reached the most efficient and humane ways of taking foxes where he hunts. This knowledge has been gained by that expensive teacher – experience. Using his insight into the fox's habits alongside his High-Tech shooting skills has brought him an open door to many a farmer's lands. His reputation is such that he is often called upon to stop predation before it becomes expensive. Any lamb that would grow into £100 is a loss. Ten killed is starting to hurt. To be willing and able to reliably nip the problem in the bud has brought Paddy a glowing reputation in Devon. He cannot be everywhere at once. This book will now spread his knowledge and skills to a wider audience.

Robert Bucknell
Essex

INTRODUCTION

Every now and then, I'm asked – usually by someone from an urban area, why I shoot animals. The people concerned are often curious as they know I'm also very keen on wildlife, having written some 20 or so books on natural history and the environment. For them it seems to be a bit of a paradox. My answer is that I'd be happy to leave it for nature to sort out, but as we have removed all the main predators, we no longer have any kind of natural balance. As a result, foxes have moved up from being effectively nature's rubbish collectors to playing the role of lions and tigers. In doing so, they have more or less doubled their size, and the bigger ones are now nearing the weight of coyotes.

Likewise, the only natural controls for the country's deer population is the availability of habitat and food Where the numbers rise too high, nature steps in – unfortunately, it can be a cruel master, and its answer is usually mass-starvations and/or rampant disease. In the Scottish highlands it is not unusual to see several hundred red deer carcasses lying together where the food has simply run out, and they've all starved to death. On reserves where hunting is not allowed, disease takes over, with tuberculosis being the main problem. This causes a slow, lingering, painful death, and those responsible for not managing it should be ashamed of themselves.

If we want to carry on seeing animals like hedgehogs, dormice, lapwings and skylarks in our countryside, then we need to protect them from predators.

Since the only meaningful way to do this is to manage their numbers, we need to find a way to achieve this. Many people consider poisoning and trapping to be distasteful, especially as both methods can also accidentally kill other animals. I think that they have their place but I don't use them myself. Some people claim that we should simply administer contraceptive

The author at work - as seen through a thermal imager, having just shot a fox on a free-range organic chicken farm.

chemicals to control the numbers of the relevant species. Unfortunately, life isn't that simple, as it's nigh-on impossible to ensure that the right individuals consume them or that the wrong ones don't. Anyone who thinks that introducing such dangerous chemicals into the environment needs their heads examining. Ironically, it's often the same people who are violently opposed to allowing such things as genetically modified crops into the countryside.

In the absence of any other practical way of controlling the populations of the relevant animals, I shoot them – here are several reasons why I think this is a good thing:

- It's very selective – I can pick and choose which ones should be taken.
- A well-placed bullet is very humane – it is a much faster and less stressful end than for the countless numbers of animals that go through slaughter houses every day.
- It is very eco-friendly – a deer shot for the table will typically only travel a few miles before it is consumed. This is in stark contrast to the meat produced in places like Argentina and New Zealand which has to be flown halfway around the world to reach us.
- The meat harvested in this manner is not only sustainable, but also much healthier to eat than that produced by modern agri-industry. No chemicals are used in their rearing, the storage times are much reduced, the fat content is lower, and until the moment the animal falls, it lives a free life.
- There is very little wastage – I feed both a cat and dog on rabbits as well as the trimmings from any deer or pheasant butchery I undertake. I challenge anyone to show me happier or healthier pets.
- With all the hills I have to scale and the amount of equipment I carry, I get a huge amount of exercise.

I live in rural mid-Devon, hidden away in the hills in the south-west corner of the United Kingdom. This is very much farming country where the vast majority of working people are involved with agriculture in one way or another. The latest model of shiny car might get a passing glance, but a really nice tractor will soon draw in a small crowd of admirers. Farmers are a

breed unto themselves though – if they see you as an asset, they will bend over backwards for you, but if you're not known to them, they can appear to be very suspicious. They do, of course, have every reason to be like this. For a start, to run a modern farm properly, they need to have many hundreds of thousands of pounds or even millions of pounds worth of equipment. A new tractor can easily cost more than a three-bedroom house.

Sadly, this draws thieves in like magnets, and few farms have managed to avoid being repeatedly burgled. Keeping a business going is very hard work, and the farmers need all the help they can get. Towards the end of the lambing season, it is not at all unusual to see big powerful men reduced to physical wrecks by weeks and weeks of little to no sleep. These people love their livestock, and get really upset to see infant animals being mauled or killed by predators, especially those which they hand-delivered a few hours beforehand. I have witnessed mother ewes standing guard over their lambs, anxiously attempting to prod them back into life, not realising that only half their infant's body remains.

Even more distressing is the sight of a pregnant ewe that has been attacked by crows after it has fallen onto its back and has been unable to right itself. Often, these cruel birds will peck the eyes and tongue out, while the helpless animal thrashes about in agony. Sometimes, they will also eat the ears away too, for good measure. Should a lamb become separated from its mother, it is in danger of being attacked by all manner of animals, ranging from foxes to badgers to dogs.

Many farmers use a small rubber ring to dock the tails from young lambs – these constrict the blood flow in such a way that after a time most of the tail simply drops off. Although it sounds a bit barbaric, it is actually done for animal welfare reasons – removing the tail helps to prevent what is known as 'fly-strike' – that is, maggots getting into the tail and eating it away from the inside. It also makes it easier to shear the sheep when they have grown, reducing cutting times and therefore the cost to the farmer and the stress levels of the animal. A direct consequence of the docking process is that when the tails drop off, they provide easy pickings for foxes. Sometimes, however, the foxes don't bother to wait, and they attack the lambs and chew the tails off. This nearly always causes the wound to become infected, and as a result they get a painful disease known as 'joint-ill', which is like a severe form of arthritis. Preventing fox attacks is obviously an important matter to every sheep farmer.

In a similar vein, young piglets can also be extremely vulnerable to attack, and it seems that once a fox has worked out a successful method of getting at them, it will continue doing so for several years: that is, unless someone manages to stop it. Fences can work, but foxes are superb climbers – a few minutes before writing this I was talking to a gamekeeper who watched one a few nights ago climbing a netted barrier as though it were a ladder. Electric fences are best, but these are not foolproof – you only need a branch to fall onto one, and the foxes will be in.

Poultry farms are especially vulnerable to this. As consumers we are (rightly) always demanding better animal welfare standards – with free-range living

conditions being considered the best. The problem with this is that a typical rearing field has a very long perimeter. As an illustration, a 10-acre field can easily need a fence that is nearly a mile long. Multiply that by several fields, and you start to see the scale of the issue. You only need a badger to smash his way through – they don't take much notice of electric fences – or a strong wind to cause a break, and you can have a massive problem. One of the farms I look after lost 175 free-range organic chickens in less than an hour to a single fox. It slaughtered most of them in a frenzied attack; the rest died from asphyxiation by smothering after crowding into a tight corner of their coop in an attempt to get away from the intruder. It was just after this that I was invited to take over the pest control on the farm.

As I don't farm myself, I don't just shoot for economic reasons. I don't even charge for my services. No, one of the main reasons I shoot foxes is to help conserve the populations of other animals. These include things like the hedgehogs, dormice, lapwings and skylarks, as well as hares, nightjars and even amphibians like frogs, toads and newts. Many of these

The remains of a free range organic chicken after it was killed by a fox. Few farmers would mind if they only took the odd one, but sadly it is not unusual for well over a hundred to die in a single attack.

No farmer can survive for very long if his crops sustain repeated damage. Here a field of oats has been badly flattened by roe deer.

would struggle to survive if their predators were not controlled. I take great pleasure in being told by a farmer that he's seen a massive rise in the amount of wildlife on his property since I started shooting there. It's not what the 'antis' would want to hear, but it's a stark fact: reduce the predation and threatened species will often recover very quickly. Indeed, several of the better-known animal charities have finally recognised this and have started fox shooting programs on their reserves – although they'd prefer it that you didn't know this. It's not just livestock that can need protection: many crops can suffer severe pest damage if they are left unattended. Roe deer, for instance, can be a serious problem to market gardeners. These lovely animals are typically browsers – that is, they carefully pick and choose their food – and then nibble it away. This tends to be the juiciest shoots on a plant, often those at the top of young trees or the ends of the branches. A small number of roe can wipe out a new plantation in no time. Red, sika and fallow deer are less fussy. They are predominantly grazers, and being much larger, need to eat vast amounts of food to survive.

A good example of the trouble they can cause occurred on a farm that lies just a couple of miles from my house. It suffered three thousand pounds worth of damage last year to a swede crop in just over a week thanks to a small herd of red deer. Some people would say that the farmer should have put up better fences. Those people have not the slightest clue as to what they are talking about. When a 250kg stag wants to go somewhere, there is very little that will stop it. It will jump most fences, and smash its way through others. The cost of truly deer-proof fencing is so astronomical as to be totally out of the question. Besides, who would want to see our countryside swathed in tens of thousands of miles of what would effectively look like concentration camp defences?

EQUIPMENT & METHODS

There are several ways in which one can hunt foxes, but these can be divided into two basic methods: by day and by night. Both rely on the same underlying principles: good fieldcraft and the ability to shoot straight being the most important ones. The main difference, of course, is that in the dark you need to be able to see the foxes, and this is where the techniques diverge sharply.

Lamping has been a traditional rural pursuit for years, with the equipment changing little in all that time. Bulbs have got brighter and the lenses better, but the main improvement has been that with the introduction of the latest generation of lightweight batteries, the weight penalty has all but disappeared. Typically, lamps are used from the back of a 4x4, with one or more shooters in attendance. It is a great way to cover a lot of ground, and can be a very effective method of shooting a lot of foxes. This is especially true in the autumn when the crops have been cut and the season's cubs have yet to associate bright lights with danger. Before long, however, a hard core of lamp-shy foxes will be left, and these can be all but impossible to control.

The recent advent of good quality night vision (NV) equipment has changed all this. It is possible for a skilled hunter to sneak up on a fox without it having any idea that he is there. Having spent many years and countless thousands of pounds on developing a successful methodology, I now have a reasonable idea as to what works and what doesn't. I've had many false starts and discovered innumerable dead ends, but I gradually learned the lessons and moved on. I should make it clear that NV kit is not for the technically inept. If you cannot use most of the features on an SLR camera, then it's probably not for you. If you're up for a challenge and have a reasonable amount of patience though, it can a very rewarding exercise.

So, let us examine the toys. Where hunting animals is concerned, vision is king. You simply cannot beat having good optics, and in daylight this essentially translates as telescopic sights and binoculars. I am a massive fan of rangefinders, and although they work very well as standalone units, I prefer to have them built into a set of binoculars. I find this invaluable, especially when I'm shooting at extended ranges. The variety of telescopic sights available these days is staggering, and to confuse the issue further, many have a multitude of reticles (crosshairs) to choose from. The most important feature for the fox shooter is probably the scope's light transmission efficiency: that is, how much of the available light it can pass through to the eye. In the middle of the day this is not particularly important, but under the lamp as well as at dawn and dusk, it is a critical factor. Having a lot of zoom can be a good thing in the day, but it's a liability at night. This is for two reasons. First, every time you increase the magnification, the amount of light that can pass through drops dramatically. Second, you need to be able to find your target quickly and easily, and if your scope is on x24, you'll really struggle to see it before it's disappeared into cover.

People have been calling foxes since time immemorial. Typically, this involves making a squeaking noise by blowing or sucking on the hand. There are also many different artificial callers that you can either blow through or squeeze. They basically simulate the sounds made by wounded prey, and they can be very effective indeed, especially on young animals. The main problem is that they really only work on foxes that you've already spotted and in countryside that allows you to track them all the way in. Any experienced foxes will do their best to disappear from sight, whereupon they'll circle around on the wind and come up behind you. Once they've scented you, they'll run away, and you'll never even know they were there. There are two main solutions to this. The first is that you find a place where you can put your back to a cliff, wide river or some large structure that will prevent a fox approaching you from behind. Unfortunately, there are few situations that allow you to do this, and if the wind is blowing in the wrong direction, there's little or nothing you can do about it.

The solution to this is to use an electronic caller. The better ones have remote controls that allow you to turn them on and off, vary the volume and change the call track. These are placed at some distance out in front of you. When the calling starts, the foxes are looking away from you instead of at you. I've had them run right past me in their haste to get to what they think is going to be an easy meal. I started out with a simple device that didn't have the remote control feature, but after having several foxes run in and away before I'd even made it back to my shooting point, I spent the extra money and haven't looked back since. My favourite caller is the Scorpion, manufactured in the United States by FOXPRO. This can carry up to 200 different sounds, and is a lethal part of my armoury.

The world of NV systems can be a minefield, with various models being available from the very cheap to the very expensive. As with so many things in life, as a general rule you get what you pay for. A budget device will give you budget performance. As time goes on they get better and better, however, and it won't be that many years before digital technology has changed out of all recognition, and high performance systems will be within everyone's reach. Until then, tubed night vision will continue to rule the roost.

One of the main problems is that there are so many different models in the marketplace that it is nigh-on impossible to know the details of every one. Frustratingly, a few manufacturers seem to make some of their products in very small batches, and as a result the designations appear to change every few weeks. I am forever being asked about my opinions on particular NV devices, and most of the time I am unable to help as I've never heard of the equipment in question.

In essence, there are four fundamental categories of NV: digital, GenI, GenII and GenIII. Each of these has specific physical features to set it apart from the others. GenII is also available in an enhanced form known as GenII+. There can be huge variations within each of these categories, with the resolution (picture quality) and light gain (image brightness) being the most important factors.

NV devices come in two basic forms: spotters and riflescopes. Spotters are typically monoculars; however, there are some binocular NV spotters available too. There is a crossover, though. Some monocular systems can be mounted on the rear of a conventional telescopic sight, giving it NV capability. The mounting bracket used for this is commonly referred to as a Direct Scope Attachment or DSA. The main issue with these is that it puts your head back so far that it can be difficult to use the rifle. Front-mount systems were developed to get around this, and the better ones work very well.

No matter what the quality of the NV device, its performance will be improved with the use of an infrared (IR) illuminator. I've heard many people claim that their NV system is so good that it doesn't need extra illumination. What they have missed, however, is that without extra light you cannot see any folds in the ground. A laser or other illuminator will create shadows that help you to see where there are rises and dips. I've seen hollows I was previously unaware of, big enough to swallow a horse, suddenly appear when I've turned my IR on. Another really helpful feature is that extra IR will create eye-shine from any animals that are looking in your direction. This can help you to identify where a fox is located in moments, saving you the trouble of inspecting every single object in the landscape. It's vitally important to remember that at close-range laser illuminators can permanently damage eyesight – both that of animals and humans – so be very careful where you aim it.

The last piece of equipment to discuss here is the thermal imager. These incredible devices work in the IR part of the spectrum, and present an image based on the temperature of all the objects, structures and

A Unique Alpine TPG-1 in .308, together with a large dog fox that fell to it. This type of rifle is impractical for every-day hunting – it is far too heavy and unwieldy.

creatures in front of them. Foxes, for example, show up as a long white shape against a dark background. Like NV, these were developed by the military for use on the battlefield; since then they have become available to the civilian market, mostly for fire-fighters and the rescue services as well as hunters. At the time of writing, they are still far too expensive for the average person to contemplate buying, but as is so often the case with technology, the price will undoubtedly come down with time. Thermal imagers vary in size from lightweight devices that can hang unobtrusively around the neck up to massive systems that are more at home on a tank or helicopter. Although the movies would have us believe that thermals can see animals through walls and trees, the truth is that you can only see things where there is a direct line of sight. A small mound of mud or a clump of wet grass will completely mask anything that is behind it. Having said that, you only need a leg or an ear sticking out to give you a warning that something is there. Thermals are especially useful for finding quarry that has fallen in partially overgrown areas, although they are far from foolproof.

The Guns

When it comes to what to shoot with, there is an enormous choice. This does, however, narrow considerably once you've outlined the purpose. Different guns do different things, so unless you have a very narrow use in mind, it is highly unlikely that any one will do everything you require.

Air rifles come in two basic formats: those which require a firearms licence, defined as anything that produces more than 12ft/lb of muzzle energy, and those which don't, because they fall under this limit. I hope it goes without saying that no air rifle should be used for hunting foxes. Shotguns are excellent for short-range use, especially for flying quarry or clay pigeons. They should not be used on foxes at any more than about 35yd though, and unless they are only a few feet away it is extremely important to ensure that a suitable load is used. Most would consider number 4 shot to be the smallest that should be contemplated. I personally favour three-inch magnum BB cartridges, but they may be considered a little extreme by some!

Most serious fox shooters use a rifle. In my opinion, rimfires are OK at sensible ranges, with the HMR being better than the .22LR, which I consider to be only suitable for very close-range work. Once you get into centrefire territory, there is a massive choice. At the smaller end of the scale there are things like the .17 Remington. While these are blindingly accurate, they are best suited to experienced shooters who reload because the ammunition can be hard to come by. Going up in size, there is a much more practical calibre: namely, .204 Ruger. Ammo is easy to come by, reloading is straightforward, they are very, very accurate, there is next to no recoil and they hit extremely hard. It is certainly one of my favourites. Above this you have the .22 centrefires. Calibres in this size include .222, .223, .22-250 and 220 Swift. Debating the merits and demerits of each is meaningless. I use a Sauer 202 in .22-250 as my dedicated NV rifle. It is flat shooting and hits very hard. I have little experience of using the others, but those who do tell me they all do the job extremely well.

Going on up from .22 CF there are the ever popular .243 and .308s, as well as things like .270, 25-06, and so on. These are really deer calibres, but they also perform very well for foxing, especially when loaded with lighter bullets. The only significant downsides are cost of ammo, recoil and noise. Some would say that safety is an issue: it should not be. If there is any doubt at all, a shot should not be taken, no matter what cartridge is employed.

One of the main changes in rifle shooting over recent years is the advent of the moderator. In the 'old days', these were few and far between – mostly due to regulations. Fortunately, however, common sense has seen the Home Office relax its stance on allowing their use. They not only minimise hearing damage for the user, but also reduce inconvenience to anyone else in the neighbourhood. I have them fitted to every one of my rifles, including my air rifles. There are two basic types: those that come back over the barrel, known as 'reflex' and those which stick out from the end. The former not only make the rifle shorter, but they help shift the balance point back, too.

I have tried most of the different kinds of ammunition on the market, but at the end of the day, it really boils down to what works for you. The main aspects to consider include cost, accuracy and availability. If you reload (not possible for rimfire calibres), the choices are even wider. Essentially, you have four components: powder, primer, case and bullet. Beyond this though are many, many fine details: case length, case weight, case volume, the amount of powder used, neck tension and so on. The most important factor is to get all the parameters of the loaded cartridges as close to one another as you can.

There are many ways to carry ammunition when you are out hunting. I've tried most of them, and have settled on using soft pouches. These generally hold about 14 rounds, which should be more than enough unless you are shooting things like rabbits or rats. Having once lost a live cartridge from one of the butt sock storage systems, I don't recommend their use. Luckily, I heard it hit the ground, and was able to retrieve it. Although cartridge belts work well for shotguns, I avoid them for rifle use for similar reasons. Having loose ammunition in your pocket should also be avoided at all times. There are not only direct safety issues, but there is an increased chance of you losing live rounds. Aside from that, they will clink together, with the obvious risk that you will alert your quarry to your presence

Shooting Rests
Bipods are two-leg rests that are generally made from metal tubing and attach to the fore-end of a rifle. Most

A Sauer 202 in .308 – these high quality German rifles are superb for deer stalking as well as taking the occasional fox. It has a bipod attached.

kinds fold up out of the way while they are not in use. Used properly and with the right place to shoot from, they can provide a very stable shooting position. Under these circumstances, they simply cannot be beaten for convenience and accuracy. Unfortunately, when foxing away from a vehicle nine shots out of ten will be from somewhere that is unsuited to a bipod. This is because of two main factors: first, the low height means that if the undergrowth is too long or the ground is of an inconvenient shape you won't be able to see anything. Second, foxes are generally creatures of movement, and trying to follow one as it runs is next to impossible with a bipod as the legs will tangle with absolutely every piece of grass anywhere near it.

After persevering with bipods for a long time I moved onto two-leg hunting sticks. Having the extra height and the freedom to swivel around was a revelation, although it took me some time to develop good accuracy at longer ranges. My fox tally went up overnight, and I was a convert. Some time later, and I have to admit somewhat reluctantly, I added a third leg. Not only did my accuracy improve, but I also found they were more convenient than the two-leg version simply because they stand up on their own. Manoeuvring the legs out as you lower them also becomes second nature after a while.

As detailed in the account 'Pimp My Sticks' (see p.96), I eventually bought a set of Vanguard tripod sticks. These allow me to sit on the side of a steep hill with the rear leg folded back up under my armpit, and the other two placed out in front. I'm right-handed, so it means my left hand goes under the rifle's butt, acting as a bridge between it and the rear leg. This gives such a stable shooting position that I have been able to take shots at ranges that I would not have been able to contemplate before.

Sticks are pretty well redundant for those who only ever shoot from a truck. For them bipods or shooting bags (typically small canvas sacks filled with sand, grain or shot) do an excellent job. Some people who hunt from 4x4s or quad bikes like to make up their own rests. These are usually constructed from things like sections of metal pipe covered with foam lagging. At the end of the day it doesn't matter what is used so long as it provides for safe and reliable shooting.

Accessory Kit

One of the problems for anyone who shoots foxes is working out just what to take and what to leave behind. For me, the starting point of hunting at night is safety, and so I not only carry a torch, but I generally take a back-up too. If a set of batteries is going to go flat, it will do so at the most inconvenient moment. If you know the ground you're going to be hunting on well, or there are sufficient navigation markers, you probably don't need a compass. If, however, you're going to be somewhere unknown or remote, take one with you. It can be on a mobile phone in the form of a GPS or other mapping system, if you like. If this is the case, however, make sure that the battery is fully charged or you'll be placing lives at risk if you get lost.

I used to carry a set of pocket scales, but I now keep a large set in the truck instead as I no longer weigh every fox I shoot. I do carry a small camera (an Olympus Mju Tough), as I photograph every one that falls to my rifle. Since I carry several different pieces of equipment that rely on optics of one kind or another – including my glasses, riflescope, binoculars, NV monocular, NV riflescope, mini thermal and so on – I'm almost obsessive about ensuring that I have several lens cloths with me. They're always kept in the same pockets, so I know exactly where they are when they're needed in a hurry. Unfortunately, they don't work on laser illuminators though, as the lenses are too small for a cloth to gain sufficient access, so I also carry several cotton buds, again in the same place every time.

One of the things that always annoys the life out of me is when things I'm carrying rattle. I want to be as near silent as I can possibly be when I'm moving, and so I try to minimise what I have in my pockets, and those things I can't do without are wrapped in thin pieces of foam. This includes my Kuhn Rikon knives. These are cheap and come with sturdy plastic sheaths, so they can be carried safely.

Although I try to minimise what I take, I always carry a mouth caller even though I'm a massive fan of electronic callers. This is because sometimes you'll spot a fox that is about to disappear and there's no time to do anything but call it straight away. In these circumstances, I find it really useful to just pull it out of my pocket and squeak away. My favourite is the BestFoxCall, which uses a thin reed, but there are lots

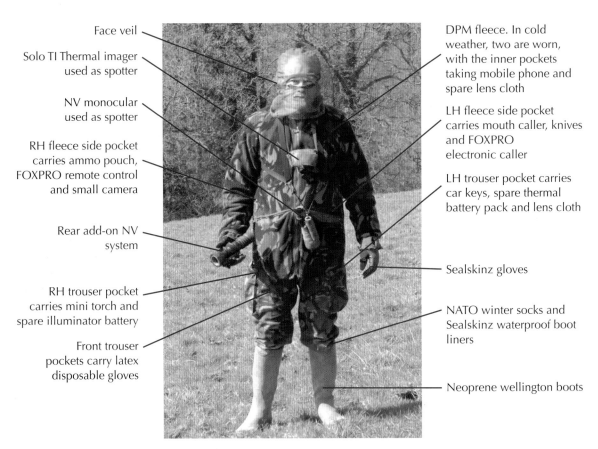

Face veil

Solo TI Thermal imager used as spotter

NV monocular used as spotter

RH fleece side pocket carries ammo pouch, FOXPRO remote control and small camera

Rear add-on NV system

RH trouser pocket carries mini torch and spare illuminator battery

Front trouser pockets carry latex disposable gloves

DPM fleece. In cold weather, two are worn, with the inner pockets taking mobile phone and spare lens cloth

LH fleece side pocket carries mouth caller, knives and FOXPRO electronic caller

LH trouser pocket carries car keys, spare thermal battery pack and lens cloth

Sealskinz gloves

NATO winter socks and Sealskinz waterproof boot liners

Neoprene wellington boots

ABOVE: If you are not really well organised, hunting at night can soon go horribly wrong. All manner of kit can get scattered around various pockets, making it far more likely that you won't be able to find what you need when you need it. Inevitably, if you can't keep track of what is meant to be there, some of it will end up getting lost. I have disciplined myself always to keep the same things in the same pockets. In the daytime I carry almost exactly the same , but with the NV spotter swapped for Leica range-finding binoculars.

BELOW LEFT: The use of hunting sticks in the standing position, here seen in night-shooting mode with rear NV add-on in place on my .204 Kimber Montana, and a NV spotter slung on a chest harness. Above it and out of sight in this photo is the TI spotter.

BELOW RIGHT: Accurately shooting into a valley from sloping ground can be a real problem. The Vanguard tripod sticks allow you to do this by folding the rear leg back so that your left hand can support your right elbow.

and lots of others out there that also work really well. These include the squeakers found in dog toys, which can be easily removed with a few deft cuts from a knife.

In the truck I keep an assortment of other things, including secateurs, an assortment of cable ties, cord and rope, as well as first aid gear and a good supply of food and water. It's only too easy to get dehydrated or let your blood sugar levels fall when you're out hunting, and you're usually having far too much fun to realise. Having a decent stash of chocolate bars and small bottles of water in your vehicle is a very good thing.

Clothing

As the famous hill walker and author of guidebooks Alfred Wainwright, once said, 'There's no such thing as bad weather,only unsuitable clothing.' If you only ever shoot from a vehicle, this is not so relevant, but for those who hunt on foot – and especially those who do so in remote places – they are vitally important words. Being properly equipped can be the difference between life and death. It's also really important to remember that it is not only you that is involved. If you get into trouble, it also imperils those who have to go out in extreme conditions and search for you, as well as placing those you leave behind under undue stress. If there is the slightest doubt about what the weather is going to do, either stay behind or go out properly kitted up. It's far better to be too hot with too much food in your pockets than the reverse! There is so much good clothing available these days that there is no excuse for being caught out. If you don't mind ex-military kit (I love it), you can often get real bargains from boot sales and surplus outlets. The desert pattern clothing is not of much use to us in the UK, but the DPM (disruptive pattern material) camouflage is superb.

Starting at the feet and working upwards: until I tried a set of Le Chameau wellington boots I'd always thought that expensive wellies were a waste of money. I was wrong. They meet every one of my requirements, and I now wear them pretty well every time I go out shooting, although I still have a pair of tough Le Chameau Mouflon leather walking boots for those occasions where I'm heading somewhere appropriate. Underneath my boots, I wear thick

woollen socks. Once again, I believe military surplus is the way to go. The white arctic warfare ones with the thin red stripe around the top are superb, and can be obtained very cheaply. I also like the Sealskinz socks, and wear them as well. These are not only very warm and comfortable, but they're waterproof too, and so act as a secondary barrier should your boots fill with water.

Above my socks I wear ex-military trousers in DPM camouflage. Some people get really sniffy about anyone who wears such things. I think they are barmy, although I will concede that camo gear is not suited to the more formal pheasant and grouse shoots. Underneath my trousers I wear thermals if it's likely to be cold. Indeed, I'll often put two pairs on if there's any doubt. It's amazing how much the wind-chill factor can rob you of body heat at the top of a hill on a dark winter's night.

I'm an adherent to the idea of wearing lots of thin layers to retain heat. The Exmoor hills can be hard taskmasters as they catch the chill winds straight off the Welsh mountains. Consequently, it is not un-usual for me to wear two thermal vests underneath two long-sleeved t-shirts when necessary. And then when it's cold I'll wear over them either two DPM fleeces, or one fleece and a camouflage jacket. The added advantage of doing this is that you get more pockets to put your various bits and pieces in. One of my pet hates is clothing that makes any kind of noise, especially those awful fabrics which rustle when rubbed together. If anyone who turns up to hunt with me is wearing such things they are likely to get a hard time.

One of the problems you will face if it's really cold is how to keep your hands warm enough to use a rifle. My favourites for the really cold nights are ex-military leather gloves known as Combat 95 pattern. They come in both green and black, and can sometimes be found in surplus stores.

People sometimes ask me why I wear a face veil at night, thinking that as it's dark, it makes no differ-ence. They clearly have little or no understanding of working under low light, when the slightest exposure of bare skin shows up like a flashlight. I always take a pair of scissors to my veil to remove the area around my mouth, however. This stops the warm humid air of my breath being ducted straight up and into my optics. If it's cold, I wear a woolly hat underneath. As my eyesight has deteriorated with age I also need to wear glasses. These are secured on a cord so they don't get lost.

Hunting Styles

There are many different ways to hunt foxes, but in essence you will either be working from foot or from a vehicle of some kind. Although I sometimes shoot from a truck, I'm predominantly a stalker. To illustrate this better, of the last 150 foxes I've shot, 149 were taken as the result of walked-up hunting. It's not that I don't like driving or being driven around – it's much easier, warmer, drier and more sociable. The stark reality about where I live is that due to the shape of the landscape and the wetness of the soil, about 98% of the ground can't be seen from a large vehicle like a 4x4. Smaller ones such as quad bikes and mules can get considerably more access; however, they are not much use if the land in question requires a 40-mile round trip through narrow lanes where a trailer is a real liability. Given the choice though, I'd probably opt for a blend of the two: that is, using a light off-road vehicle to approach my chosen hunting area, and then going on from there on foot. My personal opinion is that if you are serious about shooting foxes, then you will need to spend at least some of your time away from a vehicle, or you'll never get near the cleverer animals. I've watched lampers from afar through my NV, and it's amazing to see how all the smart foxes are already running away two or three fields ahead of the approaching vehicle. They guys on board probably thought they were doing well, but didn't realise how many animals they never even saw! I consider myself to have failed if a fox has the slightest idea that I'm there before it takes a bullet.

There are three basic ways of getting close enough to shoot to foxes: searching, baiting and calling. I like to use all three, mixing and matching them to suit the occasion. Baiting can be extremely successful, but it relies on a number of factors. Firstly, you must have somewhere suitable. It is vital that you check with the farmer and get his permission before putting anything out. The last thing you want is for him to have any concerns about his livestock being infected by some-thing you've put on his land. You also have to take care to ensure that no members of the public or their pets can be inconvenienced by any dead things you've left out. It's vital to place your bait in a location where you can creep up to check it out without being seen by foxes. If there isn't a convenient hedge, I like to place it on the far side of a rise so that I can peer over without fully exposing myself. The longer that you can bait the ground for, the more effective it is likely to be. Although you may have some success after a few hours, it's usually best to leave it for at least a day.

Since foxes are the masters of opportunism, you can use all manner of things as bait. Perhaps the easiest source is roadkill, but any vermin you've shot will do – including such things as bunnies and pigeons. The butchery trimmings off larger animals such as deer, rabbits, boar and so on all work too. The larger the bait is, the easier it will be for a fox to pick it up and run off with it. The best method is to chop it up into small pieces. These should then be scattered over as wide an area as possible so that any visitors have to search for it. This will hold them in your chosen killing zone for much longer.

You can walk about and throw the bits from a bag or tray, but it's better to distribute them from a vehicle so you won't be leaving any human scent trails from your footsteps. Likewise, it's a good idea to use dis-posable gloves both to reduce scent and the risk of you picking up any undesirable bugs. Those animals which frequent urban and suburban areas may not be so easily spooked, but true country foxes will not like to detect any human smells at all. I've seen them turn and run simply from sniffing ground that I walked across more than an hour before. Every fox is different, but it's best to assume that they're all streetwise. My favoured method of placing the bait is to leave it in a swathe at 90 degrees to the wind. If it is nicely ripe, it will generate an irresistible invitation to any hungry foxes that happen to pass downwind.

If you visit your bait and find that there are no foxes in sight, it's worth bearing in mind that any animals that have been eating it are likely to have gorged themselves, and if they did so recently, they will be lying up somewhere while their free meal digests. In my experience, they like to lie out in the open where they can easily see any approaching danger. Such individuals may be totally indifferent to any noises made by a caller, and will usually only move if they feel threatened.

On those occasions when you don't have the time to leave some bait out for a day or more – perhaps because you only visit the area infrequently – an excellent alternative is drag-baiting. This is where you take some bait – the smellier the better – and then tow it (either by hand or from a vehicle) around the perimeter of an area that is known to be occupied by one or more foxes. The idea is that they will encounter the scent trail and then follow it right up to where you're waiting for them. If you add a few zigzags into the path you take, it will give you longer to see the foxes coming in. Should you choose to do some drag-baiting on the spur of the moment – maybe because you've unexpectedly been asked to tackle a poultry or lamb killer – then freshly shot rabbits can be a convenient answer. These can simply have their back legs tied together and be pulled around on a piece of string. They will need to be 'tenderised' first. This can be done by making a series of slits through the flesh and then squashing the carcass with your boot. The more it leaks blood and gore the better. This is not a method for the squeamish! If you only have small pieces of bait to use, a spare onion bag or something similar made of netting can be used in the same way.

Ambushing can be successful, but it requires local knowledge as to where and when the foxes are moving. This information may arise out of your own observations, those of a farmer, or from the images taken by a trail camera. Whichever it may be, it's important not to walk anywhere close to the fox's expected approach route, or you risk leaving scent that will deter it. The best way is to find a position from where you can lie up and watch, ideally with the rifle ready and waiting. Vehicles and farm buildings can provide good shelter, but if none of these are to hand, then you can settle yourself into a hedge that over-looks the relevant ground. Pigeon hides and similar structures such as high seats can work very well. As part of your preparation work, it's helpful if you can use a rangefinder to work out all the distances to various salient objects – that way you won't have to stop to think about how to place your shot, as you'll already have worked it out.

Electronic Callers

There are many way of bringing foxes in to your rifle, including such things as bait, livestock and even simulated scent gland sprays. Without question, however, by far the most effective is the use of calls. These can be produced in a variety of ways. The most traditional ones typically involve sucking on the back of your hand or blowing through specially made mouth callers. Both systems can work well, but are really only suited to situations where you can already see the fox you are after. The main problem is that any wise foxes will simply disappear from sight and then go around on the wind until they are behind you. The moment they've scented human, they will run off without you ever knowing they were there. Even worse, is that they will forever associate that sound with the presence of danger.

The best way of getting around this is to use electronic callers – preferably ones with remote control operation. By locating the caller correctly with respect to the wind, any approaching foxes will be looking and sniffing at a point that may be a hundred yards away from you. Indeed, I've had them run right past me without noticing I was there in their haste to get to the caller. Sometimes, they will come in so fast that you barely have time to get the safety catch off. The types that don't have a remote control can work well too, but you have to switch them on and then walk back to your chosen shooting point with the call already running. Back when I used one of these I lost several foxes because they had come in before I'd even made it back to my sticks. By the time I was ready, they were already running off into the night. For those spur of the moment occasions when there isn't time to set up an electronic device, I still carry a BestFoxCall mouth caller,

The FOXPRO Spitfire caller with hand-held remote control.

RIGHT: A FOXPRO Scorpion in action. Note the reflective tape added to the aerial to aid finding the caller, and the home-made extension to raise it up off the ground. All the shiny parts have also been taped over to reduce the risk of a fox seeing it.

FAR RIGHT: The custom-built remote control made for me by the FOXPRO factory sits next to where I hold my rifle with my left hand. If a fox runs in, I can mute the caller by dabbing one of the buttons with my thumb. It is seen here on my Kimber Montana in .204 Ruger.

There are several manufacturers of electronic fox callers, but I've settled on those made by FOXPRO. These are available in several different models with various features. Since I predominantly shoot from foot rather than a vehicle, the size and weight of the caller are vital considerations. This is why I chose the Scorpion. The remote control works very well, so long as there's a good line of sight between the hand-held transmitter and the actual caller. Since the ground that I shoot on can be hilly, I've added a home-made mounting system to mine. Constructed from an old fishing rod, it allows me to raise the unit up to ensure better aerial reception. This is important, as I've had FOXPRO build me a one-off rifle-mounted remote control. The idea is that if a fox runs in towards the caller, I can mute the call track simply by dabbing one of the buttons with my left thumb. That way, I can not only stop the fox before it gets too close to the caller (so that it doesn't scent human), but I can also keep both hands on the rifle, ensuring a rapid shot.

I like to site my callers about 100 yards out, and unlike some who favour having the wind in their face, I like the wind to be blowing across from one side to the other. Preferably, I will choose a spot where the breeze is going into some nearby bushes or trees. The reason for that is straightforward: foxes like to get as close as they can to their prey without leaving cover. If you set things up to allow them to do this, then it narrows down the likely approach routes, meaning that you are more likely to be watching the right place when they run in. A lesson I learned the hard way is to think very carefully about where you are going to walk before you place the caller. If you leave a scent trail between the cover and the caller, the fox will smell you and run before you get the chance of a shot.

When it comes to the actual calls, the choice is almost endless. They can be broadly divided into two: prey calls and fox calls. The former would include such diverse things as vole alarm squeaks, screaming rats, distressed rabbits, wounded squirrels and so on. Some are simply synthetic noises that are not intended to sound like any living creature, but for some reason still appeal to hungry foxes. Foxes use a surprisingly wide range of calls, which is why it is well worth taking the time to study at least a little of their biology. The type known as 'squalls' are basically communication calls that are commonly heard just after dark. In effect, they're used by members of a social group to say 'I'm over here, where are you?' These calls should be used sparingly to tempt others to answer, hence revealing their whereabouts. Once you know where they are, you can go after them.

While the mating calls can be used at any time of year, they can be devastating in the middle of the breeding season. A vixen call will enrage any other females in the area, and the dominant ones will often come charging in, full of aggression, to see off the intruder. Subservient animals will often sneak around and watch to see what is going on from a distance, usually only approaching from downwind. Dominant males on the other hand will often be very curious, and may not bother about going around on the wind – after all, it's their territory, so they don't have to be afraid of any other foxes. Consequently, they can appear from anywhere. The sounds can be very convincing. I've even watched vixens throw themselves down on the ground in submissive postures in an attempt to stop their partners from approaching what they believe to be another vixen's call.

Thermal Imaging (TI)

Thermal imaging is a relatively new addition to the hunting scene which, because of the high price, is still only being used by professionals and those with strong budgets. Like so many new technologies, it was first developed for the military, and has since slowly trickled down to civilian use. Essentially, thermal imagers see in the infrared part of the spectrum, allowing you to see body heat clearly. TI can be a real benefit in many situations. Firstly, it is completely passive, so there is no light projected that could be seen by a wary animal. Secondly, it is not affected by the presence of nearby objects like tree branches or banks of fog, both of which can cause real problems for laser-equipped NV systems. A lot of people who know about thermal imagers but have never actually used them think they are some kind of magic device that can see right through solid objects like walls. In truth, the only things that will be visible are those that are in a direct line of sight. The smallest thermal imagers are light enough to be worn around the neck, while the larger ones are too heavy for anything except tripods or similar robust mountings. There are a lot of different TI systems in the marketplace, with new ones being developed all the time. The main thing to watch for is the refresh rate: anything under 30Hz will result in images that don't keep up with anything but the slowest of movement.

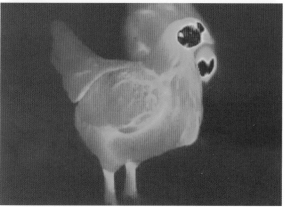

TOP: Thermal imaging typically shows up warm things as being light coloured, and cold things as dark coloured. The image shown has a warm-bodied horse on the left, and a cold metal building behind it to the right.

ABOVE: It is amazing to see just how much difference there is between the observed temperatures of different parts of an animal. Here, two chickens can be seen, with the warmth in their heads contrasting vividly with the rest of their bodies which are well insulated by multiple layers of feathers.

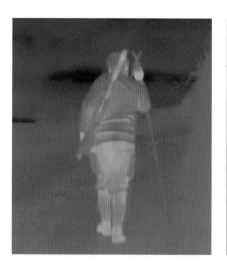

LEFT: On some systems there is also an extra setting which is known as 'black hot', where the 'white hot' situation is reversed. The two images show the author as 'white hot' (FAR LEFT) and 'black hot' (LEFT). In some situations it can be useful to switch between the two as the extra visual information allows you to build up a better mental picture of the landscape around you.

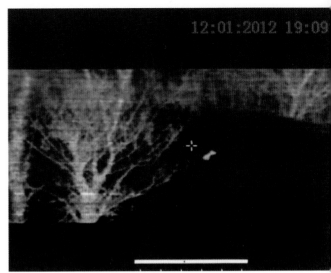

ABOVE LEFT: A fox was sitting on the knoll (**BELOW** a daylight view of the location) at about 200 yards out, viewed here via the Black Hot setting on my Thermal Lite thermal imager.

ABOVE: The fox seen again via the White Hot setting on my Thermal Lite imager. Here, it has been caught in mid-call, trying to bring in a mate, something that could not be allowed with several thousand free range organic chickens close by.

LEFT: A fox comes rushing in to the caller, as seen through the lightweight Solo TI thermal imager which usually hangs around my neck when I'm out hunting. The black box with the figure 1 indicates that the ground temperature was 1°C. Five battery segments show that the unit was fully charged.

Night Vision Systems

Using true night vision (NV) devices to go hunting is a relatively new concept – simply because the equipment has only become available in recent years. True NV equipment was first developed during the Second World War, but for many years it was exclusively the preserve of the military. Not only was it unavailable to the public, but many of the early forms were simply too big and bulky for use by civilian hunters. A secondary issue is that since these devices were developed to hunt people, the magnification was low, and so they were not well suited to the job of shooting relatively small animals.

In the last few years this situation has changed dramatically, with all manner of NV devices coming onto the civilian market. These include dedicated riflescopes, handheld spotters and various kinds of add-on units that attach either at the front or the rear of conventional daytime telescopic sights.

NV systems were exclusively based on image intensifier tubes until quite recently, but digital versions started coming out around 2006. At the time of writing, these are still a long way short of matching the higher end tubed NV systems, but they do provide a low-cost way of getting into the market, albeit with markedly reduced performance.

In many ways, NV equipment bears similarities to that used in photography. Someone who had never used a complicated camera before would not expect to be able to take first-class photographs on their first day out with it. Likewise, NV gear needs a lot of patience and thought, or there will be frustration and possibly tears. They say that you learn by your mistakes, and believe me – I've made them all!

ABOVE: My Sauer 202 in .22-250 – a fast, flat-trajectory calibre that is ideal for foxing. I don't normally use a bipod, preferring a set of adjustable shooting sticks. Here, the rifle is fitted with a Dedal D480 dedicated NV system which has had a manual-gain GenIII tube fitted. Alongside it, there is an infrared illuminator. This rig has taken hundreds and hundreds of foxes over the years.

Two options to dedicated NV systems can be seen here, both of which will allow you to shoot in the dark without altering your daytime optics. Under most circumstances you will also need a laser illuminator in order to get enough light to see anything. BELOW: A front-mounted ATN PS22 NV add-on, seen on my Sauer 202 in .308, together with an IR illuminator. BOTTOM: A rear add-on NV system. With this one, I keep a laser illuminator permanently mounted on my Swarovski scope, so that switching into NV mode takes but a few seconds. The main downside with rear add-ons is that you will need to move your head back a long way. Some people cannot get used to this, while others barely notice. It really helps if the rifle concerned does not produce any significant recoil!

JANUARY

January is a good time for the foxer. Not only does it get dark very early, but the cold nights make for hungry foxes, and the mating season is still in full swing. One of the problems with hunting foxes is that it requires time and patience. Unfortunately, spending long hours away from home does not always receive the full blessing of other occupants of the household, especially when you try to crawl into the marital bed at some ungodly hour of the morning. At this time of year, though, you can have a really long foxing session and still be home in time to watch News At Ten!

Depending on where you are located, the onset of the mating season will vary. Around here, in rural south-west England, it usually starts in November. This is heralded by the first shrill screams of the year – and for the next few months foxes that are normally extremely wary may well seemingly lose all inhibitions in the search for a mate. Used properly, electronic callers can be deadly. The dominant males will often run straight in, regardless of wind direction. Subordinate males, or those trespassing on rival territories, however, will usually go around on the wind in order to determine the size of their potential opponent. Foxes can be

Winter starts to really bite in January. Although foxes usually have a hard time trying to find enough to eat, they are generally more preoccupied with all the pressures of the mating season.

extremely aggressive to one another, and a young male risks taking a severe beating if he approaches the wrong animal, even if it's a vixen.

Likewise, vixens are usually also very careful when approaching a caller. There are no rules, however, and you really need to be on your toes in case a fox comes in from a completely unexpected direction. I remember one session in my early calling days where the snow lay thickly all around, and I was carefully watching the area downwind of the caller. The first thing I knew of a fox approaching was when I heard a loud thump. It had come in from upwind and run straight into the caller! Needless to say, by the time I'd got the rifle in position, it was long gone...

Talking of snow, one of the main challenges the January foxer faces is the weather. It's not unusual to seemingly have all fours seasons in one day – rain, snow, sun, wind and fog may all show themselves

THE FARMER'S MONTH
General farm maintenance.
Fencing and hedging.
Looking after all the livestock and poultry.
Muckspreading.
Preparing for lambing.

within hours. The main thing is to make sure you're prepared for the worst possible conditions; you can always take a few layers off if you're too hot. Getting chilled when you're out in the countryside is not a good thing, especially if you're on your own. There are not only direct life and limb safety considerations, but your performance will also suffer. That's why having good clothing is vital. It needn't cost the earth: ex-military kit can be picked up from surplus outlets and car boot sales for next to nothing. It's also worth taking a thermos of hot drink and a few chocolate bars if there's any chance that the temperature will drop.

In many places January provides the last chance to get on the foxes before lambing starts in earnest – so it's a good time to earn some Brownie points, but it's also important to remember that the pheasant season is drawing to a close (it ends on 1 February). It's worth staying in touch with any local keepers to make sure that you don't inadvertently tread on anyone's toes. Most are delighted to have the foxes shot, but others can be worried about having their birds spooked at night by people creeping around and firing guns.

From the farmer's point of view, January is mainly concerned with looking after livestock, most of which will be over-wintering in sheds. This can be quite an intensive exercise, as it not only means moving large amounts of food, but also clearing up all the slurry that results. One of the best ways of using it is as a fertiliser – an estimated 90 million tonnes of manure and slurry are spread on the land in the UK every year. One of the problems with this is that if it isn't done carefully, the residues wash off into rivers and streams. The incredibly high nitrogen content then kills more or less everything that lives in them. As a consequence of this, the regulations tighten ever more as each year passes, making life increasingly complicated for every-one involved. A good coating of slurry makes a massive difference to the quality of the hay or silage that grows, however, getting onto the land with any kind of equipment is next to impossible if the ground is very wet. This is where a series of hard frosts are welcome, as it hardens the soil up enough to take the weight of a tractor.

Those farmers who keep a lot of sheep spend much of the month getting them ready for lambing. Checking the ewes' feet is important to make sure their toenails haven't grown too long whilst in the artificial surroundings of their winter quarters. Those breeds that have long hair may also need their wool trimmed back to provide the young lambs with good access to the teats. Aside from looking after cattle and sheep, the other main activity is doing general maintenance. This includes fencing and hedging – it's the right time of year to be doing it as there is no longer any wild fruit to worry about, and the birds have not started building nests yet.

January is a tough time to be living out in the elements. In midwinter, many wild birds rely on the generosity of humans – this robin certainly enjoyed its free peanuts. When it thinks no one is looking, the bank vole (**BOTTOM**) also sneaks out of its hiding place to join the feast.

A FRANTIC TIME IN THE FOG

DATE:	2 January 2011	WIND DIRECTION:	Westerly
PLACE:	Robert's Farm	RIFLE:	Sauer 202
TIME:	19:30	CALIBRE:	.22-250
SUNSET:	16:22	AMMO:	55gr PPU SP
STATE OF MOON:	Morning crescent, not visible	RANGE:	All around 100yd
		CALL TRACK:	Vixen mating call
WEATHER:	Dry, cold, very foggy	OPTICS:	D480 GenIII NV riflescope

The New Year had just started, and as I was keen to keep the owner of a recently acquired permission happy, I headed out to check their place over. I'd been given the introduction by Rob, a mate who lives a few houses up the road from me. He was doing some electrical work for Robert, the farmer there. I'd been told by him that there were a few foxes about, and that one of them had an unusually dark coloration. The property in question was only a couple of miles away, and as the weather on the way over didn't seem too bad, I was hopeful of a good session. When I got there, however, I could see that the fog was settling in, and immediately realised that I wouldn't have long before I'd have to jack it in and go home. As there was no time to head out onto the main part of the farm, I simply chose the nearest pony paddock and positioned the caller about 50yd

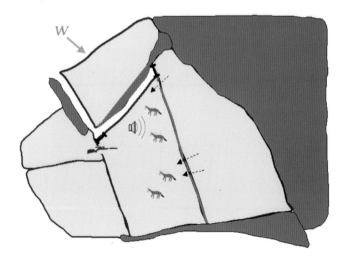

out. By placing myself to one side of the gate, I would not only have the benefit of a dark background, but it would also mean the breeze would be blowing across from my left towards a break in the hedge on the far side. Beyond this is a field which borders some extensive mixed conifer and broadleaf woodland.

Once I was in under the tallest section of the nearby hedge, I set my rifle up on the sticks and checked the focus on the NV riflescope. The fog wasn't helping me see with it, but there was more than enough visibility to shoot anything that came into the field. I decided to start with the vixen on heat call, and had barely got it going when I was amazed to see a set of eyes appear at the gap in the hedge. It can't have taken more than about five seconds to appear! The fox proceeded to run in a sweeping arc towards the caller, circling around so that it could approach the 'vixen' from downwind. When it got to about 20yd from the sound, it paused briefly, and in that instant it took a .22-250 softpoint in the chest.

A few seconds after I'd checked he was down, another fox came through the same gap in the hedge taking almost exactly the same path towards the caller. Again, he was smacked down courtesy of a Prvi Partizan round. I switched back to the spotter, only to see another fox running in. It was a bit more cautious, and came a bit further around on the wind – presumably, this was because it could smell the other two foxes that I'd just shot. When it got to about 80yd from the caller it paused to sniff the air again. At that point I dropped it.

Having taken three shots the magazine was empty, so I fitted the spare and decided that I'd better reload the first one just in case I needed more rounds than expected. I therefore set the caller to 'mute', but just as I was about to get the ammo wallet out I thought I'd better have a quick scan around. As I raised the monocular to my eye, I saw there was yet another fox coming in. I immediately moved back to the riflescope and got myself ready. It ran almost right up to the caller, even though it'd been off for about a minute, but as it got close, like the others, it paused to see what was going on and in that fleeting moment I shot it.

Barely a minute later the fog came in so thickly that I had a hell of a job finding all four carcasses. It's amazing just how much a pile of horse poo can look like a dead fox through the NV! Anyway, the cautious one turned out to be a vixen, with the other three being dogs. The smallest was about 14lb, and the biggest just shy of 20lb. Interestingly, although one of them had black belly fur, none fitted the description of the unusually dark individual. I'd have liked to stay a bit longer to see if I could find it, but as the fog was so thick I had no choice but to return home. Luckily the drive home went without any mishaps, and when I spoke to the farmer the next morning he was delighted with my efforts.

These four foxes all came to the vixen mating call within a few hectic minutes; three were dogs, the other a vixen. By the time this photo was taken, the fog had come right down.

DARK FOX

DATE:	7 January 2011	**WIND DIRECTION:**	Westerly
PLACE:	Robert's Farm	**RIFLE:**	Sauer 202
TIME:	20:30	**CALIBRE:**	.22-250
SUNSET:	16:27	**AMMO:**	55gr Win SP
STATE OF MOON:	Evening crescent, not visible	**RANGE:**	Around 100yd
		CALL TRACK:	None
WEATHER:	Dry, cold, cloudy	**OPTICS:**	D480 GenIII NV riflescope

My first visit to Robert's farm had been on Christmas Eve, following an invitation from him the day before. On my introductory walk around the place, Robert told me that both he and his wife had seen a fox several times that appeared unusually dark. I expected it to have been amongst the four I'd shot in the fog in the previous account, but although one did have a dark belly, the other three had the typical reddy-brown coats and white throats/underbellies that you would expect of a fox.

I decided that it'd be worth going back over for another try. When I phoned beforehand, Robert said that he could hear a fox calling in the woods below his house. This whetted my anticipation, and I was keen to get on site ASAP. Before I left, I checked the wind direction on the Met Office's website, and realised that the best way to approach the farm would be from the lane which runs down the far side, so that is where I headed. I backed my Disco into the chosen gateway, taking care to avoid the deep ditch on either side. Once kitted up, I did my best to make a covert approach towards the woods, but with the field so wet that it made a good simulation of the Somme, every footstep resulted in a loud sploshing/squelching sound. My progress was, therefore, painfully slow.

I eventually reached the hedgeline above the woods, and set the caller out with the wind going from my left to my right. I got the sticks in position with the rifle on top and my feet in a suitable

BELOW: A daylight view of the location. I was just setting up under the trees by the far gate when I saw the fox coming from the right, straight towards me.

RIGHT: The camera's flash was deceiving. The fox was actually much darker than it appears in this photo. It was also large – my Sauer is just under four feet long, and it was easily the same length.

shooting stance. I then rechecked the field with my NV monocular, worked out the likeliest fox approach routes, and set the vixen on heat track going. I was half-expecting another rapid response (the last time I was there a fox had come in within about five seconds), and so I was on tenterhooks for the first minute or two. After five minutes nothing had appeared, so I switched to 'vixen mating call', as this can sometimes bring a wary fox into view when the other track fails, but some 10 minutes later I'd still seen nothing.

I decided to move on, so packed the caller up and started walking towards the woods. As I did so, a fox started calling loudly from deep within the trees. I could see a couple of nervous bunnies and two or three woodcock take off into the safety of the night but there was no sign of the fox, which I could hear was moving around quite quickly. I chose a new ambush point and tried the caller again, but with no luck. At one point, I heard what sounded like someone blowing a police whistle but this gradually morphed into a shrieking fox call: very strange, especially as it was within 100yd of me!

The originator of the sound was again moving quickly, and appeared to be going away from me, so I moved to another calling spot. This appeared to be ideal, with a tall hedge behind me and the wind crossing from my right to my left. The field in front was wide open, with very little dead ground, so I knew I'd have good visibility.

I counted out 50 paces, and put the caller in a clump of grass, then had a quick scan around with

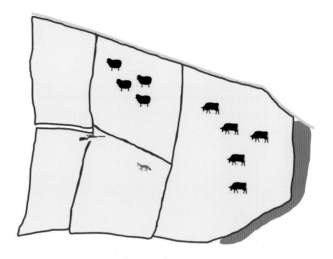

TIPS & TRICKS

If you're about to set up a calling session, don't just walk up to the location, there may already be a fox nearby. It's a good idea to creep up and have a good look around first.

the NV. The only animal I could see was a small bunny about 150yd away, so I quietly made my way back. As the previous owners bred horses, all the fields have sturdy wooden fences about three feet in from the hedges. I negotiated the one by my chosen shooting point, and then had another quick look with the NV. Much to my surprise, there was a fox coming straight towards me, about 60yd out! Thanks to my laser illuminator, its eyes were glowing like they were on fire. I didn't have time to set the sticks up, so I rested the rifle on the fence and when the reticle was over its chest I gently squeezed a round off. There was a convincing 'whop', and it fell on the spot.

I checked around to make sure there were no other foxes about, then walked over to look at my fallen quarry. On examination, I was pleased to find that I'd dropped the dark fox that I'd been told about. It was black from its chin all the way along its throat and underbelly to the end of its tail, and had a thin smattering of black hairs covering the rest of its coat. At 17.5lb it wasn't the largest fox I've shot by a very long way, but its highly unusual coloration and lack of shot damage made this an ideal candidate for taxidermy. As I write this, it's lying in my bait freezer as I wait for the taxidermist to tell me that he's got a free slot. It's been in there nearly two years now, so I'm hoping that it'll be done soon.

A GAME FOR TWO

DATE:	17 January 2011	**WIND DIRECTION:**	North-easterly
PLACE:	Aubrey's Farm	**RIFLES:**	2 x Sauer 202
TIME:	18:30	**CALIBRE:**	.22-250 and .308
SUNSET:	16:42	**AMMO:**	55gr Win BT
STATE OF MOON:	Waxing gibbous	**RANGE:**	Around 150yd
WEATHER:	Dry, cold with full cloud cover	**CALL TRACK:**	Grey squirrel distress
		OPTICS:	D480 GenIII NV riflescope

Late one winter's afternoon I set out on one of my combined deer/fox stalking sessions on the edge of Exmoor. After walking a mile or so from the farm, I settled myself into a Devon bank and began surveying the area. I soon spotted a herd of around 10 red deer but they were about ¾ mile away, on land that I don't have access to. Since they showed no signs of moving on, I realised they'd have to wait for another day. I therefore decided to sit back and enjoy the wildlife around me instead. I'd recently given the farmer an owl nesting box, so I was delighted to see a beautiful barn owl swoop over the hedge and down across the thick tufts of moorland grass. It didn't stay long, but about quarter of an hour later, a sudden flash of white announced its return. It started out by fluttering at a slow walking pace along the side of the moor, at maybe 10–15ft off the ground. Every now and then it would go back and double-check a particular tussock. At one point it swooped up in the air, did a sort of owl equivalent of a handstand, and dived back down into the grass. It missed whatever it was after though, and took off again. Almost immediately, it plunged back into the grass and, having caught something, fanned its wings around itself and began eating its hapless victim. Within a couple of minutes, however, two carrion crows started mobbing it. It managed to avoid them for long enough to finish its meal, whereupon it took off and began hunting again.

The crows weren't done though, and soon started cawing like mad and trying to dive-bomb the owl. I was delighted to see that the little chap was made of plucky stuff. He clearly wasn't worried that he was outnumbered four to one, as the next time they

attacked he suddenly rocketed up like an Exocet missile, making a very convincing attempt at trying to take one of his tormentors down. The would-be bullies realised they were pushing their luck, and cleared off before things got painful.

As the light had nearly gone, it was time for me to get going too, so I stood up and looked into the field behind. Just as I did so, a fox came running along the hedge below me – literally about five feet away. Unfortunately a blackthorn branch chose that moment to scratch loudly across my jacket, and within a millisecond the fox had run off. Now this really frustrated me as I'd been smelling a strong vulpine scent around the old barn, and knew that if the owl was to have any chance of successfully raising a brood, this was a predator I had to remove. As I was now upwind of where it had disappeared, I realised that I'd be wasting my time trying to go after it, so I made my way back to the yard, checking around every so often with the hand-held NV monocular. Apart from some woodcock, however, I didn't see anything but sheep. Once there, I retrieved my 'proper' NV rifle from the firearms cabinet in my truck, and set off back to where I'd been. While the NV add-on attached to the stalking rifle is good, its performance is nowhere near that of a dedicated NV rig. At the end of the farm track I tried the FOXPRO with a vixen call, but nothing seemed interested, so I moved on towards the old barn.

Once there, I set the caller out again, but to my frustration there was no response. I then tried a screaming rat call, and eventually spotted a pair of eyes glowing brightly a couple of hundred yards away out on the moor. It was a fox and due to its position, almost certainly the one I was after. I then tried a string of different distress calls, none of which

> **TIPS & TRICKS**
> If you accidentally spook a fox and it runs off it may well end up on a rival's patch. If that's the case, it will want to get back to the safety of its home territory as soon as possible. If you can work out where this is and cover any likely access routes, you may well get a result.

seemed to interest it. All of a sudden it disappeared from view, and a few seconds later a flash of eyes told me it had run in and was now just over the hedge. But that was it for about 10 minutes – not a sign of activity. Then, just as I was starting to think it'd gone, it jumped out of the bushes. Instead of heading towards the caller, it turned and ran up the hedgeline towards the top of the hill. This was clearly an experienced fox, as it was obviously going around on the wind to check the scent before approaching. I knew that would ruin it for me, as this would take it downwind of my position. Sure enough, the moment it winded me, it was gone...

I was not going to give up there, though. I knew that if the fox was going to return to its home ground, it had to loop around and back down the hill again. I therefore decided to play it at its own game, and walked some way off to the other side of where I expected it to travel. That way I'd be downwind of it at all times. I checked with the monocular every few paces, and two fields further on, I spotted it trotting out of a hedge. It was a fair way out and, seemingly confident of its safety, was heading back to its home territory. Fortunately, it was still within range of a careful shot, so I set the rifle up on the sticks and waited to see if it would pause for anything. Sure enough, it suddenly turned and went back to sniff at something it had just passed. A barely perceptible movement from my trigger finger launched a soft-point round, and a loud 'pop' coincided with it dropping on the spot. It turned out to be an old dog fox, with the top left and lower right canines missing. The rest of its teeth were in a terrible state, so it had been going for a good few years. It was definitely a candidate lamb-killer, if there ever was one.

THREE SHOOTS IN A DAY

DATE:	24 January 2011	**WIND DIRECTION:**	North-westerly
PLACE:	Aubrey's Farm	**RIFLE:**	Sauer 202
TIME:	19:00	**CALIBRE:**	.22-250
SUNSET:	16:53	**AMMO:**	55gr Win SP
STATE OF MOON:	Waning gibbous	**RANGE:**	120yd
WEATHER:	Dry and cold with full cloud cover	**CALL TRACK:**	None
		OPTICS:	D480 GenIII NV riflescope

At two minutes past nine this morning, the phone in my home office went, ruining my attempt at a slow start to the day. It was my mate asking if I wanted to go driven pheasant shooting in half an hour... Now, it's not really my type of thing, but I like him and a couple of the others who were going, so I agreed on the basis that he'd have me home in time to go deer stalking at 3:00pm. Fortunately, most of my business is done via email and can therefore be dealt with when it suits me.

As it's only about 15 miles away, we were soon on site. We did a number of drives and shot some birds, and I was duly returned home about a minute before I was due to leave the house to go stalking. I swapped the shottie for my brace of Sauers (.22-250 NV rig and .308 stalking rifle) and set off. Luckily, I got there a couple of minutes before my mate so I was able to get everything organised to my satisfaction before he pulled up.

As we set off, there was still about an hour and a half's worth of light left. The sky was clear, and there was a chill wind blowing from the north. Before long, I decided to put a pair of Combat 95 leather gloves over my thin shooting items in order to ensure that my fingers would still be warm enough to move, should the opportunity arise to shoot something.

Once at the top of the hill that overlooks the valley where we stalk, we closely scanned the landscape through our binos. We quickly spotted a group of five red deer: a large stag, three pricket stags, and a hind. They were, however, about a mile away, several fields into someone else's land. There wasn't anything immediately obvious on our shoot, but we didn't let that put us off, wishing each other good luck before splitting off to our chosen shooting areas.

When I arrived at my spot, I settled in for a long wait. On my last visit I'd been entertained by a barn owl, but sadly it didn't show itself. The crows were still there, and at one point they dived down and chased an unidentified bird of prey from their patch.

The deer we had seen earlier had moved on across the river, and every now and then one of them could be seen through the trees. I scanned every millimetre of the ground in front of me, and before long found four hinds grazing in one of the few fields where the grass was still green. They were also the best part of a mile away though, so were only of passing interest. Gradually the light faded away, and I decided to have a brief wander about to see if any deer were to be found. Within about a minute of doing so, however, a contractor drove a tractor and muck-spreader into one of the fields on the other side of the valley. The northern side of the valley: that is, directly upwind of me... Within a couple of minutes, the air was thick with smell of rancid slurry. I realised that with all the mechanical and olfactory disturbance, any further hope of finding deer was futile so I gave up and set off to hike back over the hill back to the farm. My attempt to hold my breath for the quarter of an hour it took was hampered somewhat by the steep incline, and before long I could actually taste the manure.

When I got back to the farmyard, I was able to catch my breath again. Both the farmer and his son said that they had smelt fox scent nearby, so I packed my stalking gear away and set out again armed with my NV set-up. As they were still feeding the sheep and cattle, the yard was lit up like a landing strip, so I chose a route around the far side of the farm. Some bait had been left out in the nearest field, so I planned things to ensure that on my return I'd be approaching it from downwind.

> ### TIPS & TRICKS
>
> If you spot foxes in the act of mating, they will – somewhat understandably – be a little preoccupied. If you decide to take a shot, be ready to reload quickly, because if you're fast enough, you may well get both of them.

The first field I went through was badly lit up by adjacent houses, so I quickly made my way over the brow of the hill to get the benefit of the truly dark night. Although the moon was still quite full, it wasn't due to rise for several hours. I tried the rat distress call for a few minutes, but nothing seemed interested, so I carried on through another couple of fields. All was quiet though, at least until I spotted eyes glowing in the reflection from the laser. They were just above some dead ground on the other side of the field. A quick readjustment of the NV monocular's focus confirmed that I had a fox for company.

I moved forward a few yards and set the sticks out then settled the rifle on top. Flicking the dedicated NV on, I quickly got things adjusted. I then realised that the strange shape I was looking at was a double-decker fox. Yes, I'd caught a pair in the act of mating! I lined up on the lower one and squeezed off a shot. There was a loud 'pop' and it fell over. The other one made a panicked dash before stopping to try and work out what had happened. As it did so, a loud smack in the chest ended its deliberations.

I performed my usual inspections and set off to finish my circuit. Nothing else showed, so I called in on the farmer to give him the good news. He was delighted with my efforts, which always gives me a boost. Believe me, after 11 hours of more of less continuous shooting, I needed one!

This dog fox was somewhat preoccupied as I crept up on him and his partner. All's fair in love and war!

A FOXY TALE OF LAMBS' TAILS

DATE:	24 January 2012	**RIFLE:**	Sauer 202
PLACE:	Roy's Farm	**CALIBRE:**	.22-250
TIME:	20:30	**AMMO:**	55gr Sierra BlitzKing SP
SUNSET:	16:53	**RANGE:**	130yd
STATE OF MOON:	Evening crescent, but set	**CALL TRACK:**	BestFoxCall mouth
WEATHER:	Dry and cold		caller
WIND DIRECTION:	Westerly	**OPTICS:**	D480 GenIII NV riflescope

One evening, just as I arrived home from a day's pheasant shooting with a mate, I spotted two blokes getting out of a pick-up truck. It was my neighbour together with his brother-in-law, a local farmer. The moment he saw me, he called out 'Ah, I wus gonna come and zee you.' After a brief chat, it transpired that his newly-born lambs were being attacked again. Every year it happens, and every year he always blames it on badgers. Until last winter that is, when I spent endless hours up there trying to find the culprits. All the time I was on his land, however, the ground was frozen solid. The winter of 2011–2012 saw several weeks of bitter temperatures, and there was not a badger to be seen. I reminded him of this, and said that I was surprised to hear of another attack, as I'd been up there the night before checking the lambs carefully to make sure they were alright.

I was seriously hacked-off to hear the bad news about the lambs. Each of the little things has a compressive ring fitted to the base of its tail. This constricts the blood supply and eventually causes it to wither and drop off. It's a humane way of tail-docking. The trouble is, however, that if a predator rips the tail off before it's ready to go, the resulting wound gets infected very quickly, and the poor creature gets what is known as 'joint-ill'. This is not only very painful, but is there for life. In spite of what townies think, most farmers are extremely conscientious about their livestock, and get very upset to see any of their animals suffer. This is particularly true for anything they've raised and possibly hand-delivered themselves.

I couldn't understand it, as I'd been hammering the foxes on the farm all year in order to make sure this didn't happen again. I'd been scanning the fields for weeks without seeing any sign whatsoever of Charlie. You can normally tell how many foxes there are in an area at this time of year simply by listening for them after dark. Their mating calls carry for miles, and so it's relatively easy to know that they're there. And yet I hadn't heard any calls anywhere close.

I told the farmer that I'd get on the case. The problem was that I was dead on my feet. Not only had we been walking around all day, but the combination of cold winds and getting soaked to the skin had really taken it out of us. No matter how upset I was, it'd have to wait for another night. I then spent the next couple of hours sorting out the day's business emails and after that retired to the sitting room to watch some telly with my Good Lady. As I walked into the room, however, she glowered up at me and said 'I do hope you're not coming in here.' She was watching some dreadful wedding program, and knew that if I saw any of it I'd only start ranting about what a feckless bunch of prats they were. She clearly knows me rather well... I can take a hint though, and knew that in spite of my tiredness, I'd be better off heading out to see if I could find what was attacking the lambs.

The first thing I needed to do was find some dry hunting kit as the stuff I'd been wearing earlier was still soaked through. I have loads of it, but in no sort of order. The first three sets of DPM trousers turned out to be ones that I'd bought for my stepson when he was about 14. The fourth set were, however, the right size, so on they went. A dig in the cupboard found me a new set of camo gloves, albeit super-lightweight summer ones made from thin netting

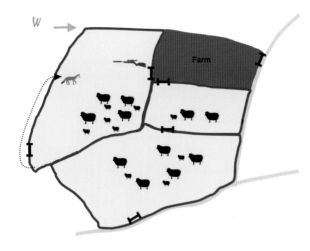

around. Once again, however, there were no foxes to be seen anywhere. Satisfied that I had no option but to walk up the lane and into the field that overlooked the sheep, I slung the rifle over my shoulders, grabbed my sticks and locked the truck.

One of the things I hate most about hunting in the dark is closed gates. It's amazing just how much they can vary. Some farmers make sure that every gate on their property is good and solid. Others think that a delicate tracery of rust held in place by a couple of pieces of baler twine will suffice. While the former present few problems, the latter can be a serious risk to life and limb. The moment one foot touches a rail, the structure either tries to fall over or gives way and collapses. If you're lucky, any semblance of covert movement is lost. If things are not going your way though, you could easily end up with a broken leg or a smashed rifle. So I was not amused to find that the gate before me was shut. Fortunately, I knew that it was a heavily built one in good condition, and that it wouldn't clang when I scaled it.

Things got worse as I climbed down though. The field, which is normally nice and firm underfoot, was so sodden that every step of the way I sank. It's easily the worst I've experienced on that property, and I really feel for any farmers who have to try and work through it. As if that wasn't bad enough, I then found that the light outside his garage was illuminating the rest of the field. There was no way that I could make it to the far side without being seen – and with all the sploshing around, being heard. Still, I wasn't there for my own pleasure: I had lambs to protect. In the end I made it to the far gate – this led into the area I was most interested in – but that bloody light was now right behind me, exposing me to anything that looked in my direction.

The one thing in my favour was that the wind was now right in my face. Well, I say that it was in my favour: it should have been, but it was carrying a strong mizzle. This is the unpleasant combination of mist and drizzle that soaks everything in minutes – except NV illuminators, of course, which it swamps in seconds. As I leant on the gate, I did my best to scan the field, but every time I cleaned the laser, it was covered again in less than five seconds. I constantly fumbled through my pockets trying to find fresh cotton buds to stay ahead of the game.

material. Still, they'd be better than nothing, and as it was getting late, I didn't want to waste any more time looking for a thicker pair. The rest of my shooting gear came together easily, and I set off. I'd decided to travel light, so left all the bulky things like the electronic caller behind..

The farm is less than a mile from my house, so I was there in moments. The first field lies across the side of a steep valley, and has been the scene of many of my hunting sessions. I killed the lights and switched the engine off as I rolled into the lay-by, which sits opposite the main gate. I was already wearing my face veil and gloves, so didn't need to faff about before climbing out. Since I was only planning on a quick look around, I left the rifle in its case. A few steps took me to the middle of the lane, and my usual vantage point. The field was full of ewes and their lambs, but no matter how hard I looked, there wasn't a fox to be seen. I stayed where I was for several minutes, scanning with both the NV monocular and the mini-thermal, but in the end realised that I wasn't going to see anything.

A quick blast up the hill saw me pulling in near the farm buildings – not too close though, the last thing I needed was the cacophony that the farmer's small pack of collies makes. The area I parked on lies to the side of the road, and is often used by the council to store huge piles of gravel. Some of this still lies at one end, and its gentle slope provides a useful method of getting high enough to look over the hedge. A quick scramble saw me in position to have a good scan

I'd already checked the ewes and their lambs several times with the NV mono when I spotted an unidentified light source at the top of a hedge about 250yd away. It was only just below the street lamps from the village, so at first I wondered if it was someone's porch light. But the next time I saw it I put my hand over the laser and it disappeared. When I removed my hand, it returned. I could now be reasonably sure that it was an eye reflecting back at me – but what did it belong to? Was it simply an adventurous sheep that had climbed the hedge? The conditions were so bad that everything was screaming at me to call it a night and head back to the warmth of the house. But I couldn't leave the lambs. I had to press on.

Halfway across the field there was a telegraph pole. I figured that I might be able to gain enough shelter from it to use the NV mono without having to keep drying the laser off, so I made my way over to it. The going was still dreadful: thick gloopy mud that slowed any progress to a crawl. I finally got to the pole and steadied myself against it while I had another look with the NV, but that turned out to be a complete waste of time as the brightest lights in the village were directly in line with where the eye was last seen. I had a look around and decided that I had little choice but to loop around towards the far hedge by way of the ground to my right which was, at least, not lit up by that dratted garage light.

Every time I moved, some of the lambs bleated in alarm, and many of the ewes were trotting to and fro unsure as to whether I presented any kind of a threat. When I'd made it about halfway to the hedge, which was now only about 50yd from me, I stopped for another look. The eye was still there, but so far I'd only seen a single reflection. Whatever it was seemed to be sheltering out of the wind, and sticking its head up every now and then to see where the lambs were. It appeared to be checking if any of the mothers had left their babies unattended. I now needed to prove whether it was a predator or not, so I pulled the BestFoxCall mouth caller from my pocket and placed it between my teeth.

A quick squeal from it caused all the sheep to stampede across to the far side of the field. This caused the owner of the eye to sit up and look around. Bingo! I now had two eyes looking straight at me and as they were situated on the front of its face, it was clearly a predator, and not a miscreant lamb. Whatever they belonged to was still a long way off though, so I needed to get it closer – the area between us was too brightly lit by that garage light for me to risk walking towards it. I tried another more sustained series of squeaks, but there was no sign of the creature in question.

By now both the laser illuminator and the mono were awash, so I switched over to using the mini-thermal. Looking through it can be a bit disheartening, though. This is because I've fitted dark film over the eyepieces to reduce the amount of glare. Previously, I'd be blinded by the damned thing in no time. The end result is that unless there's an object with some kind of heat source in view, it looks as though you're watching a more or less black screen. At times like this it's very easy to get completely disoriented, and mistakenly start looking above the horizon or even down at the ground beyond your feet.

If you're going to be successful, you have to discipline yourself to keep checking back to a known reference point. Luckily for me, there was a sheep trough that was a degree or so warmer than the surrounding area, so it gave a faint glow. This was enough for me to stay on the right axis, and so I scanned back and forth along the hedgeline to see if I could pick anything up. All of a sudden, there was a huge white thing almost on top of the hedge right in front of me, some 45yd away. Everything about it shouted 'Fox!', but I needed to double-check with the dedicated NV riflescope.

I set the sticks out and slipped the rifle off my shoulder. In doing so, I pulled the covers off the front lens and the laser. What a difference: nice dry optics! And now I was looking face-on at my fox, which had made it halfway down the bank. With the crosshairs sitting steadily between its eyes, I gently squeezed the trigger. There was an immediate 'smack', as though I'd shot into a rock. 'Blimey!', I thought to myself (or words to that effect), 'That hit something hard.' A quick check with the thermal showed the fox lying where it had been hit. With adrenaline coursing through my body, I slung the rifle back over my shoulder and sploshed over to inspect what turned out to be a small vixen. It had taken the round to the right of its skull, and some of this, together with most of its shoulder and parts of its chest had been replaced by a massive hole. Full marks to the 55gr Sierra BlitzKing: this fox didn't know what had hit it, which is how I like things to go.

Since I wanted to check its stomach contents as well as show it to the farmer, I needed to carry it back with me. So I pulled the glove off my right hand – which by now felt as though it had been in a freezer for a couple of hours – and swapped it for a disposable vinyl version. The trudge to the farmhouse was much easier than it had been on the way over, as I no longer needed to remain covert. This meant that I could also use the torch to see where I was going, which helped me navigate around all the pieces of discarded equipment that always seem to gather around farmyards. A quick knock on the door brought the farmer out – as well as his gaggle of barking dogs – or 'dugs' as they're known locally. Fortunately, a fierce shout from him shut them up instantly, and I was able to recount my experiences. To say that he was pleased would be an understatement, not only because of the result, but because I'd

TIPS & TRICKS
Remote control electronic callers can be a real boon to foxers, both by day and by night, but there isn't always time to get them in position. It is a good idea to keep a small hand-held mouth caller in a handy pocket.

responded to him so quickly and in such appalling conditions.

As I drove home I stopped at the first field for another check – but by then a thick mist had arisen in the depths of the valley – and I couldn't see a thing. Luckily, the thermal doesn't care about such things, and I was able to satisfy myself that the lambs there were all safe and well. A minute or so later I was back in the warmth of my house but not before I had slung the fox onto the roof of the log store. Today, having spent all morning dealing with VAT papers, I performed my autopsy. Whilst doing so, I also emptied the contents of its bladder into my fox urine jar for later use as a scent attractant. To be honest, I was unable to conclusively identify anything I found in its guts, although there was a pile composed of something that may well have been partly-digested lamb's tails.

This vixen had been tearing the tails off young lambs, which is not only an extremely distressing experience for the youngsters involved, but it also leaves them with lifelong medical problems.

FEBRUARY

February can be a difficult time for foxes. If the weather has been harsh, there may be precious little food available. When times are hard, foxes will live up to their reputation as superb opportunists, and will seek out all manner of unlikely food sources. I've seen them jump up into feed bins out in the fields in order to vacuum up the last crumbs left behind by the cattle. I've also seen them hunting frogs on marshland as well as raiding farm buildings for anything they can find. One old farmer I know walked into a room off his kitchen to find a fox chewing on the carcass of a dead lamb. As it was dark in there, the first he knew it was there was when it growled at him when he got too close! It turned and ran as soon as the light was switched on, but it just goes to show how brazen they can be.

Although winter can be a time of real austerity for both farmers and wildlife, 2012 was most unusual in that it was more like late spring. In Devon, the rabbits didn't even stop breeding – one farmer told me that his cat was bringing baby ones into the house throughout January and February. Consequently, the foxes had far more food around than is usual. This appears to have

Mid-Devon in early February after a brief fall of snow. Although such conditions can be harsh to operate in at night, it can be a very good time to use both distress calls and vixen mating calls to bring foxes in.

stimulated the dominant vixens to allow one or more of their subordinate females to breed. The results were seen later in the year. As normal, the first cubs showed on top in March. These would have been the progeny produced by November/December matings. Most unusually, however, we then saw a new batch of cubs produced from another series of litters in June/July.

Even though the daytime temperatures can get quite high in February, when the nights are clear they can really plummet. This often creates a thin coating of ice over the ground, and when this happens, it is nigh-on impossible to move covertly. Every step produces a sound like breaking glass. Ice can also make it very dangerous to drive, so every consideration needs to be given to the risks when venturing out, especially as few councils bother to salt country roads any more.

> ### THE FARMER'S MONTH
> Spring ploughing,
> chain harrowing and rolling.
> General farm maintenance.
> Slurry spreading.
> Feed livestock.
> Lambing.
> Calving.

February can be a good time to drive along the lanes between the fields, stopping at the gateways if the area you have to shoot over makes this possible. The lack of crops means you have a far better chance of seeing any foxes moving around than you will later in the year. Once again, however, you need to be well aware of the local conditions. You can be reasonably sure that if the ground isn't frozen, it'll be wet – and that usually equates to mud – and vast amounts of it. When that's the case, anything heavier than a quad or mule (a light agricultural vehicle) will tear the turf apart, and that won't please the farmer. One of the pleasures of the month is seeing all the woodcock and snipe about. Their eyes really stand out with the NV, and it's not all uncommon to see the same birds in the same places, night after night.

February can be a busy time for farmers, especially those who start lambing then. The actual time this happens will depend on a number of factors, including when the ewes were tupped (mated), the breed, and the farm's location – particularly its altitude. The annual average temperature falls by 1°C for every extra 100m in altitude. Lambing can require a huge amount of work. One farmer I know sees his flock produce around a thousand lambs, and by the end of this time he looks like a ghost, having had very little sleep for around two months. Anyone who thinks farming is easy should see how hard he works to keep his infant lambs alive and well.

Lambing is essentially done in two ways: in sheds, or out in the open. As a general rule of thumb, the healthiest method is out in the fields, as this minimises the risk of any disease spreading. The downside, however, is that it leaves the youngsters extremely vulnerable to attack by foxes, badgers, rooks, crows and magpies. Most farmers try to get around this by moving the ewes in close to the farm just before they give birth, but while this may provide a little more shelter and makes it easier to check them, it won't deter hungry foxes which will even climb into stalls to get a tasty meal. Watching a desperate ewe trying to revive a lamb that has been killed by a fox is heartbreaking. Consequently, many farmers will be very nervous about the welfare of their new arrivals. In some cases foxes will attack the youngsters and chew their tails off; in others, they will kill the defenceless new-borns. The ones at least risk are those whose mothers have done it all before. They know the score and will do their best to protect their offspring. New mothers, and those with more than one lamb to look after, however, are far more likely to be attacked. In some cases, foxes will work in pairs. One distracts the mother while the other goes around behind and seizes the unfortunate baby.

Even those farmers who don't start lambing for another month will still have a lot of work to do, including performing such tasks as pregnancy scanning. On some farms the cattle will begin calving – again, when it happens will depend on the type of cows, when they were served, and so on. There are also many other jobs to be done, weather permitting. These include spring ploughing, chain harrowing and rolling pastures, spreading slurry and, of course, more general farm maintenance.

If the temperatures rise above freezing for any length of time, the ground will soften, making it ideal for tracking. Here (BELOW) a set of roe deer 'slots' can be seen. But if there is much ice around (BOTTOM), it is almost impossible to move quietly.

' 'EE AIN'T GOING TO BE BEAT, I'S SURE 'O THAT'

DATE:	7 February 2011	**RIFLE:**	Sauer 202
PLACE:	Roy's Farm	**CALIBRE:**	.22-250
TIME:	19:30	**AMMO:**	55gr Win SP
SUNSET:	17:17	**RANGE:**	About 180yd and 190yd
STATE OF MOON:	Evening crescent	**CALL TRACK:**	Various fox
WEATHER:	Dry with full cloud cover		communication calls
WIND DIRECTION:	North-westerly	**OPTICS:**	D480 GenIII NV riflescope

Two foxes had been seen on a local farm where the newly born lambs were due to go out. As a result I'd spent six nights and one morning after them, but in spite of getting near them on a couple of occasions, none of my sessions had paid off. The pressure was definitely on. Several people had seen the foxes in question, and given the time of year, it was assumed that they were ones that had paired up.

The moon was coming up later in the week, so I knew I had to make the most of what could be the last dark evenings for the best part of a fortnight. I also promised myself that I wouldn't simply trudge endlessly around the farm, up hill and down dale, without having at least a reasonable idea as to where the foxes were. The problem with this is that the ground is far too wet to drive over, and only a few of the fields can be seen from the road. On pondering the matter further, I decided that I'd modify my original plan. I'd scan the farm as far as I could, but if nothing was visible, I'd continue on to some other land that lies nearby. Promising my Good Lady (who was lying on the sofa incapacitated by Woman Flu) that I wouldn't be long, I packed my gear and set off. As I drove out of the village, I thought to myself that it was a damn good job that 'not long' wasn't clearly defined in law...

As the farm is less than a mile from my house, I didn't have time to reflect any further on my domestic bliss. There was work to be done, and I pulled up at the first gateway, from where most of my recent forays had started. I killed the lights, and quietly opened the door. Much to my annoyance, one of the rear load area lamps (which had been taped over) had come out of its holder and was now illuminating the interior of my Disco. I'd already made sure that none of the others could produce any unwanted light, so, not wishing to waste any time, I simply pulled one of the wiring connectors off and the problem was solved.

Having made sure that I wasn't drawing any other kind of unwanted attention to myself, I then leant against the truck and scanned the landscape with my NV monocular. I was parked in the bottom of a small valley, with a brook babbling at my feet – this was running away at 90 degrees from the lane, with the main sheep field stretching up from there to the top of the hill. I could see lots of ewes and lambs, but no foxes. My surveying was briefly interrupted by a car driving past: as I was clad in camo gear from head to foot, I made sure that I was out of sight until it had gone. No point in needlessly frightening the locals...

At this point the moon was hidden, so it wasn't a problem but I could see that the cloud cover was sporadic, and that there would be periods of time when it would be fully exposed. Even though there was only a sliver showing – what is known as a waxing crescent moon – I knew that it wouldn't take much for my presence to be revealed to a wary fox. Care would be needed.

After checking out all the other fields, hedges and rough ground, I moved on to the next gateway. Again, there was nothing to be seen. My next stop saw me looking out at the fields behind the farm itself and within moments, I caught sight of a dark shape snuffling in the paddock. As it was about 400yd away, I couldn't be sure what it was at first, but from its movements I did know that it was either a fox or a badger. Then it raised its head, and I got strong eye-shine. Game on: it was a fox!

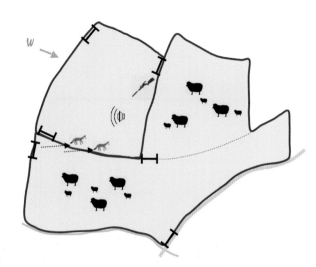

As I couldn't leave the truck where it was, I drove on to a lay-by next to the farmer's house and parked up. Like so many others in the area, he has a pack of mental sheepdogs that seem to be pathologically addicted to barking at the slightest excuse. And they are not into just normal, everyday style barking – no, this is a shrill, frantic, 'Oh my God, the world is ending' kind of barking. Sure enough, as soon as I pulled up, they erupted into a furious bout of aural violence. I find it very stressful, as I hate causing anyone any kind of disturbance. Still, I was away in moments, and before long they quietened down.

I made my way back to the gate, and had another look. The fox was still there, and fortunately appeared totally unconcerned by the row from the dogs. I had two fields to cross to get to it, and as both had metal gates that I'd not gone over before, I knew I'd have to take care that they weren't noisy ones. The wind was very slight, and blowing from the west meaning it would be in my face. While that was ideal, the farmyard was lit up like a landing strip, and it was quite clear that I would have my work cut out to get anywhere near the fox without being seen by it. Still, nothing ventured, nothing gained...

The sheep in the first field were a bit worried by my sudden appearance, but luckily stood their ground without charging about all over the place. There was a huge amount of mud – in places I was struggling to avoid my feet making loud sucking noises as I pulled them free – but I made it to the first gate without any significant dramas. I was pleased to find it had been properly hung, with nice solid mountings.

As an aside, it never ceases to amaze me just how many people simply don't know how to climb a gate. If you do so at the latch end, all your weight is magnified by the leverage effect, and over time it can do enormous damage to the hinges. So don't do it! It's always best to climb as close to the pivots as you can. If it's dark and you don't know the gate in question, it is extremely important that you suss it

out before attempting to climb it. Farmers have all manner of pressures on them, and sometimes for reasons of haste, they will hang a gate with baler twine. Or they will leave one in place that should have been replaced in the Napoleonic era. Consequently, crossing gates in the dark can be very dangerous, especially if your feet are covered in wet mud. So do take care!

By the time I was over and back on firm ground, I was in the full light from the yard. There was nothing I could do about it, and there was no other approach route, so I carried on. Before I reached the next gate, however, the fox started to move down the field and it wasn't long before it came level with me. I spotted its eyes through the hedge, and realised that I had next to no chance of getting any further without being sussed. Sure enough, when I got to the gate it was nowhere to be seen. Damn! How was I ever going to get onto these blasted creatures?

I made a thorough check of the area before crossing the paddock and approaching the gate into the first of the big fields. This had a large flock of ewes and lambs in it. I cautiously stuck to the shadows under the hedges, and scanned the landscape as I moved forwards. I soon picked up eye-shine but this was too small to be what I was after. When I got closer, I confirmed that I was looking at three woodcock – every time I'd been there over the previous two or three weeks, they'd been in that part of the field. These beautiful birds are night-time feeders, using their long beaks to seek out and devour worms and grubs from the soft ground. I go out of my way to avoid disturbing them – life is hard enough at this time of year for these long-travelled creatures – so I skirted around and carefully picked my way towards the next gate. Looking back behind me I was pleased to see that they hadn't moved.

The field in front of me was where I'd nearly trodden on a fox the last time I was there, so I made a very thorough scan of the area before approaching it. Apart from lots more ewes and lambs, there was nothing visible, so I climbed over and had another look. The land dives away as it falls to the river below. In so doing, it undulates with great rolls. This provides lots of dead ground for foxes to move about in unseen and gives me no end of hassle, as every bit has to be checked and double-checked. All the while, I'm being given the evil eye by protective sheep, wary in case I'm bringing trouble to their precious babies.

After a few minutes, I selected a route that would cause minimum disturbance to the flock and wended my way to the hedge that runs down the left side of the field. This has two gates in it: one into a field that borders the river, the other into a comparatively flat field. After scanning them both, I chose the latter. I could see that there was a small bird – probably a snipe – about 50yd out, but nothing else. By now I was well away from the farmyard lights, however, the cloud cover had gone, and the moon was illuminating the landscape. This meant that I had to take care to stick to the shadows. As I'd not seen any further sign of the foxes, my plan was to set the caller out to see if I could lure them in.

> **TIPS & TRICKS**
> If one or more foxes are causing problems, don't give up. Try everything you can think of: vary the time you visit, use bait, approach from different directions, and try different calls. Remember: the fox has to get lucky every time – you only have to be lucky once!

Since I had to take the wind direction into account, I chose the far hedge as my ambush point, and duly counted out 50 paces before placing the caller in the long grass. I then retreated to cover and got my sticks up, with the rifle on top. I could see that the moon would shortly be covered by clouds again, so I took the opportunity to check everything over. I used a cotton bud to clean the laser on the riflescope, and a spectacle cloth to wipe the scope lenses, then got everything focused to my satisfaction.

Within seconds of the clouds reaching the moon, everything went nice and dark. At this point, I started the caller on screaming bunny. I chose this track as I'd not used it on that farm for at least a year. After about five minutes with no luck, I paused it, and tried vixen on heat as I could hear another fox calling across the valley (where I also have permission). This didn't bring anything either, so I decided to try getting a bit of a fox conversation going, and played a few seconds of each of several different calls – squalls, yells, etc. In between, I had a good scan around, but saw nothing. Since the foxes had been attacking lambs, I decided to try a helpless kid goat call, figuring this might tempt them in as it sounds very similar.

A few seconds later, I spotted a bright eye and a small body right down by the far hedge – about 200yd away, and about 50ft lower than me. This was either a hare or a fox partly obscured by a dip in the ground. I gave the area some intense scrutiny, and realised very quickly that this was a Charlie. My identification was further confirmed when a second fox jumped out of the hedge/bank to join it. They

then had a bit of a squabble – making similar sounds to the ones I'd just played. They were clearly interested in my call, but were in no real hurry to approach it. To make matters more complicated, the moon had started to show again.

I carefully swapped from the monocular to the riflescope, and got my feet into a nice stable position. I set my arms where they'd give the sticks the best support, and held the reticle over the nearer of the two foxes until it stopped moving around. When I was satisfied that I'd got the best possible point of aim, I touched off a shot. There was a long 'seeeeiiioou' as the bullet flew through the air, followed by a loud 'dooopsh', along the lines of the noise a golf ball would make if it was dropped into a well.

At this, the other fox jumped up onto the top of the bank, ran a few feet, and then turned to look back at me. Normally, it would not have been possible to take the shot, but this was one of the few places on the farm where there is another hill running close-by on the opposite side. Around here these mini-valleys are called 'goyles'. I could see that the back stop was clear, and so got the reticle in place and launched another round. Once again, I heard the bullet singing its way to its target, and there was an identical thump when it struck home. There was no doubting that these were both perfect hits, so I slung my rifle over my shoulder, and counted out the distances involved. The nearer one was at 180 paces, with the other at 190. Both were hit smack in the heart, and had literally fallen on the spot. I was amazed to see that they were both dog foxes. I, and everyone else who'd seen them assumed that at this time of year they would be a mating pair. From their coloration and markings, it is probable that they were siblings.

These two foxes had been seen on the farm for several weeks – given the time of year, everyone assumed that they were a pair. When they finally succumbed to the rifle, it transpired that they were both male.

All in all, it was a satisfying end to what had been a frustrating couple of weeks of trying to get a couple of elusive foxes under very difficult circumstances. These included ice, fog, rain, mud, wind, the moon, floodlights from both the local sportsfield and the farmyard – not forgetting, of course, also having to do it all on what is really challenging landscape. I spoke to the very grateful farmer the next morning. He said that he had been talking about my quest to get the foxes in the pub while he was playing skittles. He'd told the others ' 'Ee ain't going to be beat, I's sure 'o that.'

THE FLYING SQUIRREL THAT BIT BACK

DATE:	11 February 2012	**RIFLE:**	Sauer 202
PLACE:	Jim's Farm	**CALIBRE:**	.22-250
TIME:	19:30	**AMMO:**	55gr Nosler BT
SUNSET:	17:24	**RANGE:**	85yd
STATE OF MOON:	Waning gibbous	**CALL TRACK:**	Flying squirrel distress
WEATHER:	Dry with full cloud cover	**OPTICS:**	D480 GenIII NV riflescope
WIND DIRECTION:	North-westerly		

One of the big farms I look after had been in the run-up to full-on lambing. There had been a few early arrivals, but the peak of activity was still a week or so away. I'd only started shooting there at the end of the previous lambing season as the result of the foxes killing a lot of the new-borns. Consequently, I'd been doing my best to stay on top of them to minimise the risks of it happening again. A few days before I'd shot two, but I knew that I still had more to deal with as I'd heard at least another two shrieking at each other down in some cover near the farm buildings. I'd tried again in the week, but the conditions had been awful, and I'd

ended up on my backside in some deep mud. I could have coped with that, but as my rifle had been soaked too I needed to go back to the truck to clean it off. On the way there the heavens opened, so I decided it'd be better if I just went home and gave it a full going over there.

A few nights later I decided to have a prolonged session at the farm, so set off in midafternoon with the truck loaded to the gunwales. Not knowing what I was going to find, I took the .17HMR in case I saw any corvids, the Sauer .308 - my stalking rifle – in case Charlie showed in daylight and, of course, my beloved Sauer .22-250 NV rig. I also packed the big

thermal imager and a crate of really stinky bait. This was composed of various roe deer bones, four bunnies and a big heap of pheasant bits: wings, heads, feet and guts. By the time I got to the farm, the truck was rather unpleasant inside.

On arriving at the yard I had various options open to me, but chose to drive down a long track to get to some relatively high ground. This would allow me to make the most of the thermal rig, which is an excellent area observation system. I set it up on its tripod and then search for my intended prey. With it I can spot a fox at huge distances, probably 800yd or more if there's nothing in the way. When I've spotted something I want to shoot, I then switch it off and set out in pursuit.

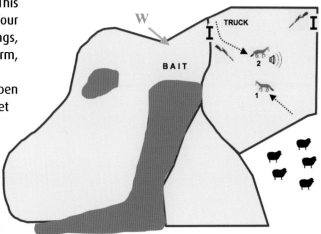

This was all very well in theory, but the stark reality was that within about five minutes of getting it all unloaded and set up, I began to freeze. Now I'm used to getting cold on my hunting forays, but this was different. My exposed position meant I was being hit by a razor-sharp wind that cut straight through several layers of thermals. I knew that I could grin and bear it for a while, but dusk was still some two hours away, and I wanted to still be fit to shoot with the NV. It was obvious that the amount of time I could spend watching the landscape was going to be severely limited, so I spent a few minutes using

the thermal rig to record some footage of the sheep, and then packed it all away again.

My next task was to set the bait out. A set of disposable gloves helped me fill a carrier bag from the crate without getting covered in any of the stinking goo. I then walked up and down the hedgelines, chucking a tasty morsel here and there until the bag was empty, whereupon I refilled it and repeated the exercise until there was none left. I'd intended to set the caller out but before I was able to do so I heard the unmistakable sound of the farmer's quad bike coming up the hill. Within

This fox tried to make off with my precious caller – it even left tooth marks on the case!

moments, he and his wife were in the next field tending to their flock, clanging and banging the feed troughs around.

About half an hour later, they finished their work and moved on: peace finally returned. At that stage, the sun was sitting just above the horizon, casting a beautiful golden glow over the landscape. Every now and then a crow landed in the field, but for some time they stayed far too far out for any chance of a shot. I had considered driving around while it was light to see if I could spot any foxes on their travels, but the ground was so sodden that there was a real risk that I'd get the truck stuck. This idea abandoned, I made the most of the time by getting stuck into a large chunk of date and banana cake that my Good Lady had recently made for me. As I chomped my way through the tasty treat I enjoyed the large number of brazil nuts that she'd included in the mix. The DAB radio was tuned to Planet Rock, and I had the latest copy of *Shooting Times* spread out on my lap. Oh well, I mused to myself, life could be worse!

Gradually, the sun sank behind the hills and the light slowly dimmed. As it did so, a glorious red band formed along the western horizon. While this was happening, I got myself ready for darkness. The .308 rounds came out of both magazines (as they fit both rifles) and were replaced with ballistic tipped .22-250 Blitzkings. I slipped on the chest harness which carries my NV mono, and temporarily removed my face veil while I got my woolly hat in place. A second pair of

gloves went on, albeit after a bit of a struggle. Now I was ready for a quick scout around; in particular, I needed to check whether anything was already at the bait. A few paces saw me in the gateway which overlooked one of the stretches where I'd laid out the smelly pheasant entrails. As it wasn't really dark enough to switch the NV on, I used my mini-thermal instead. This hangs around my neck like a small pair of stalking binos. But nothing was doing and with the loss of daylight the cold really came in hard: it seemed that anything sensible was lying up in shelter.

A short wander saw me back in the original field and looking out over the next one where there were yet more expectant ewes. As a result of the cold wet air, a freezing mist was now forming in the valley below. Although this plays merry hell with the NV, fortunately, the thermal simply ignores it. Scanning around, I could see the white silhouettes formed by the sheep, most of which were stood around grazing. Down by the far hedge, though, I spotted another white shape, but this one was running in a manner most uncharacteristic of anything that wears a woolly jacket. Fox. But before I could do anything, it'd gone.

A minute or two later, I heard a dog bark in the woods. That's strange, I thought to myself, who's out there at this time of night? And then the most ungodly shrieking began: that's when I realised that it had been a fox barking, not a dog. Now I have to say that the sounds it was making were unlike those of any other fox I've ever heard – and believe me I've heard a lot – except that is, for the one I'd heard on the same farm on my abortive trip earlier in the week. Undoubtedly, it was the same animal. The calls were comprised of a more or less constant wailing, interspersed here and there with shrill yaps. The whole scene was made all the more eerie by the staggered echoes reverberating back and forth in the mist-covered goyle.

Realising that the wind direction meant that there was no possibility of me getting anywhere near it, I retraced my steps, hoping that the stinky treats I'd left out would instead bring the fox to me. I did another tour of the furthest bait before carefully making my way back towards the truck. In doing so, I had to scale a steel gate; that was when I discovered just how cold it was. Each time I placed my foot on a rung, it immediately iced up and stuck fast. The low temperatures combined with the wind chill were making this a bitter place to be. Still, better to be there than vegetating in front of a brain-sapping TV.

Some 50yd or so before I reached my vehicle, I had another quick scan with the thermal. There, some 100yd in front of me, was what looked suspiciously like a fox. In one smooth movement, I had the sticks up and my rifle in place. The NV riflescope confirmed it: there was, indeed, a Charlie making straight for me, and within moments it would be downwind of me. There was no time to waste. Luckily the safety catch on a Sauer sits just above the trigger finger, and so I was ready to fire in an instant. The fox, however, was jinking back and forth

– I think the Disco's presence was making it nervous – and I took the opportunity to adjust the focus. The moment it paused, I sent a Blitzking on its way. The crunchy 'pop' that resulted sounded like a solid skull hit, and the fox fell on the spot. When I reached the carcass, as I suspected, the round had made a real mess of the large vixen's head.

Dragging the dead fox back to the truck, I changed the batteries on the thermal – luckily they're rechargeable, since it eats them – and got ready to use the caller. I carefully assessed the wind direction, the likely approach routes of any foxes and placed the caller out at 85 paces. Since I'd used it there many times in the past, I didn't want to play any calls that the foxes could have heard before, so I trawled through the menu and picked out a series of tracks based on high-pitched squeaks of one sort or another. With my rifle up on the sticks and my feet in my preferred shooting stance, I started the caller going. A few minutes later – with no sign of any action – I switched to a different track. A couple of times I heard a strange sound to my right, on the other side of my Disco, but couldn't place it. I thought nothing more of it, and carried on working my way through the sound tracks.

About the fourth call I tried was flying squirrel distress. It had only been running for about 30 seconds when a fox ran out from the direction of my truck. This was from upwind and thus totally unexpected. I hit the instant kill switch on my NV mono (a new innovation I'd recently fitted), and slipped the safety off. Meanwhile, the fox was still running at full speed. As it reached the caller, it went into a classic leap and dive manoeuvre, its jaws closing loudly on the caller's plastic casing – as if this wasn't enough, it then tried to make off with it. This put me in a quandary – do I shoot the fox and risk blowing my treasured FOXPRO apart, or do I let it go? Luckily, the fox was even more confused than I, and it paused sideways on, clearly unsure as to just what it had captured. I wasn't going to waste the opportunity, and peremptorily shot it. It flipped over and fell. As it did so, for an instant, its eyes glowed fiercely in the light from my laser.

I wasted no time in going out to check that the caller was OK. Fortunately, it was – albeit with a couple of pronounced tooth marks! The fox was a large male. Before long, I hope to have his skull mounted on a plaque in my office. I dragged him back and draped him on the bonnet, then placed the vixen over the spare wheel, which is mounted on the rear door. With everything safely accounted for, I began my slow journey back up the track. Not only did I have gates to deal with, but the thick mud and rapidly reforming ice made the going treacherous. I figured it'd be better to take more time and arrive in one piece than rush things! As I did so, I ran back over the series of events as they happened. That's when it clicked: the sound I'd heard earlier was that of the fox crunching its way through some of the roe deer bones I'd chucked in the hedge, but because the Disco was in the way, I hadn't been able to see it!

I made it back to the yard without skidding off into the mire, and then began a round of the nursery fields, but with no foxes to be seen, I called in on the farmer, who was absolutely delighted with my results, and headed off home.

Another successful mission accomplished!

MORE DEADLY THAN THE MALE

DATE:	16 February 2012	**RIFLE:**	Sauer 202
PLACE:	Jim's Farm	**CALIBRE:**	.22-250
TIME:	19:30	**AMMO:**	55gr Nosler BT
SUNSET:	17:33	**RANGE:**	50yd
STATE OF MOON:	Morning crescent	**CALL TRACK:**	None
WEATHER:	Dry with full cloud cover	**OPTICS:**	D480 GenIII NV riflescope
WIND DIRECTION:	North-westerly		

As Kipling said, 'The female of the species is more deadly than the male.' Well, whether this is true or not, one little foray showed me that she can certainly be completely heartless. Just over a week before, I'd been asked to deal with the foxes on a large farm where they were about to start lambing. I'd gone over and not long after arriving, started scanning two long fields across a small valley with my mini-thermal imager. These run alongside some coniferous woodland, and are often used as motorways by the local wildlife. More or less immediately I saw two white shapes in the first field – they were too big to be rabbits, too small to be sheep, and from the way they were moving, more likely to be foxes than badgers. A quick switch over to the NV confirmed this. One of them had just begun heading off down the valley away from me, while the other turned and trotted left, towards the flock of sheep that I was meant to be guarding. To cut a long story short, I shot it: a big dog fox, at 265 paces off sticks.

The other fox, which I took to be his vixen, didn't show again that night, so my mission now was to find her. On the way over, I was more than a little concerned at the amount of fine mizzle. Some 20 minutes later I pulled in by the barn, but could see straight away that things were going to be very difficult indeed. A lighthouse-like halogen lamp illuminates the cattle sheds and this showed the mizzle was blowing sideways. In fact, it was so fine that I had to double-check that it wasn't smoke.

A few paces out into the first field confirmed my fears: there was so much water in the air that the thermal was struggling to see anything. A quick scan with the NV mono showed that it was suffering even more. I couldn't even see the sheep that were a mere 100yd or so away. At that point I was really glad that I'd fitted both the NV riflescope and its laser illuminator with home-made covers. These are simple constructions made from sheet foam and camo tape, and work really well at keeping any moisture off the lenses. Had the farm been closer to home, I may well have aborted the session there and then, but I wasn't going to undertake a 16-mile round trip without at least having a try.

After some careful studying with the mini-thermal, I could just make out that there were five sheep sheltering in the lee of the nearest hedge. I decided that some smaller white shapes were probably rabbits, feasting on the meadow's lush grass. Meanwhile over the lane, the herd of cattle were much more prominent in the viewer. As there was nothing fox-like to be seen though, I moved on. The first gate I had to cross is a nice substantial affair that makes no noise at all when you scale it. The second one, composed of the remains of two old gates loosely tied to each other with absolutely no support at either end, belongs to a neighbouring farmer and is an accident waiting to happen.

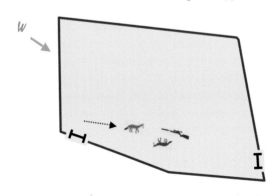

In the end, I squeezed through between two broken rails, not an easy task as I was covered in kit. My NV mono was sitting on its chest harness, and above it was the mini-thermal. To make matters worse, my pockets were stuffed with all manner of extra bits and pieces. Even though I was really careful, I couldn't avoid the gate's loose pipes banging and clattering into each other. I hate making any kind of noise when I'm out hunting, so wasn't in the best of moods by the time I was back on my feet again.

A minute or two earlier, I'd spotted something from the other side of the valley but couldn't be sure what it was, so I wanted to get close enough to make a positive ID. I soon saw that what I'd been looking at was two rabbits sitting close to each other. Nearby was a cluster of small birds – probably snipe – but not wanting to disturb them, I didn't go any closer. I was sheltered from the elements while near the hedge, but the moment I moved away I was enveloped by the horizontal mizzle. The NV mono was OK if I looked downwind, but within seconds of pointing it anywhere else, the illuminator was covered in small droplets, and the image soon disappeared under black spots. The thermal fared better, but still struggled. Anyone sensible would have called it quits, but I carried on all the same. I could hear two foxes squabbling somewhere far off, so I tried the caller for a while. There was no response so I moved on again.

As there didn't appear to be anything about, I went to see if I could find the remains of the fox I'd shot the week before. Even though I'd given him precise details of where I'd put the carcass, the farmer hadn't found it. It proved to be exactly where I'd left it – at least some of it was. Pretty well everything edible had been eaten and quite obviously some of it had been taken by a large carnivore, as most of the ribs were broken away. The most likely candidates for this were badgers or foxes. There were also indications that birds – probably corvids or buzzards – had also been feeding from it as the eyes had been pecked out. At least the fox had been dead when this had happened, unlike the defenceless young lambs that commonly suffer the same fate.

Before heading back to the farm, I thought I'd have a check nothing had snuck up on me. The thermal takes a few seconds to boot up, and as the picture swam into view, I found I was looking straight at a fox less than 50yd away. Luckily, it was upwind, but there was no time to waste as it was running back and forth sniffing the ground, presumably trying to locate the carcass.

I had the sticks up and the rifle in place in an instant, but couldn't switch the scope on straight away as the lens covers were still in place. Somehow, I slid these off and got them into a pocket without making any noise. I pointed the rifle away from my target before switching the scope and laser on so that the sudden appearance of the IR wouldn't spook it. As soon as I was ready, I swivelled the rifle around until I found my quarry. It obviously knew I was there, but was clearly totally unaware that I was any kind of a threat as it was skirting around looking at me sideways. I quickly placed the reticle high on its shoulder – at that range you have to allow for the fact that the scope sits nearly four inches above the barrel – and squeezed the trigger. There was a resounding 'whop', and it collapsed in a heap without a twitch. Counting my steps, I found that the body was a mere 40yd out, and was that of a large and very pregnant vixen. I can only presume that it was her that had been feeding off what was probably her late partner's carcass. I guess that's the vulpine equivalent of a divorce settlement. I certainly know a few women who one suspects wouldn't bat an eyelid at doing the same, given the opportunity!

TIPS & TRICKS

You simply cannot beat patience when it comes to foxing. People who rush about will never be able to compete with those who take their time to observe what is going on around them.

BIRTH NIGHT

DATE:	25 February 2012	RIFLE:	Sauer 202
PLACE:	Jim's Farm	CALIBRE:	.22-250
TIME:	19:30	AMMO:	55gr Nosler BT
SUNSET:	17:49	RANGE:	90yd
STATE OF MOON:	Evening crescent	CALL TRACK:	Vixen mating call
WEATHER:	Dry	OPTICS:	D480 GenIII NV riflescope
WIND DIRECTION:	South-westerly		

My next session was back on Jim's sheep farm. His animals are spread out across various pieces of land, some of which he owns, some of which he rents. As the lambing season begins to get into full swing, he not only works his socks off during the day, but gets little sleep at night too. As an illustration, when I got there I found he'd worked late the previous day, and then gone out again at 04:00 that morning to check how things were going. It's a good thing he did so, as he discovered that two lambs which he'd expected to be delivered safely had got their legs tangled up, and were both half out of their mothers and very close to death. Fortunately, he got to them in time, and they both survived. Not only does he have to dash to and fro constantly trying to deal with all the complications that lambing brings, but once they've arrived, he also has to do his best to keep them alive.

One of the more obvious problems is that of foxes, some of which will sit within a few feet of a pregnant ewe that already has a lamb, and wait for her to start giving birth. While this is going on, they will watch for the right moment and then run in and snatch the unguarded youngster. At other times, they will simply dive in and bite the tongue out of a lamb that is halfway out of its mum. Nature can be such a cruel beast. I do my best to clear any foxes from the most sensitive areas in the run-up to lambing, but just when you think you've got things under control, more Charlies appear, seemingly from nowhere. Apart from the numbers of pheasants left over from the winter shoots – most of which have by now learned to look after themselves – there's not much else for them to feed on in mid-February. It's no surprise, therefore, that they're relentlessly drawn to the lure of defenceless lambs, piles of afterbirth and where tail-ringing has started to take effect, lots of cast-off tails lying around for the taking.

It wasn't exactly unexpected therefore when I got a call from Jim, asking if I'd be prepared to visit some of his more far-flung rental grounds. Not only is keeping my landowners sweet a top priority, but I love a specific challenge – especially when it gets me even more places to shoot over! I asked him how he wanted me to prioritise the different areas, and after a brief discussion, we got the order of importance sorted out. That night I visited a smallholding that lies in a narrow valley near some of my other permissions. I had a dreadful time: not only was the terrain mostly near-vertical, but the mizzle was so thick that I couldn't see a thing – either with the thermal or the NV. After a couple of hours of wallowing in mud, scaling unnecessarily high barbed-wire fences, and trying to avoid being lit up by car headlights, I was beginning to seriously overheat. With the humidity being so

TIPS & TRICKS

Lambing can be an anxious time for sheep farmers, especially those who choose to leave their animals out in the fields. In many ways this is the best method as there is a much reduced risk of infection. It does, however, leave the infant lambs very vulnerable to attack. Some foxes can be really brazen, and will sit a few feet away from a ewe that is about to give birth – even in broad daylight – and will patiently wait until she is completely defenceless before attacking.

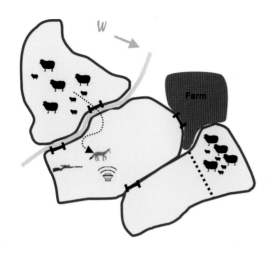

was a rogue fox around. Looking through the thermal, I could clearly see the white shapes of the sheep some 300–400yd away on the other side of the lane. Near them, however, were also two slightly smaller shapes. There was too much foliage in the way to get a positive ID with the NV, but I suspected they could well be foxes. Sure enough, when I started the caller with a vixen mating call, both shapes started running towards the lane.

A few seconds later, a white form appeared in my field, and it was game on. I turned the thermal off and got the NV riflescope and laser operational in moments. Almost immediately, I picked up a bright set of fox eyes coming in at speed, ducking and diving between the rows of maize stubble. Before they got very close to the caller, however, they suddenly changed direction and swung around to get fully downwind. This put the fox at about 90yd from me, but somewhat frustratingly, it kept disappearing from sight in the deep furrows. At some point it must have crossed where I'd walked out to position the caller, because something spooked it and it suddenly turned to run away. Just as it did so, it presented itself to me side-on, and I dropped it with a perfect chest shot.

The loud 'whomp' in response to the hit was all the confirmation I needed, so I waited to see if the other fox would show. In spite of all sorts of tempting calls nothing came in, so I collected the fox and walked back towards the gate. Before I got there, however, I found a hidden tractor rut. The first I knew of its existence was when I went smack down into the mud, and milliseconds later my rifle swung off my shoulder and joined me in the mire. I was not best pleased, to put it mildly. It took me some ten minutes with cotton buds to get the laser clean enough to use – luckily, everything else seemed OK, if a bit mud-encrusted.

With the fox carcass stashed in an accessible place, I then spent the next ten minutes standing balanced on top of the gate trying to see into the nearby fields. Although I couldn't have shot anything there as I didn't have the necessary permissions, it would have given me an excellent excuse to speak to the relevant farmers. Having convinced myself that there was nothing more to see, I packed up and went home.

high, it meant that every time I tried to look through the NV monocular, it instantly misted over. In the end, I realised that I'd be better off going back another night, so packed up and went home.

Luckily, the forecast for the next evening looked more promising, so I was hoping that I'd have more success then. In due course, I got everything arranged and drove over. When I got there, I was delighted to find that I could actually see everything properly, and having thoroughly worn myself out there the previous night, I now knew the lie of the land. Instead of beating myself to death climbing up and down all the hills again, I parked up at the top and worked around what I hoped would be the more productive areas. No matter what I tried though, I couldn't find any foxes, either with the thermal or with the caller. Admittedly, the wind wasn't helping, blowing as it was from the most awkward direction, but I was mystified as to where they could be.

As I made my way back to my truck, I realised that there were some sheep close by on a neighbouring farm. I wondered if they were already lambing, and if so, whether that was where the foxes had gone. I decided to try putting the caller in a location that might tempt anything lurking there out. My first problem was finding a position that wouldn't leave me lit up if a car drove by on the road below. That done, I placed the FOXPRO out in the field, got my rifle up on the sticks, and set to with a quick burst of vixen squalls to announce to the world that there

MARCH

March is a busy time for foxes and a very difficult one for anyone trying to control them. Those vixens with litters are underground and will stay there until the cubs have weaned, so they will only be seen rarely. If the weather was warm enough early in the year some late matings will have taken place. As a result, there might well be a few pregnant vixens still around until the middle of the month. The first cubs may well show: usually the first evidence of them being about is when they are seen lying dead at the side of the road. The dog foxes and subordinate vixens will be running back and forth with food for the growing cubs. If they had the chance to bury significant food reserves in the previous weeks, these foxes may well prove difficult to find, as they won't be doing their usual territorial patrolling and opportunistic hunting. They may also ignore the calls that normally bring them in.

From my perspective, where foxes are concerned, March is a month for baiting. There's usually not much food about, so if you can find some really smelly meat, it can be a very effective way of getting foxes in. I usually use ripe bunny, pheasant and deer trimmings.

March is lambing time, a period that is often accompanied by huge amounts of stress for the farmers concerned. Thanks to the need for orphans and weak individuals to be fed or medicated every few hours, they often have to endure several weeks with very little sleep.

If they are cut into small pieces and liberally distributed, it can hold foxes in the chosen area for some time. Sometimes I simply put it out in likely places, other times I drag bait: that is, I tow it around the area to leave an enticing scent trail; the remains are then staked out in my chosen killing zone.

Since lambing is often in full swing, it can pay dividends to lie up and watch over a suitable flock, especially if you can do so from the comfort of a convenient building or vehicle. Trail cameras can be invaluable, as they can tell you what animals are moving about and when. Some foxes will travel in from miles away, and unless you know when they're likely to be crossing the ground in question, you'll never get near them.

As you're going to be spending significant amounts of time in the dark, it's really important that you have a good torch to hand at all times. I also carry a back-up in case the first one fails for some reason.

THE FARMER'S MONTH
Lambing.
Calving.
Scraping out slurry.
Slurry spreading.
Crops sprayed and fertilised.
Fields chain harrowed.
Fences repaired.

The more remote the location you're working in, the more important this is. For the same reasons, it's also good to carry a mobile. You may not have an accident, but someone else (possibly a passer-by) might, and you'll be able to call the emergency services more quickly if you don't have to rush back to you vehicle. Likewise, if your vehicle sinks in the mud or spins out on the ice, you'll be glad that you can call for help rather than have to trudge miles to find it.

March sees the days beginning to lengthen, and the hour also changes back to BST. The longer days and higher temperatures herald the start of spring, and the world takes on a much more positive feel, with vivid yellow celandines and daffodils thronging the hedges and woodland edges. Above them dangle hazel catkins, and many trees are in flower with apple and plum blossom bringing special splendour to the countryside. Joining in with the spirit of things a wide variety of songbirds are trilling their way to the start of a new season's romance.

Many cows calve at this time of year and sadly, on occasion, they abort. While there are many reasons why this can happen, two of the main ones are of interest to the pest controller. Firstly, there is neospora, a protozoan parasite infection that is spread in fox dung; secondly, leptospirosis or Weil's disease, which is closely associated with rats. The former is best dealt with by skilled foxers as there is currently no remedy available. This is fortunately not true of the latter, and so a combined stance of rat removal and vaccination can remove the problem. Although poison and trapping can be very efficient, sometimes the rats seem able to steer clear of them. In this instance, shooting can be the best method of getting on top of the problem. High-powered air rifles are, in my experience, the best tools for the job: they not only deliver a fatal blow, but there is little risk of ricochet injuries or damage to buildings. My favourite is a Theoben Rapid in .25 calibre. This runs at 50ft/lb, and when coupled with an add-on NV unit, makes for a very efficient ratting rig. Having the right equipment won't do you any good if there are no rats visible – and the best way to draw them out is to use bait. As with foxes, you need to be able to get them to stay in position for long enough for a shot to be possible. The solution to this is to use something that they have to lick up, rather than simply grab and run. Peanut butter

and cat food are excellent for this – they can be daubed onto lumps of wood a few days in advance of your session. Before long the rats get used to the presence of this food, and you are far more likely to experience success.

Farmers have a variety of other jobs to do during the month, depending on their business. Those who grow sugar beet, for instance, usually start drilling it in now. Potato fields and other crops will also need fertilising and/or spraying. If the weather has been good, the ground may be sufficiently dry for the livestock to go out. Before this can happen, all the fences, hedges and gates need to be checked to ensure that the ravages of winter haven't rendered them unfit.

For farmers lambing is often accompanied by huge amounts of stress. Thanks to the need for orphans or weak individuals to be fed or medicated every few hours, many farmers have to endure several weeks with very little sleep. Mervyn keeps a few sheep (**BELOW**) – these are mostly Zwartbles (pronounced 'Swartblay') and Dorset breeds. Although the pheasant season is over, the gamekeepers will still be out doing vital maintenance work on equipment such as this feeding station (**BOTTOM**).

DOGGED PURSUIT

DATE:	6 March 2012	**RIFLE:**	Sauer 202
PLACE:	Roy's Farm	**CALIBRE:**	.22-250
TIME:	19:30	**AMMO:**	55gr Nosler BT
SUNSET:	18:06	**RANGE:**	100yd
STATE OF MOON:	Waxing gibbous	**CALL TRACK:**	None
WEATHER:	Dry with full cloud cover	**OPTICS:**	D480 GenIII NV riflescope
WIND DIRECTION:	South-westerly		

Once again, it was lambing time on Roy's farm, and he was somewhat understandably keen to see that all his young charges survived. The previous week I'd started baiting the field next to the main lambing area after I'd seen a fox in with the ewes. I'd put a load of tempting bits out and went off to another site. On the way back home, some two hours later, I'd stopped off to see if anything was around. Within a couple of minutes I'd managed to shoot a very pregnant vixen that was contentedly noshing away on some of the extremely smelly pheasant guts I'd left there. The next night, however, I briefly saw another fox in the same place, but it had spotted me at the same time as I'd spotted it, and by the time I'd got the rifle ready it was long gone. The same sort of thing happened several times over the next week. The moon had been so bright and the land so difficult that I just couldn't get the drop on this wily character.

Since the bait was continuing to disappear, I knew the fox was unlikely to go far, and there was no way I was going to give up. On the night in question, I set off more hopeful than I'd been for days: the moon had at last been covered by rain clouds. There was still a lot more light than I'd have hoped for, but it was a vast improvement. The land is very steep, with tall hedges every couple of hundred yards. These are mostly composed of tightly packed bramble and thorn bushes and are a complete nightmare to cross, a problem made worse by various generations of barbed wire and unfriendly ditches. At the bottom of each hill there's usually a stream or small river of some kind, often bounded by seemingly random areas of swamp. While the habitat is a nightmare for hunters, the foxes love it.

I pulled my Land Rover off the lane and drove straight out onto the muddy pasture. Luckily, the farmer leaves the gate open for me when the live-stock are all secure in the subsequent fields. As soon as I was clear of the road, I killed the lights and coasted to a stop. I was already wearing my face veil, gloves and NV gear, so all I had to do was retrieve the rifle and sticks and I was off. The baited area lies just over the brow of the hill, and as the wind was in my face I was able to sneak up and take a peek at what was about. My first check was a quick scan with the mini-thermal – but as there was nothing there, I was to be disappointed. Damn.

My money was on the fox being somewhere near the sheep, so I snuck up to a gap in the hedge and peered over. There were several ewes watching over their young lambs, but still no sign of Charlie. The only other sheep I knew of in the area were on the other side of the lane, at the top of another steep hillside. Luckily, I knew I could get a reasonable view of them from near where I was, although having said that they were some 300–400yd away, and thus not easy to distinguish accurately in the damp air. No matter how hard I tried, though, I couldn't see any hints as to the presence of a fox. The sheep all looked peaceful enough, and there were no tell-tale glowing eyes hiding anywhere.

I decided to back-track and look over the bait area again, but when this again proved to be devoid of anything of interest, I had to stop and think things through. As there were few options, I figured it might be worth a look over the gate on the lower side of the field – this looks down over rough grassland to the stream below. I've never seen a fox in there before,

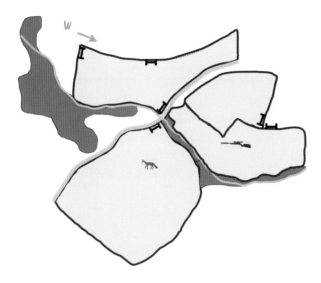

but nothing ventured, nothing gained. As I got closer, however, I realised that rather unexpectedly, the farmer had put a flock of sheep and lambs down there. I stopped in the gateway for a quick look with the thermal, and checked the ewes which were by now standing looking back at me. Round their feet were various lambs nuzzling away.

As I watched, one of white hot spot shapes suddenly jumped up and raced around the outside of the tightly huddled flock, running from my right to my left, some 20yd away. As it did so, I realised that instead of having a lamb's face, it had a long pointy snout. It then ran straight over the brow and disappeared into the depths of the goyle (small valley) beyond. Yep – I'd blown it again. The damned thing had only been a few feet away, and I'd spooked it. Cursing myself, I tried to work out where it might have gone. The most likely answer was it'd taken cover somewhere in the thicket down by the stream. I didn't want to risk going into the field to look for it though, in case the sheep stampeded around and blew my cover.

At this point, I invoked the 'discretion is the better part of valour' rule, and withdrew back up to the hedge-line. For once, the wind was in my favour, so I hoped that if I left it a few minutes, the fox might show itself somewhere near the flock on the other

> **TIPS & TRICKS**
> One of the best ways to improve your success rate is to pre-bait an area. Since it can take a day or so for the bait to be discovered, don't expect it to work wonders straight away. I like to bait for at least two or three days in advance.

side of the lane. I therefore slowly made my way to the best vantage point – and in doing so tried to avoid frightening a large woodcock that was resting in the long grass. Once in position, I set the sticks up and began scanning with the NV riflescope. The six times magnification and wide field of view of its superb optics made the job much easier than with the hand-held NV spotter. After some ten minutes or so, I had to accept that my vulpine target wasn't there, and that it didn't seem to have any intention of showing itself on the ground below.

I tried to get a sneak view of the hillside where I'd seen it earlier by walking down the length of an adjoining field, but the hedge in between was too high and too thick. Frustrated, I followed my previous footsteps and made my way back to where I'd first seen the fox. This time, however, I stayed out of sight while I worked out the best way to get a decent idea of what was in the field. I then realised that there was a short stretch of heavy wooden fencing by the gate. This made an ideal ladder, and I slowly climbed up it, scanning the area beyond with both the thermal and the NV spotter as I did so. I ended up standing on the second highest rung without having seen anything other than yet more sheep.

So, the fox wasn't in the field in front of me, and it wasn't over to my right on the other side of the lane. The area to my left held nothing of obvious interest to a hungry fox, so the only logical place was the large meadow ahead of me on the far side of the stream. This held a small herd of cattle, but I could see with the thermal that they were some half a mile away, sheltering from the cold breeze under the lee of some large oak trees. Once again, I began scanning for signs of Charlie with the NV. Sweeping back and forth, my attention was drawn to a dark shape on the far side of a large ash tree. It certainly looked promising, so I put the sticks up and had a closer look with the riflescope. Sure enough, there it was, and from its size it looked to be a dog fox. He was busily snuffling around in the grass – presumably looking for voles. He was a long way out – the best part of some 300yd or so, and at least 100ft below me.

I considered taking a long range shot, but there were too many things against this course of action – most noticeably, the light foliage in the hedge in front of me. It wasn't really noticeable without the laser illuminator, but the moment I switched it on my view disappeared in the strong reflections. At that point I had two basic choices: to give up and try again another night, or to go off down the hill in pursuit. There was no way that I was going to stop now though, so I scaled the gate, made my way around the sheep and down towards the stream.

Every 20yd or so I stopped and checked the fox's position. He was moving to my left along the side of the opposite hill. At first he was a long way below me, but as I lost height, the angle began to level out. By keeping the biggest of the trees between us, I did my best to ensure that he couldn't see me. The wind was still directly in my face, and with the gentle tinkling sounds of the stream as well as the noises from the sheep moving around, he certainly wasn't going to hear me unless I made a big mistake. I was worried that he might hear the

snorted warning signals that some of the ewes were making.

When I'd closed the range down to about 100yd, I got the sticks up and the rifle ready. There was only one gap in the trees that I could shoot through, so I had to get everything right. I moved a couple of times to make sure I was happy that everything was in my favour. At this stage the fox was completely unaware of my presence, and I patiently waited as he gradually made his way into the chosen killing zone. By then I'd got the focus just right, the laser adjusted perfectly, and was ready and waiting. At the appropriate moment, I slipped the safety off and released a round. On its impact, he leapt into the air but in doing so went into a forward somersault and was already dead by the time he fell a couple of feet further on.

I then had the small problem of crossing the stream and climbing the hill on the other side to retrieve my kill. Although I normally refuse to switch the torch on for anything short of an emergency, I decided that prudence was the order of the day, and duly navigated my way over under its light – and without any further problems. The carcass was, as I'd thought, that of a large dog fox. I suspect that he was probably the partner of the vixen I shot last week. I have to confess that the slog back up the hill – carrying the fox, rifle, sticks, NV spotter, thermal and so on – required a few brief stops to allow me to catch my breath. Still, I had a great sense of satisfaction when I finally got there. This fox had been a direct threat to the lambs, and needed dealing with. Needless to say, the farmer was delighted, which is always a bonus!

This fox was a definite candidate for a lamb killer. I'd seen it a few times, but every time it had been lucky with the wind direction. Its good fortune ran out one night when I found it in with the sheep – although it ran off, I caught up with it a few minutes later.

A BIT OF A DRAG

DATE:	26 March 2012	**RIFLE:**	Sauer 202
PLACE:	Cyril's Farm	**CALIBRE:**	.22-250
TIME:	21:30	**AMMO:**	55gr Nosler BT
SUNSET:	19:39	**RANGE:**	Both at about 80yd
STATE OF MOON:	Evening crescent	**CALL TRACK:**	Vixen on heat
WEATHER:	Dry	**OPTICS:**	D480 GenIII NV riflescope
WIND DIRECTION:	South-westerly		

Working from home has its pros and cons, but one of the upsides is that I'm generally around if any farmers need to contact me in a hurry. One day in late March I arrived at my desk to find a phone message waiting for me. A local chap, who keeps a hundred or so sheep, had discovered that one of his lambs had been torn apart in the night, and its remains dragged into the lee of a hedge, where it had been partly consumed. The poor man was very upset by this, and was somewhat anxious for me to do something about it.

What surprised me was that the field where this happened was right next to a farm where I'd shot some 20 foxes over the previous year. I'd been really diligent, and had thought I'd got the area well under control. That was until rumours surfaced about a consignment of foxes being dumped nearby by a supposed animal charity. Ever since then, the damned things had been popping up all over the place. One

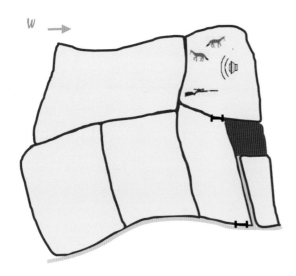

night I shot two that looked distinctly out of place. On inspection, one of them had a large bald patch which appeared at some stage to have been caused by a serious case of mange. As far as I know, this very rarely clears up on its own, and so one has to suspect that it'd received human help.

Still, whether or not that was the case, I had another lamb-killer to deal with. I called the farmer back and arranged to meet up with him so that I could see on a map where the crime had taken place. He'd already decided to move the sheep back to his own land where he could keep a closer eye on them, so that meant I'd have the area to myself. I'd not shot over the fields in question before as he rents them, so I was keen to ensure that I was absolutely certain where the boundaries were. That done, we agreed to meet on the site that evening so that I could be introduced to the landowner. It was handy that the hour had gone forward, as it gave me time to see everything in daylight and still get home for a bite to eat. The ground was essentially two fields, the first being almost level (unusual for around here), whereas the second dived steeply down to a small brook. The lamb had been killed about halfway down and then dragged through a patch of mud over to the upper hedge. The amazing thing is that this was only about 50yd from the owner's house. The place is less than a mile from where I live, so I was able to wait until it'd got dark before returning.

Before doing so, I'd made a plan: I was going to drive around the fields towing a smelly piece of meat in the hope that it would help draw any foxes in. As it happened, I'd had a minor tragedy the previous week, The trip had gone on the panel that feeds my walk-in chiller without anyone realising. Sadly, it meant that the red deer carcass in there had got warm. Although it looked and smelt fine, my wife had been going through chemotherapy, and I just couldn't risk her catching a bug – either directly or from me. Consequently, I'd decided to consign it to the category of fox bait, which meant I had a large haunch all bagged up and ready to go.

The gate had been left open for me, so I drove a few yards into the field before killing the lights and coasting to a halt. I was already wearing my face veil, NV monocular and mini-thermal, so as soon as I was out of the truck, I had a quick scan around. With nothing of interest in sight, I opened the back door and passed a length of thin Nylon rope through the haunch where it'd been hocked. The other end went around the tow bar, and after making a few extra cuts into the juicy bits to release the maximum possible scent, I was ready. Keeping the main lights off, I drove slowly around the field, then through the gateway into the one beyond. As this was where the lamb had been killed, it was where I was expecting the action to take place. I had to be careful, though. Not knowing the ground I couldn't be sure that there weren't any marshy patches, and so I stayed well away from the steeper gradients. Having looped around to my satisfaction, I unhitched the bait and drove back through the gate and parked up.

With my trusty Sauer over my shoulder, I grabbed my sticks and returned to the bait. Just as I cleared the gateway, a fox began calling in the next field. There's something about the sound that just gets my heart going, and I immediately feel the hunter instinct kicking in. Another scan with the thermal showed that it wasn't anywhere near me so I quickly set about getting everything ready. Now that there was a decent scent trail in place, I needed to ensure the bait itself was in a suitable position. As I did so, I discovered a problem: there were two bright lights on the wall of the owner's house, and these were illuminating most of the field. Damn. If I'd known them better, I'd have gone over and asked if they could switch the offending lamps off. As it was, I'd only met the husband, and thought the wife might take fright at the sight of an unknown and heavily armed bloke dressed head to toe in camo turning up in the dark on her doorstep unannounced...

So, I had to persevere. In the end, I found that if I went far enough down the hill, I could get out of the lights. In some ways one could have considered them to be an advantage, as any approaching foxes would almost certainly avoid the illuminated area too, and so this narrowed down the likely access routes I had to watch. Once the bait was down, I had to find a site for the caller. This proved to be a little more difficult – even when I was out of sight of the house, there was still too much moonlight for comfort. The combination of this and the wind direction gave me very little choice, but in the end I was happy that I'd have sufficient warning if a fox came in. I wasn't sure if the breeze had already given me away, as it was blowing towards where I'd heard the calls a few minutes earlier. I was hoping that because of the close proximity of the house any foxes in the area would have been well used to the smell of humans.

Still, nothing ventured, nothing gained, and I got myself nicely ensconced in the shadows cast by the hedge. I set my sticks out, very pleased with the fact that they were now quiet. I'm a real stickler for minimising any unnecessary sounds, and over the previous weeks had been getting increasingly annoyed by the creaks and groans they'd begun making whenever I leant on them. On close examination, I'd found that the bolt holes had become elongated with use, and it was here that the creaks were coming from. A brief trip out to the workshop had found some aircraft aluminium bar of the right dimensions, and a few minutes with the lathe and drill press resulted in some suitable reinforcing slugs being knocked up. These were then pushed up inside the sticks and bonded into place using rapid-setting Araldite. Once that was fully cured, I applied a few dabs of Molykote grease to the bolts and reassembled everything. A quick check showed that they seemed to be as smooth as silk, but I wanted to see how they performed in action before considering the job to be a success. Now that I was out in the field, however, I was happy – no matter how much pressure I put on them, they stayed completely silent.

With that all sorted out, it was time for me to make some intentional noise, but the question was what I should start with. My concern was to avoid using a sound that I'd already used in the area, as I regularly hunted over the adjoining farmland. To this end, I settled on flying squirrel distress call, and duly set the FOXPRO going. I already had my rifle up on the sticks, and scanned continuously with the thermal. After about five minutes, my initial enthusiasm had begun to wane. If there's a fox about, it usually shows pretty quickly. After 10 minutes, I hit the mute button and waited while I pondered my next move. As the rodent squeaks hadn't worked, I reverted to the old faithful and tried two short burst of fox squalls, before starting the vixen on heat call. I left this running, and after about a minute a white shape suddenly ran in from downwind. There was no time to switch the thermal off, so I just let it dangle around my neck while I switched the NV riflescope on. The fox was still running as I caught it in the reticle, and the moment it paused to sniff the air, I dropped it with a ballistic tip. It fell on the spot. Result! 'The farmer will be well pleased', I thought to myself.

Only one fox had been seen in the area, and I had no reason to suspect that there might be any more around. I still left the caller running for a few more minutes though, but as nothing showed, I decided to move on. I pressed the mute button again, and made

my way over to the carcass using the thermal to make sure I was going in the right direction. I counted the range at 80 paces, and when I got there found it was a very scrawny and barren vixen. If there was a brood nearby, she could well have been a helper. Typically, these are one of the mother's sisters or daughters, whose role would be to provide as much food as possible for the hungry pups. In the event of the mother's demise, the helper would usually take over rearing them but only if they'd already been weaned. As I'd shot a very pregnant vixen in a nearby field less than 10 days previously – together with a large dog fox – I thought it unlikely that there was a brood earth or any other foxes around.

Having taken a series of photos for my records – lighting everything up with my torch whilst doing so – I was ready to make my way over to retrieve the caller. Before doing this, however, I had another quick look around with the thermal. I could see that there was an animal of some description beyond the hedge, but as there was too much vegetation in the way, I couldn't identify it. I therefore decided to walk over to see if I could find a gap of some kind to get a better

view. In the end, it was a false alarm – I was actually seeing some cows way off in the distance. Shrugging it off as one of those things, I turned back and used the thermal to locate my caller. The moment I did so, however, my heart jumped into my mouth, for there was a large fox running up the hill straight towards the bait. I fumbled the sticks into place and got the rifle up.

The fox dived onto the venison with a ravenous leap, but as it did so it must have heard me, for it suddenly stopped and stared straight at me. I was completely downwind, so it certainly hadn't scented me. Anyway, it had about it what I can only describe as a look of sudden realisation of the serious position it was in. It clearly knew it was in real trouble. Its synapses were obviously telling it to move, but those connecting my brain to my trigger finger were faster, and it went down with a convincing 'whump'. Again, the range

TIPS & TRICKS

When there isn't the time to bait in advance, an alternative method is to 'drag-bait'. This is where some particularly smelly meat is dragged across a wide area, leaving a scent trail that a marauding fox cannot fail to find. The bait may be dragged by hand, or from the back of a vehicle. The latter is better where possible, as it reduces the smell of human presence. The bait itself is then left where you want the fox to end up.

was about 80 paces, but as I got close, I could see that this was no ordinary fox: it was absolutely enormous. I would say that it was the best part of 25lb, and is easily the biggest I've seen for some time. There was no doubting that this was a dog fox: his white-haired scrotum was sticking out prominently from between his back legs. On close inspection, I found that his upper right canine had been broken at some stage, but other than that he was in good condition – apart from the bullet hole, of course! If there was ever a candidate for a lamb-killer, this was it.

A quick call to the farmer was answered by his wife – around here Monday evenings are for skittles, and he was off with the local team in a pub enjoying himself. She was delighted to hear the news though as the sheep are mainly her responsibility. It's always good to have another satisfied 'customer'!

The small vixen (BELOW LEFT) came in to the caller, but it seemed an unlikely lamb killer – unlike the huge dog fox (BELOW) which ran in to the bait a few minutes later. Although its upper right canine was missing, it must have weighed the best part of 25lb.

THREE DOG NIGHT

DATE:	29 March 2012	RIFLE:	Sauer 202
PLACE:	Brian's Farm	CALIBRE:	.22-250
TIME:	19:30	AMMO:	55gr Nosler BT
SUNSET:	19:44	RANGE:	All three at about 80yd
STATE OF MOON:	Evening crescent	CALL TRACK:	Distressed rabbit/rodent
WEATHER:	Dry with full cloud cover	OPTICS:	D480 GenIII NV riflescope
WIND DIRECTION:	Westerly		

The black plastic bin liner rustled occasionally as it brushed against the odd piece of vegetation. My mission was to spread its contents – the hide, bones and trimmings from a roe carcass – out as fox bait before the sun went down. It was a new shoot for me, and I wanted to make a good impression on the farmer. The ground there is typical of the area to the north of Exeter – absolutely beautiful countryside made up of low-lying hills interspersed with numerous small brooks and streams. Where the plough has been in action the archetypal red Devon soil can be seen. This makes for superb agricultural land, with tracts of rich pasture and meadows running for miles in every direction. The higher bits tend to drain well, but some of the lower areas can stay boggy for most of the year. The field I was in ran along the side of what is normally a fast-flowing stream: due to the lack of rain, however, it was little more than a trickle.

The mix of lush grass, light woodland and small areas of cover combine with the relatively mild climate to provide an ideal habitat for all manner of wildlife, including bunnies, roe deer, badgers, crows, rooks, ravens and so on. Wherever there is such an abundance of prey, of course, there are also foxes – lots of them. I had been called in by the farmer as he needed someone to sort them out. Although the year's lambs were by then big enough to be out of immediate danger, if one had got tangled in a fence or separated from its mother, it would have been in serious trouble.

I felt honoured to receive the invite as many others had asked to shoot on the land, but had all been turned away since the farmer doesn't like the idea of 'strangers' on his property. The introduction had come about because I've been shooting for one of his neighbours for several years, and this gave him the confidence to allow me in. I'd had a meeting in Exeter the previous afternoon, so had arranged to meet up with him on my way in so that we could discuss such things as the positions of the boundaries, and so on. He was a little reserved at first, but it was good to see just how much he relaxed when I listed off the names of some of the other farmers I look after, many of whom are very highly respected in the local farming community. By the time I left, I felt as though I'd had a red carpet laid out for me, and was especially pleased to find that I'd not just scored one farm, but two, as he rents a second property just up the road!

I'd returned with the sun lying just above the horizon. There was about half an hour of daylight left, and the western reaches ranged from orange to crimson which contrasted well against the vivid blue sky elsewhere. My intent was to get the bait out before dark, and then to leave it for an hour or so before going back to check it. The wind was in the north-west, and so was blowing diagonally down and across the valley. The moon was clearly going to be a problem though. The clear skies meant that there'd be no cloud cover whatsoever, and as it was also very high in the sky, there'd be very little chance of being able to hide in the shadows. A follow-on issue was that as many foxes are very reluctant to show themselves when there is a lot of moonlight, I knew I'd have my work cut out.

I'd driven my Land Rover down the winding farm track and hidden it in a deep fold of ground between a hedge and a stream. From there I'd walked to the far end of the field, and then ripped the bin liner open

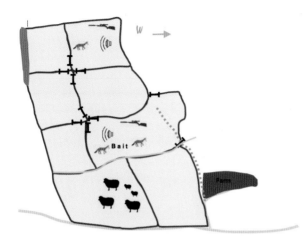

– having first put on a disposable vinyl glove. I'd stopped every few paces, pulled out a handful of suitably smelly bones and then thrown them around to leave a wide trail of what I hoped would be considered choice morsels by any nearby foxes. This reached across the field almost as far as the upper hedge, and given the wind direction would have broadcast the scent to most of the valley beyond. I had my Sauer .308 over my shoulder in case anything of interest showed itself, but as it happened it wasn't needed. Had I left it behind, Sod's Law would undoubtedly have had it that a group of roe deer would have walked out in front of me!

By the time I'd looped back to the truck the light was starting to go, so I unlocked my gun safe and switched rifles. My Leica rangefinding binos were swapped for the NV monocular, but the mini-thermal stayed hanging around my neck. The magazines were emptied of .308 ammo, and a series of .22-250 rounds went in their place.

Once all that was sorted out, I went and sat on an old farm trailer and enjoyed the last few minutes before darkness set in properly. All around me were the noises of a late evening in springtime. I leant back and tried to see how many different sounds I could pick out. First and foremost were the noisy ewes in the next field, calling constantly to their lambs. These replied with tiny bleats that sounded both pathetic and endearing at the same time. Between them and the rooks at the top of the hill, which were making a real racket, it was hard to distinguish anything else. I could also hear several crows shouting their angry

protests at whatever it was that had upset them. I knew it was probably just domestic politics as there were several magpies a couple of fields away, and since they hadn't made any alarm calls, it was unlikely that any foxes were about yet. As the light fell and the world slowly went dimpsy, a thrush loudly staked out its territorial claim from the top of a tall ash tree. A little further away a barn owl produced the occasional shriek from somewhere just over the brow of the hill. Closer to hand, a number of cock pheasants were trying to entice the numerous hens to come and roost on their respective patches. Rounding up the show, there were innumerable small songbirds chattering away the last moments of the day. Where else but rural Devon could a man possibly want to live?

When the last vestiges of blue sky finally turned to grey, I put an end to my reverie and slowly began making my way up the hill. At this stage it was still a bit too early for the NV, so I scanned with the thermal as I went. When the sun has been out all manner of unlikely objects give out heat signatures – mostly, these are things like tree roots and areas of baked soil. One initially unrecognisable white shape gradually morphed itself into a hen pheasant as it appeared from behind a dip in the ground.

Exploring an unknown farm in the dark can be rather challenging at times, particularly when you don't know where the gates are, or how robust they're going to be when you finally find them. Whenever I found a gap in the hedge I scanned around for potential quarry, but apart from a frightened bunny that ran into some bushes a few feet in front of me, I saw nothing. Now that the birds had gone to roost it had become deathly quiet, and as a result every blade of grass I trod on made what seemed to be an unbearably loud crunching sound. Even though the moon was still only half-full, it was incredibly bright, casting short but sharp shadows. Having scanned several fields without any sign of Charlie, I decided that the only thing for it would be to try the FOXPRO caller. I needed to find the right location though, as the grass was already long enough in most places to hide a cautious predator.

In the end, I found a relatively flat area in a freshly sown field. Hiding myself in the shadows of a small oak tree, I tried the distressed rabbit call. There were some woods about 200yd ahead of me, a hedge to my right, and the field dived away to my left some 50yd or so beyond the caller. As this was the down-wind direction, it was where I was expecting any approaching foxes to come from. I was more than a little surprised when one suddenly ran out from the hedgeline on my right: they're not meant to come from upwind! I let the thermal go without attempting to switch it off, and got the NV riflescope in action. The fox ran right in to the caller, but jumped back in surprise when it discovered that the helpless creature was, in fact, made from hard plastic and not tasty flesh. It paused for a moment to reconsider and then went back in again for a second look. Before it got there, however, it was hit hard by a .22-250 bullet, and down it went.

I left the caller running for a few minutes, but when it became clear that nothing else was going to show, I muted it and went to inspect the carcass. Sometimes it can hard to see where a bullet has struck a fox, but in this instance there was no uncertainty - the ballistic-tip round had made a real mess. It proved to be a medium-sized male with a scattering of pale spots across its upper flanks. Since the farmer said he'd collect any foxes I'd shot, I left it where it was and continued on my way. It was now about an hour

and a half since I'd left the bait out, so I thought it'd make sense to go back see if anything was there.

As I worked back across the field I could see that about half a mile further up the valley someone was out lamping. Every now and then a beam of light flicked around and a shot or two rang out. Since they were actually on the far side of the hill, I was happy that my safety (and theirs) wasn't going to be an issue. I was also conscious that their activities could well help to push any foxes towards me, so I forgot about them and returned my attention to what lay ahead. I was soon in a position to use the NV mono to look down to where the bait had been laid out. Almost immediately, I got the unmistakable glint of fox eyes reflecting back from my laser. Thanks to the moon I was now somewhat exposed, and I was reasonably sure the animal in question could see me. I had no choice though; all I could do was carry on to the far side of the field so that I could circle around and ap-proach from downwind. It took me about 15 minutes to do so, but when I checked the area over, there was nothing to be seen. I wasn't too worried: if the fox had found the bait, it may well have been ferrying pieces of it back and forth to various safe hiding places, and so could easily return at any moment.

This large dog fox couldn't resist the lure of the trimmings from a roe deer carcass which I'd scattered over a wide area just before it got dark.

Before it could do so, I carefully placed the caller in a likely spot. Back by the hedge I got into a small pool of shadow under an ash tree and set the sticks up. After pondering the matter over, I decided to try the rat duet call. This is a sequence of two increasingly distressed rodent calls, and the shrill squeaks seem to carry well on the night air. The main issue I had to deal with was that there was a lot of dead ground behind the caller, so I was going to get very little warning of any foxes running in. I normally scan with the mono or the thermal and then switch over to the rifle, but on this occasion it wasn't an option: I was going to have to use the riflescope from start to finish. Before I set the caller going, I had another thorough scan with the thermal for safety reasons. Satisfied that all was clear, I had good back stops everywhere and there were no human access routes except for where I was standing, I pressed the button.

TIPS & TRICKS

If you're planning to put bait down, it's best to place it somewhere that you can get reasonably close to without being seen. That way, you can creep up, check the area and move away again without spooking any foxes that may be lurking nearby. Remember that when foxes find a surfeit of food, they will carry away anything they can't eat and bury it for later retrieval. So if there's nothing about, it may just be that a fox is off hiding his finds. Come back a little later, and you might get lucky.

Within a minute of the rat sounds starting, a fox ran in from downwind and briefly stopped to stare at the caller. It went down to an engine-room shot. A quick swivel around with the riflescope picked up another set of eyes running up from the stream. They disappeared as they got to the dead ground behind the caller, so I had to gamble that they'd go around on the wind. Sure enough, a few seconds later the fox reappeared some 30yd further out from the one I'd just shot. It also fell where it stood. Both turned out to be males, so in honour of the 1970s rock band of the same name, I called this account 'Three Dog Night'. I spoke to the farmer's wife and she said they were very pleased, but I knew that unless some decent cloud cover showed up I'd struggle with the moon over the next week, so decided that it was a good excuse to give the foxes a break and go and do some daylight roe stalking on the other farm instead. Happy days!

APRIL

April is another difficult month for the foxer. Across most of the country the vixens are still staying close to their cubs. Their helpers, which are usually comprised of the dog and one or more of the vixen's sisters, aunts or daughters, are kept busy running back and forth with food. As a result, they can be very difficult to find. In 2012 I shot 19 in February, and 15 in March. Despite being out almost every night, I only managed two in April and one in May. In the warmer locations the first cubs will be venturing above ground. At first the vixen will be reluctant to leave them, but as they get older she'll start to leave them for longer periods. If there are any young lambs in the area they will be vulnerable to attack as there will be a lot of pressure on the adult foxes to keep the cubs' voracious appetites sated.

Any vixens that are shot at this time of year need to be checked to see if they are in milk. This is easy to establish as the nipples will be swollen and when squeezed, some milk may issue. If this happens, then significant attempts should be made to find the cubs. This is for humanitarian reasons, although most vixens will not leave

April sees the world beginning to warm up – here, the gorse is in bloom, and the first blackthorn (sloe) flowers can be seen on the far side of the valley. It is, nevertheless, a busy time for gamekeepers – this photo shows a new pheasant pen under construction.

them until they have been weaned, this is not always the case. Cubs that have moved onto solid food will usually be fed well by the helpers and so can survive without their mother. It is not fair to rely on this though, and so if it is possible to find them, they should be culled to prevent any suffering. One method that has been used for many years is to dig a hole nearby and then place the dead vixen in it. If the cubs smell her, they will follow the scent and then jump down to be with her. If the hole was made deep enough, they will not be able to get out again. This works equally well with vixens that have been killed by cars as for those which have been shot. Dealing with orphaned cubs is one of the less pleasant aspects of fox control. Sometimes vixens will be found that have clearly been in milk, but the nipples have shrunk and fur around them has begun regrowing. This shows that

THE FARMER'S MONTH
Cattle back out into the fields.
Calving.
First silage cut.
Lambing nearly finished.
Fertiliser spreading and
crops sprayed.
Potatoes, oil seed rape
and peas planted.
Apple in blossom.

the individual concerned recently had cubs, but that she had lost them. The most likely cause is disease, but it is also possible that they were killed by a badger.

In England and Wales, the end of March sees the red, sika and fallow deer hind seasons finish, together with those for roe does and both sexes of Chinese water deer. Conversely, it is the beginning of the roe deer buck season. Most of the pregnant hinds and does will start moving off to their summer breeding grounds where they stay largely solitary until their calves and fawns are big enough to rejoin the other adults. Keeping the youngsters from other deer helps to minimise the risks from predation and disease.

April can be a tough time for the farmer. Although the weather can appear to be good enough to turn the cattle back out into the fields, it can revert to a winter-like state very quickly. Where the temperatures are high enough, the grass starts growing very quickly, providing good fodder for them. In the warmer areas, farmers will be hoping to get their first cut of silage before the end of the month. Animals that have been cooped up for several months often demonstrate their joy at being out in the open again by running madly about and skipping around like baby lambs. Some herds will start calving around now, and where this happens it is always worth keeping an eye out for foxes feeding on the remnants of the afterbirth. Likewise, any lambs will need to be guarded until they are big enough to fend off any attacks. Sadly, no matter how big they are, they will always be at risk from domestic dogs. I have seen many otherwise healthy animals mortally wounded or killed by out of control pets, and it is heartbreaking for the farmer to see his beloved charges needlessly attacked in this way.

Another source of worry for the shepherd comes from corvids – crows, rooks, ravens and magpies. If a young lamb is left unprotected or a pregnant ewe is cast (rolls over onto her back) and cannot right herself, they will be extremely vulnerable to these vicious creatures. Anyone who has seen the results of such an episode will not forget it in a hurry. Typically, they will peck the eyes out first, then if they can get at it, they will eat the tongue. Ears are often ripped apart, too, all this while the helpless sheep can do nothing more than lie there. Even worse is when these birds start at the other end, and tear the anus and vulva apart, slowly eating their way towards the poor animal's

major organs. If they are allowed to continue, they will carry on pecking away until their victim dies. This can take a considerable time though, and the pain and fear they undoubtedly go through is beyond imagination. It is little wonder that farmers hate these birds with a vengeance. The massive upsurge in the raven population has been matched by large increases in the number of attacks, but they still have protected status, and so nothing can be done about them. The other corvids are fair game though, and should be controlled whenever possible. Larsen traps which use a live magpie as a decoy can be very effective, and carry on working even when you have other things to do. You need to check them regularly though, as all sorts of other creatures have been known to be trapped. These include sparrowhawks, tawny owls, cats, foxes and so on. Fortunately, with these traps it is easy to release anything that you don't want unharmed.

As spring gets into its stride and the sun shines once again, so all the creatures that have been in hibernation soak up the welcome rays. This skinny robin has got a lot of catching up to do after the lean times of winter if it is to put enough weight on to make it through the rigours of breeding.

HELPING A KEEPER

DATE:	1 April 2009	**RIFLE:**	Sauer 202
PLACE:	Critter's Shoot	**CALIBRE:**	.22-250
TIME:	21:30	**AMMO:**	55gr Nosler BT
SUNSET:	19:48	**RANGE:**	100yd
STATE OF MOON:	Evening crescent	**CALL TRACK:**	Distressed rabbit
WEATHER:	Dry with full cloud cover	**OPTICS:**	D480 GenIII NV riflescope
WIND DIRECTION:	South-westerly		

A friend of mine, Critter – Devonian for Christopher – is a keeper on an estate with a newly established pheasant shoot. It lies in a steep valley hidden in the hills of deepest mid-Devon. The big house dates to medieval times, and has recently undergone a revamp after being bought by a city trader.

Critter is known as an expert terrier man, and has hunted in one form or another all his life. One April Fool's Day evening I went over to show him my NV set-up, as he'd shown great interest when we'd spoken about it a couple of week's before. After a long chat about all things foxing-related, we decided it was dark enough to give the caller a try, so we gathered our things together and went out into the yard. The estate's owner was away, so we didn't have to worry about disturbing anyone – consequently, we set the FOXPRO caller up close by. I started it on the distressed rabbit track and began scanning around to see if anything would come in. A couple of minutes later, I spotted a set of eyes, high up on the hill above us. I adjusted the spotter and got a better focus – this gave me the positive ID I was looking for. Switching over to the NV riflescope, I tracked it as it wandered along the old sheep path. Even though it'd come to the caller, it wasn't keen on coming in any closer – presumably it knew the house was a source of potential danger. I waited until it got to about 100yd away, then held back until it paused. At one point it looked back over its shoulder to check that nothing was approaching from behind. This was my cue, and I immediately squeezed off a shot. There was a thump, and it crumpled on the spot.

It took us ages to find. The long grass and large number of gorse bushes threw us off, and we started searching an area well below where it had been. Once we'd realised this and started looking in the right place we found the carcass relatively easily. It was a dog fox that weighed 14lb on my pocket scales. Critter and I checked it over, and between us we agreed that by the look of its teeth it was probably about two years old. Another interesting feature was that it had unusually sharp claws. This meant it wasn't having to travel very far to feed itself, or they'd have worn down a lot more. All in all, it was a good fox to remove as it was almost certainly one of the individuals that had been attacking Critter's pheasants. He was both pleased with my efforts and impressed with the NV equipment.

> **TIPS & TRICKS**
>
> Local knowledge is worth its weight in gold when it comes to hunting – knowing where and when an animal is likely to appear beats every other trick going.

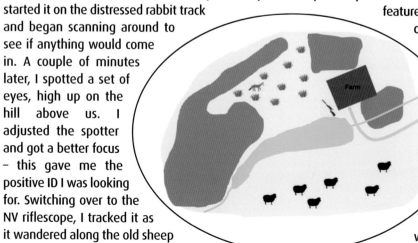

DAYLIGHT MARAUDER

DATE:	7 April 2010	**WIND DIRECTION:**	Westerly
PLACE:	Mrs. B's Farm	**RIFLE:**	Sauer 202
TIME:	19:30	**CALIBRE:**	.308
SUNSET:	19:57	**AMMO:**	180gr Norma SP
STATE OF MOON:	Daylight (morning crescent)	**RANGE:**	90yd
		CALL TRACK:	Distressed rabbit
WEATHER:	Dry	**OPTICS:**	Swarovski Z6 2.5-15x56

Mrs. B bought 100 acres of rough pasture and moorland with a small cottage where she tended her new family: one composed entirely of bantams, chickens, ducks and geese. To her they are more than just animals, and when a fox manages to get in and kill any of them she gets upset. It is vital that I keep on top of the problem. Luckily for Mrs. B, I now shoot across a lot of the surrounding countryside too, so her birds tend to live a lot longer than they used to.

One spring evening I decided to try a calling session on the moorland a few hundred yards from her house. The ground there can be tricky to cross in the dark, so I went for a daylight shoot. I had to fight my way through the thick blackthorn bushes that made up the hedge to keep the wind in my face on the approach to stop being scented. It was my first time through the area, so I didn't know it and had to search for the right spot for my caller. I had to fight my way across some boggy terrain. While this was a bit of a mission, I was pleased to see that some of the more pond-like stretches were full of wriggling tadpoles. Since foxes like to feast on young amphibians, I knew that my vulpine control efforts should help to boost their populations too. As though to emphasise they weren't the only things that needed conserving, a hare rose up and ran off, another of the animals that would also do much better with fewer foxes around.

Having regained a decent footing, I had another look around. There was a level area of about 150yd

> **TIPS & TRICKS**
>
> Calling in daylight can work well, especially at dawn and dusk. Remote control electronic callers are excellent for this, as they focus the fox's attention on a spot well removed from you. I've had them run within a few feet of me, even from downwind, in their haste to get to what they think will be an easy meal.

across in front of me. Beyond that, there was scrubby undergrowth; to either side, swathes of reeds – so there would be no point in trying to site a caller there. I decided to stick where I was. I would be able to hide myself among the lower branches of the pussy-willow trees, and still get a good view. I counted out 100 paces and positioned the caller, before retiring into my natural hide. I set it going on the distressed rabbit call. A couple of minutes later, I heard an animal running in close behind me. Surely no predator would approach from downwind? A quick glance told me I was wrong. A fox was running looping round to what it hoped was easy meat. It ran to about 10yd of the caller, before halting suddenly, confused at what it saw. Before it could jump away, my .308 barked and my quarry folded where it stood.

I told Mrs. B when I got home. Delighted, she promised some chocolates. Result!

HUNT FOR A LAMB KILLER

Having climbed out of bed at 05:45 in order to go to the car boot sale in Exeter, I was more than a little tired when I got home. So I sorted out the things that needed doing, such as unloading the truck and presenting my wife with the plants I'd bought for her, and then hitting the sack for a couple of hours' kip. Whilst enjoying the catch-up on my beauty sleep, the phone rang in my office. Fortunately, Her Lady-ship was within earshot and ran through to answer it. The call was a plea for help from Jim, one of my favourite farmers. On waking up, I found a garbled message lying on my desk scribbled on a piece of paper and ending with 'little paddock behind house'. This needed further investigation...

It transpired that a lamb had been killed overnight by a fox in the small holding paddock right next to the farmhouse. I always do my best to respond to any such requests, and as it was a relatively new permission for me – I'd only been to the place about five times – I was keen to get stuck in to see if I could sort the problem out. I spent the

next hour or so going through my kit: charging the batteries in my caller, checking the ammo wallets, and so on. Once everything was loaded up, I set off in my trusty Disco to wend my way through the lanes to the scene of the crime.

On inspection, it was clear that because the paddock was so close to the house, the wind was in the wrong direction, and there was a distinct lack of cover for me to shoot from, I'd be better off waiting until after dark. Since I had about an hour and a half of daylight left, I decided to use the opportunity to see if I could suss out where the roe deer were feeding in the area to the south of the farm. I had a quick chat with the farmer's son about the best approach routes, and with the directions all sorted out, I drove off down the track towards the isolated valley where I hoped to see the deer.

One of the problems that one meets on a live-stock farm at this time of year is that the gates need to be kept shut, and since I was on my own, this meant repeatedly leaping in and out of the truck as

DATE:	10 April 2011	RIFLE:	Sauer 202
PLACE:	Jim's Farm	CALIBRE:	.22-250
TIME:	21:00	AMMO:	55gr Nosler BT
SUNSET:	20:02	RANGE:	50yd
STATE OF MOON:	Evening crescent	CALL TRACK:	Vole squeaks
WEATHER:	Dry	OPTICS:	D480 GenIII NV riflescope
WIND DIRECTION:	North-westerly		

I slowly went from field to field. In some places, the sheep charged off as soon as they saw me. In others, they came running up, presumably hoping for a free feed. In one meadow there were a lot of black cows, which can be a real pain if they're feeling inquisitive. Trying to get a vehicle through a gate without them escaping can also be a hassle. Fortunately, on this occasion they were more interested in the fresh grass than in seeing what the strange bloke dressed in camo was up to.

Eventually, I got to the chosen area – a truly beautiful piece of ground. Although I'd seen aerial photographs of the land I was now surveying, they did not do the place justice. It had been a very hot day, and the sky was still crystal clear. As the sun was by now lying near the horizon, its rays were almost horizontal, creating long shadows over the rolling hills and verdant fields. A few bunnies were sunning themselves along the hedges, and the songbirds were chattering their little hearts out with the joys of spring. Every now and then, however, the peace and tranquillity was pierced by raucous shouts from some crows that seemed determined to lend an air of menace to the scene. Their efforts were in vain though, as it felt as though everything else – from the bright yellow celandines at my feet, through to the newly emerged leaves at the tops of the trees – was truly glad to be alive.

After parking up, I did my best to merge with the landscape, and quickly snuck off into the shadows. Every 30 seconds or so, I paused and checked the ground with my Nikon binos. There were the aforementioned bunnies, as well as some amorous pigeons and a few territorial blackbirds, but sadly, there were no deer to be seen. After about 10 minutes' walk, I reached a point where I could watch over a long field that ran along the side of a hill. On its lower side there was a small stream bordered by various scrub – mostly hazel. At the far end the grass gave way to thick woodland, and at the top there was a thick hedge; all ideal roe habitats. On the other side of the stream there was another large sloping field stretching off into the distance. This also had woodland along two edges, and appeared to be perfect deer country. Within a few feet of me, I noticed that the cattle had made themselves a refuge from the weather by hollowing out the vegetation in the hedge. This proved itself to be a nigh-on perfect hide, and so I settled into it, with my sticks and rifle to my side. The gentle breeze was blowing down the valley towards me, and as I was now almost entirely hidden from view, I was confident that if anything was about, I'd stand a good chance of seeing it.

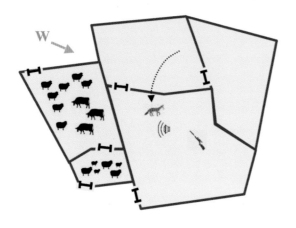

Over the next hour, I watched as the sun slowly sank below the skyline. I scrutinised every bush, twig and tussock for signs of life, but there were still no deer anywhere in sight. In the end, I realised that it was getting too dark to continue, so made my way back to the truck. A few minutes of jarring and jolting over the rough ground saw me back at the yard – thankfully, the route I chose only featured three or four gates, so was far less painful than it'd been on the way out.

I swapped the binos for my NV and set out again. Unfortunately, thanks to the wind direction, the paddock where the lamb was killed was still a non-starter. To make matters more difficult, the only way around it would take me upwind, so I hoped I could get to the higher ground above the farm without compromising the hunt. I had several noisy metal gates to negotiate just to get out of the yard, but once the last was out of the way, I was in a large meadow that I figured would be an ideal area for the caller.

The field started by rising steeply before me. I knew that it then fell into a shallow dip some 100yd across before rising again on the far side. Although I couldn't yet see them, I could hear a large number of sheep and lambs calling, but hoped that they wouldn't get in the way. Picking my way slowly along the hedgeline, I was disturbed to see how distinct my shadow was – the damned moon was obviously going to be an issue. As I passed the top gateway into the paddock, some ewes jumped up, surprised at my sudden appearance. They soon settled again though, and I continued on my way. Every few feet, I scanned the landscape with my NV monocular – this kind of shooting is not for the impatient, and it's always better to see the fox before it sees you...

When I made it to the crest of the rise, I was disheartened to see that along with the sheep, there were also about 20 cows in the field. That blew my plans for the caller – I couldn't risk using it there as the cattle would almost certainly go charging about the place as soon as I turned it on. That left me wondering just how I was going to get on the fox. The bright moon, wrong wind direction and difficult terrain were all conspiring against me. There was nothing for it. Even though there was no gate into the next field, I'd have to climb through the hedge and try there. Going back and around would take me half an hour. The only point where this is possible features several runs of barbed wire, numerous blackthorn bushes, a steep bank and all manner of other obstacles. It's hard enough to do in the day, but it's really difficult in the dark. Everything seems intent on either sinking a spike into your flesh, or clawing at your clothes – especially your face veil – with grim determination. Still, with measured patience and taking great care of the rifle and my monocular, I made it safely through to the field beyond.

Other than a lack of cattle, the one advantage my new location gave me was the fact that I was now able to get into the shadows cast by some small trees. A quick scan around showed that the field was devoid of any animals – apart from two bunnies about 100yd or so from me. With my back to the hedge, I double-checked the

TIPS & TRICKS

Safety is always a vitally important part of shooting. Aside from all the obvious issues to do with handling guns, it is always important to know what the other risks are. One of the most potentially dangerous aspects of wandering around farmland concerns livestock. Some animals will only be curious, but others – especially cows protecting their calves or aggressive bulls – are well worth avoiding. A good rule of thumb is always to stay uphill of any unknown cattle as it makes it much harder for them to trample you, either by accident or intentionally.

landscape. I was almost at the highest point – there was a continuation of the dip from the field I'd just come from – but from where I was standing, some of it was dead ground. Having satisfied myself that nothing was nearby, I started scanning the area on the far side of the dip. This featured a hedge and then a field which rose to a crest – after that, it fell away into thick woodland.

Whilst doing this, I spotted movement some 400yd away. The animal in question was too fast and too big to be a bunny, but as I didn't have time to get a good focus, I couldn't get a positive ID on it. My NV mono only has 3x magnification, so I set the sticks up and settled the rifle into place. My dedicated NV has 6x mag, and I quickly ascertained that I had, indeed, seen a fox. It was darting back and forth chasing something with determination – presumably a rabbit – so it was quite clear that it was in killing mode. I knew that if I cocked up the opportunity to call it in, it'd probably kill another lamb, so I got my act together quickly. I counted out 50 paces, and put the caller in position.

Retiring to the depths of the shadows, I started the caller on vole squeaks. Even though the fox had been some way off, within moments it came in from downwind like a steam train. I was tracking it with the reticle, but it just kept going. I started to worry that it'd reach the caller before I got a chance to fire. I knew that the instant it scented me, it'd run off. Just as I feared, it turned and ran within what seemed a millisecond. Luckily for me – and unluckily for the fox – it paused briefly to look over its shoulder after about 30yd. That was all I needed, and a .22-250 round immediately smacked it down.

Very pleased with myself, I counted out the 50 paces and retrieved the caller before walking over to see the kill. Switching on my torch, I was amazed to see how big it was. There was no doubting that it was a dog fox and it was not the biggest I've shot, but still a heck of a beast. Stretched out, it was the same length as my Sauer 202 with moderator – which measures 48 inches end to end, with teeth to match its bulk. 'The farmer has got to see this', I thought to myself, so I dragged it back to the yard – through the hedge and all. As I was doing so, I jokingly reflected that it was bigger than some roe deer I've shot in the past.

ABOVE: If a lamb is killed and left behind by a fox, its mother will stand over the body for several days, hoping against hope that it will somehow revive.

BELOW: The lamb killings stopped when this large dog fox, which weighed 23lb was shot. It came in to the vole squeaks track on my FOXPRO Scorpion electronic caller.

In the end, it weighed in at 23lb, and as the lamb killings stopped, I think we can be sure I shot the right animal. Needless to say, the farmer was very pleased indeed – as were his lambs and their mothers!

REDS IN THE NIGHT

DATE:	13 April 2011	**RIFLE:**	Sauer 202
PLACE:	Robert's Farm	**CALIBRE:**	.22-250
TIME:	21:00	**AMMO:**	55gr Nosler BT
SUNSET:	20:07	**RANGE:**	100yd
STATE OF MOON:	Waxing gibbous	**CALL TRACK:**	Fox squeals after vixen
WEATHER:	Dry		on heat
WIND DIRECTION:	North-westerly	**OPTICS:**	D480 GenIII NV riflescope

Since the season for roe does and red hinds ended at the beginning of the month, I was limited to bucks and stags while it was daylight – then after dark, I could go after the foxes.

Before I left the house I checked the weather forecast, paying particular attention to the wind map as its direction would be critical to the success of my session. But after arriving in the yard, I got all kitted out and set off towards the woods. Before I'd got more than 30yd, however, I realised the wind was behind me. This wasn't obvious while I was in between all the barns, but the moment I left their cover, it became evident.

Muttering various swear words to myself about the veracity of the weather forecast, I packed everything back in the truck and drove off to the other side of the farm. Once there, I was much happier that I was not going to be upwind of my intended prey. I had about 45 minutes of light left, so was keen to get on my way. Before I did though, I had a quick scan around with the binos. A momentary flash of white through the trees some 600yd away gave away the presence of a red hind. Closer examination showed that there were several other animals with her, and that something had spooked them, as they were dashing about all over the place. Although it's always nice to watch deer in their natural environment, this was not what I wanted to see as it meant that the main herd in the area was well away on someone else's land.

I wasn't about to give up yet though, and slowly made my way along the hedges towards the field that I felt was likeliest to have deer on it. This is a meadow which lies on the north side of a stretch of mixed pine and broadleaf woodland. The grass there is lush at the

moment, and the site is rarely disturbed by anyone – especially so near dark. Consequently, the deer seem to like to feed there. A few startled bunnies scuttled away from me: they weren't a problem, as they were nice and quiet. The pheasants were a different matter. Every few feet I'd spot some more, and every one of them had to be treated with care, as a wrong move would see them clattering off and shrieking.

Luckily, I made it within sight of my chosen observation point without being compromised. Not everything was in my favour. In the 20 or so minutes it'd taken me, the wind had changed direction, and I now had to take a different route over the last few yards to ensure that I didn't get upwind of the field. All my efforts were in vain, though. When I eventually got in place, there wasn't anything to be seen. I scanned every possible tree, bush and hedge but alas, it was indeed, a deer-free zone.

Not wanting to waste any time, I made my way upwind towards another possible site – but yet again, there were no deer anywhere. By then the light was going, so decided it'd be best if I made my way back to the truck for a rethink. On the way there, I was able to see that the herd I'd spotted earlier was still in the same field, still well off my permission. By now they'd settled down and were grazing away merrily. Oh well, they'd have to wait for another time.

Back at the yard, I discovered that the farmer was now home, and that he'd been roped into helping his wife with some DIY. They'd not owned the place for very long, and the move from their last farm had almost crippled them financially, so they were desperately trying to finish off a small holiday cottage that adjoined their house so that it could be rented out.

I did my best to stay out of the way whilst catching up on all the important gossip – where they'd seen deer, what damage had been done to the crops and fences, etc.

Once all that was sorted, I set out for a foxing session. I wasn't at all hopeful that I'd be successful, as I'd already shot most of the foxes on the farm, and they don't seem to move about very much in March. Within seconds of leaving the yard, however, I heard a fox calling from some way off. I hoped it was a good omen!

The field I was aiming for was on the other side of the woods from where I'd been looking for the deer earlier. It was a long piece of land, that constantly rises and dips along its length. The farmer had said that I might well see some deer while I was there as they'd been crossing it most nights to get to some other ground. On page 26 there's an section about how I called in four foxes in five minutes ('A Frantic Time In The Fog'). Well, the field I was now in was where the foxes had appeared from.

Unlike that time, when the fog was coming in really heavily, on this occasion the sky was completely clear – which was not good news as the moon was very bright. I therefore spent some time trying to find some shadows to hide in. In the end, I found a tree to lurk under that was growing out of a particularly thick part of the hedge – while it wasn't perfect, it was the best I was going to get under the circumstances. I stood back for a minute or so to gauge the wind, the

> **TIPS & TRICKS**
> If you're using a remote-control caller and/or bait, check the lay of the land very carefully, as foxes are masters of using dead ground. If there are any approach routes that you cannot see properly from your chosen shooting position, it is likely that the fox will be in and gone before you can do anything about it, so take the time to find another vantage point before you start.

lie of the land, and the possible directions from where a fox could approach. I then walked 50 paces into the field and placed the caller.

Back at the hedge, I set my sticks up and focused the NV on the caller, checked the illuminator was working OK and got my feet into a good shooting stance. A quick scan around with the mono picked up a set of bunny eyes, but nothing else, so I started the caller going – set to vixen on heat. After about two minutes with no action, I muted it and waited for a while.

Still nothing showed, so I tried again with a quick burst of fox squalls. About five seconds later a set of eyes appeared above the grass for a moment. They then reappeared as a fox running in at speed. I rushed to turn the mono off and get the rifle ready. As soon as I'd got the riflescope switched on, however, I saw that the fox was now running away from the caller up the field. It was looking over its shoulder down towards the corner of the wood. Something else had spooked it big time.

I thought it was probably another fox and just as I was thinking this, my intended prey made the mistake of stopping for a better look, about 100yd out. The moment it did so, I squeezed off a round. A fraction of a second later there was a loud 'pop' and the fox fell face first into the grass. Just as the echo resounded, it was joined by the sound of a stampede to my immediate right – immediately on the other side of the hedge. I swung the scope across the field in time to see two red hinds diving back into the woods. I couldn't see the ones beyond the hedge – I can only assume that they were reds too – if so, there must have been about 25 of them. Since the big herd I'd seen earlier numbered about that, I think it's likely that they were the same animals.

On inspection, the fox – which had been hit right in the engine room – was a vixen. Her teats were swollen, but there was no sign of milk, so she must have already weaned her pups. When I got back to the yard, the farmer and his wife were still at the DIY – he was very grateful for my efforts, and urged me to get back after the deer as soon as I could!

DEALING WITH A LAMB-KILLER

DATE:	20 April 2009	**RIFLE:**	Sauer 202
PLACE:	Critter's Shoot	**CALIBRE:**	.22-250
TIME:	19:30	**AMMO:**	55gr Win SP
SUNSET:	20:19	**RANGE:**	100yd
STATE OF MOON:	Morning crescent	**CALL TRACK:**	Adult rat distress
WEATHER:	Dry	**OPTICS:**	D480 GenIII NV riflescope
WIND DIRECTION:	South-westerly		

Not long after I'd been over and shot a fox near the big house on the estate where Critter works, he called me up and said that he'd been asked to deal with a multiple lamb-killer on a neighbouring farm. He went on to say that it would be a difficult one for him to deal with as it was lamp-shy, and so my NV gear could be just what was needed. I agreed to help out and drove over that evening. I left my truck at his place and jumped into his Toyota pick-up. That way there'd be no confusion with the farmer suddenly finding an unknown vehicle on his land. We wound our way up the steep hill and before long we were there. Parking up as quietly as we could, we gathered our things and slowly tiptoed to the gate to look out over the flock that had been repeatedly attacked. No matter how hard we looked though, we couldn't see any foxes. That was just as well, as the wind, which was blowing from the south-west, was

> ## TIPS & TRICKS
> I always give top priority to farmers who are having livestock killed by foxes – young lambs represent such an important part of a farmer's income that any losses are not only extremely upsetting, but are also very damaging from an economic perspective too. In such circumstances, you cannot beat putting the hours in. Patiently watching a lambing flock will usually pay dividends sooner or later.

completely wrong for us. It was very dark though, so at least we wouldn't be fighting a bright moon.

We decided it would be much better if we moved to the next field which was further down the hill. If we took the easy route and walked along the lane, the wind would be behind us, so that was not an option. The only way for it was to go right across to the other side and work in from there. On the way over Critter shot a bunny with his .22RF so that we could use it as bait. We found a spot with very little dead ground that looked suitable for an ambush, so we set ourselves up in the shadow of the hedge. The next job was to split the rabbit open and place it next to the caller, about 100yd out. When all was ready, I switched it on using the screaming bunny call track. We had a good view across the field over to where the sheep were grazing in a tight huddle. This is usually a sign that some kind of predator is around, so we were hopeful of a result. Sure enough, about five minutes later, a fox appeared from the direction of the lambs, but to our dismay it sat a long way back and just watched.

After a couple of minutes, it jumped up and ran to our right towards the nearby woods. Before it got there, and for no apparent reason, it sat down again and watched over the area. It did this about four or five times, and then appeared to head off into the woods. In an attempt to bring it in, I then switched the call to distressed adult rat. Within about 30 seconds or so, the fox suddenly appeared from nowhere and ran in at speed. It circled around on the wind to get the safest approach angle and rushed in. I tracked it all the way, and when it paused to sniff the air, some 20yd from the caller, I shot it. It fell where it was hit.

We checked that no other foxes were around, then walked over to inspect it. There was little surprise that it was a big dog that tipped the scales at 18lb. Critter felt the stomach, which was very obviously full, and said that as it contained a lot of large pieces of meat; we had almost certainly found

I was called in to deal with a fox that had been killing lambs. Although it soon showed itself after I started the caller, it wasn't in a hurry to come in close. In the end it couldn't resist sound of the distressed rat call. I had been experiencing problems with light reflecting back off the moderator from the laser illuminator, so I fitted an experimental shroud to it, as can be seen in this photo.

the lamb-killer. Since there were no more killings after that night, there is little doubt that we were correct.

HALF FOX, HALF RAT

DATE:	21 April 2012	**RIFLE:**	Sauer 202
PLACE:	Roy's Farm	**CALIBRE:**	.22-250
TIME:	21:30	**AMMO:**	55gr Nosler BT
SUNSET:	20:21	**RANGE:**	90yd
STATE OF MOON:	New	**CALL TRACK:**	BestFoxCall mouth
WEATHER:	Dry		caller
WIND DIRECTION:	North-westerly	**OPTICS:**	D480 GenIII NV riflescope

For a couple of months I kept getting reports of a particularly mangy fox that had been seen in various places. One call concerned it hanging around some very valuable rare breed lambs on a local farm. I went over that evening and successfully called in and shot two, neither of which was mangy though. I went back a couple of times, but the one I was after had vanished. It's unusual to see any around here that are in anything but the best of health – except, that is, when the supposed animal charities have been dumping their unwanted guests on us, so they were the prime suspects for its appearance.

About a week after that, another farmer on the other side of the village said that a very mangy fox had been seen in the field next to his young lambs. I was already keeping a close eye on them for him, but again, it was nowhere to be seen. I can only assume that being in such poor condition, it was being constantly pushed off any established territories by the resident foxes.

One night, however, on the way over to another permission, I decided that it was not quite dark enough to start using the NV, so I stopped and quickly checked a meadow where I've shot loads of foxes with the thermal imager. There was nothing there, but before jumping back in the truck, I scanned across another field that runs along the top of a hill on the other side of the lane. Bingo! A bright white shape was running back and forth behind a tree. I dived back and grabbed the rifle and sticks. Since I would be facing east, I figured the light levels should be OK to switch the NV riflescope on. Just to be sure, however, I also cranked the manual

TIPS & TRICKS

Mange is a horrible and very infectious affliction, so if you shoot a fox that has it, make sure you dispose of the carcass carefully. Don't just throw it into a nearby hedge, as it will pose a risk to other wildlife as well as to any dogs that are walked in the vicinity.

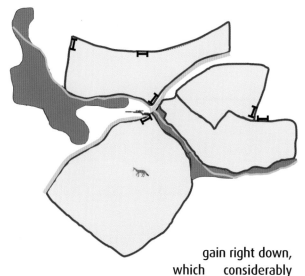

gain right down, which considerably reduces the tube brightness. I couldn't see the fox at first, as there were some large branches in the way, so I shuffled forwards a few feet. Once I was clear of the tree, I was able to see my intended target, sitting up and clearly silhouetted against the skyline. Not only was the shot unthinkable, the fox was directly downwind of me.

Just as I was wondering what to do, it got up and sauntered off over the brow and out of sight. Damn! I moved a bit further forwards and checked with the thermal, but it had gone. I therefore whipped the mouth caller out of my pocket and quickly blew a few plaintive squeaks. Within moments, the fox was back, but once again it was skylined, making the shot anything but safe. I waited, hoping against hope that it couldn't scent me, and although it was obviously being cautious, a few seconds later it began heading down the slope towards me. At one point it paused, presumably to sniff the wind, and in that instant a .22-250 round hit it hard. The sound was that of a bullet smacking something very solid, so I suspected a direct skull hit. This was backed up by the fact that it fell without a twitch.

When I got to it, I discovered it was the mangiest fox I've ever seen. I'd clearly done it a big favour. Its tail looked as though it belonged on a giant rat, much of its body fur was missing, and its flesh appeared to be very flaccid. It was a large dog fox that in spite of its dreadful condition still weighed a lot. It must have been massive when it was healthy. As I'd thought, it had been hit by a perfect head shot. I have to say that I was very pleased to have finally caught up with this sorry creature. Not only would the livestock be that much safer, but a potentially major source of sarcoptic mange infection had been removed from the locality – as it was only yards from one of the most popular dog walking routes in the area, its demise cannot have come soon enough.

I'd been getting reports of a mangy fox from all over the place. It was clearly being pushed out of every territory it entered, because it ended up on this hill, at least two miles away from where it'd first been seen. It went over the brow, but I managed to call it back, and shot it about half way down. The detail photo shows the extent of the mange.

MAY

From my perspective, May is probably the hardest month of the year for foxing. No matter what I try, or how hard I look, I find that most of the foxes have just disappeared. Even the usually productive callers are generally ineffective, and if you aren't careful, it is easy to start questioning your abilities. The longer days, however, do give you a chance to get out in the evenings. The older and more adventurous cubs will start to appear, especially towards the end of the month. Any late lambs will need to be kept under a close eye, as they will be vulnerable, because in many areas there's not much food around.

Before long the young birds and baby rabbits start showing in significant numbers, and that is good news for hungry foxes. Unfortunately, both eggs and nestlings can take a real hammering from predators – once again, the main threats come from foxes and corvids. I have watched as a jay flew down in front of a blackbird hen sitting on her precious nest of young birds and then deliberately antagonised her. As she got more and more worried about the safety of her babies, she attempted to chase it away by flapping her wings and

By the start of May the world is abounding with life – the trees have all grown fresh verdant leaves, the birds have broods of hungry nestlings on the way to fledging and the hedges are full of wild flowers in bloom.

squawking loudly. All the while, the jay's partner sat patiently in the branches just out of sight behind her. The moment she left the nest to chase the scurrilous intruder away, the second bird swooped down and grabbed several of the chicks. I have shot many foxes that had just raided a nest or killed a tiny fledgling – one of these occasions is recounted in detail later in this chapter.

The roe bucks start getting territorial in May, and the does can get very aggressive towards anything they think might be a threat towards their fawns. I've had them come charging in to the caller when it's been on a prey distress sound, clearly intent on chasing the 'predator' away.

As the sunlight warms the ground the vegetation grows taller and taller, until it becomes impossible to see anything hiding within it. Sadly, this often includes young deer and leverets (baby hares) on fields that are being

THE FARMER'S MONTH
First haylage and silage mown.
Livestock buildings cleaned through.
Sheep and lambs tagged and marked.
Fertiliser and muck spreading.
Crops sprayed.

mown. Unless the tractor driver is careful, the first thing he knows about them being there is a sudden bang from the cutters – tragic but the numbers accidentally killed in this way are tiny relative to those killed by predators. Scientists now believe that about half of all roe fawns are taken by foxes, for instance.

Although the lambing is mostly finished by now, there is little rest for the farmer. All the new arrivals need to be attended to – they will all be ear-tagged, and the male lambs are castrated. Both adults and young need to be protected against fly-strike – this is where eggs are laid on the wool, and the resulting maggots eat into the living flesh. Most sheep – especially those on hill farms are also marked to help with identification. The first haylage and silage crops will be cut – the only real difference between hay, haylage and silage is the moisture content, and how the cut material is stored. All grass crops respond well to fertiliser, and so the livestock is removed from the fields in question before spraying takes place.

The nutritional value of the grass is directly linked to the amount of sunlight it has received, and so every farmer is thankful to see blue skies. It is an anxious time, as there is the perennial gamble as to when to cut – leave it too long, and there is the risk of rain ruining the years crop. Conversely, mowing it too soon risks losing out on valuable extra growth. There is also the added problem of access to the machinery – generally, when one field is ready, so are all the others, and as a result getting everything organised needs significant planning and preparation. Many of the bigger farms implement a one-way system, so that all the silage trailers are able to get back and forth without getting tangled up with one another. Yet again, this is a time of little sleep – in this part of the world it is not at all unusual for the silage foragers to be run late into the night. More or less as soon as the fields have been mown, the farmers will be back in spraying with an after-cut fertiliser to encourage enough growth for second and hopefully third cuts.

The world really starts to come alive in May. The trees all have fresh green leaves and the hedgerows are filled with wild flowers in bloom. Close inspection can reveal all manner of wildlife – things like lizards and snakes will find quiet spots to bask in the sun, and out on the twigs caterpillars that have over-wintered will be frantically trying to fatten up before crawling off to somewhere secluded to pupate. Some of these can be spectacular, with the large hairy larvae of the oak eggar, drinker and lappet moths being my personal favourites. Orange tip butterflies can be seen flying in most rural areas when the sun is out. The males have the distinctive orange patches on the end of their wings from which their name derives. The females are much harder to distinguish – looking much like cabbage whites to the average person. They do not lay their eggs on cabbages though, for their most common food plants are Cuckoo flower – also known as Ladies Smock, and Garlic Mustard and often referred to as 'Jack By The Hedge'.

Wasps will also be building nests – they can often be seen rasping wood pulp from fenceposts, trees and dried plant stems. Left unchecked, the rabbits will breed like mad, so it is a good time to reduce their numbers if you get the time. Rabbit meat is very good eating – both for humans and pets, and the guts as well as the trimmings also make excellent fox bait.

Common gorse flowers from autumn to spring but when the Orange Tip butterfly appears, you can be sure that summer is only just around the corner. Only the male has the distinctive wing-tip coloration.

CARRION FEEDERS

DATE:	1 & 2 May 2011		**RIFLE:**	Sauer 202
PLACE:	Jim's Farm		**CALIBRE:**	.22-250
TIME:	Both around 22:30		**AMMO:**	55gr Nosler BT
SUNSET:	20:35		**RANGE:**	80yd and 60yd
STATE OF MOON:	Morning crescent		**CALL TRACK:**	None
WEATHER:	Dry		**OPTICS:**	D480 GenIII NV riflescope
WIND DIRECTION:	North-westerly			

I was working in my office when I got a call from Jim. He was anxious for me to go over as he'd had several lambs killed by foxes in the orchard paddock just opposite his house. There was also a dead ewe in the same field. Before ending the call, I asked exactly where it was, so that I'd know where to look.

When I got there, I couldn't see any sign of foxes, so I did a quick tour of the fields on the other side of the farmyard. After half an hour or so, I crept back and circled around to the gate at the top of the orchard paddock. This meant the wind would be in my favour. From there I spotted a fox tearing at the ewe's carcass. It wasn't going to be an easy shot as there was a rise in the ground between us, so I waited until it moved into a better position, and dropped it with a round from my Sauer. With the sound of the discharge, another fox popped out from behind the dead sheep and ran into the bushes. I was keen to get to grips it, but although I spent a couple of hours trying to find it, I had no luck. The vixen was milky, so clearly she had pups somewhere. By then it was too late to try to find them, so I left it for the night.

I went back the next morning in daylight to see if I could find the cubs. I searched the top woods as well as all the hedges and covers, but with no luck. I went back again that evening to see if I could get to grips with the second fox. I had another attempt at finding the cubs, but drew another blank.

As darkness had fallen, I went back to the yard to see if my intended prey was anywhere near what little remained of the ewe's carcass. I used the NV to look over the gate into the orchard paddock and immediately saw a fox under the hedge in the far corner. It was lying down and feeding on the last of the dead sheep. Once again there was a rise in the way, so I climbed over the fence as quietly as I could and made my way towards it. The wind was strong, and I had trouble keeping the rifle steady. Unluckily for the fox, it was blowing my scent towards the top gate, so it didn't know I was there. I waited until it turned sideways, then knocked it to the floor. Surprisingly, it proved to be another milky vixen – I wasn't expecting this as I didn't think two litter-bearing females would tolerate each other as close as they'd been the night before. The question therefore, was whether they were co-suckling the same cubs, or whether the two vixens were closely related, and thus able to exist happily side by side?

> ### TIPS & TRICKS
> If you are approaching an area that might well have foxes on it, take great care to ensure that you do not become silhouetted against the sky, as you will show up really easily, even in very dark conditions. To avoid this, try only to move in front of suitable cover – hedges, bushes, walls or buildings.

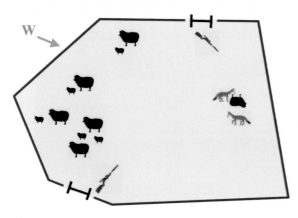

DUCK KILLER

DATE:	11 May 2011	**RIFLE:**	Sauer 202
PLACE:	Reg's Farm	**CALIBRE:**	.22-250
TIME:	23:00	**AMMO:**	55gr Nosler BT
SUNSET:	20:51	**RANGE:**	Around 150yd
STATE OF MOON:	Waxing gibbous	**CALL TRACK:**	None
WEATHER:	Dry with full cloud cover	**OPTICS:**	D480 GenIII NV riflescope
WIND DIRECTION:	North-westerly		

One morning in mid-May, I got a call from Catherine, who runs the livestock side of her father's farm, to say that she'd found a dead lamb that had been killed recently. It was a large one – at least a month old – and so not the typical behaviour of foxes, although every now and then you do get a rogue dog fox that grows large enough to kill correspondingly larger prey.

I agreed to go over to inspect the carcass and see what I could make of the matter. I waited until late evening before I left so that it'd be dark enough to use the NV equipment. The remains of the lamb showed it was far larger than one would expect for a fox to take down. It was impossible to say what had killed it though, as the farm dogs had found the carcass first, and they'd had a good chew on it, masking the hard evidence. My feeling was that it was most likely to have been the result of a dog attack. Still, I'd agreed to take a tour of the farm to see if there were any foxes about, so that is what I did.

I set off down the farm track but got to the bottom without seeing anything, so I climbed up on a bank to look into the next field. I scanned around the edges of the big woods, but all I saw were rabbits. I decided to stay where I was and observe. This proved to be sensible, as about five minutes later I spotted a set of fox eyes shining back at me from low down in the opposite hedge – although there was no way that I could take a shot at it. The fox crept out and spent a good ten seconds looking up at the bunnies and then disappeared. Knowing how wily they can be, I guessed it was going to circle around and then come back into the field downwind of the rabbits ... and that gave me 30 seconds to find a way through the hedge. Easier said than done! Just as I made it onto stable ground, the fox reappeared where I thought it would. It advanced downhill and I realised I only had a few seconds before it would be directly downwind of me. As I got the sticks set up, the fox sussed something was going on, and sat back, looking straight towards me. I wasted no time in lining up on its chest and shooting, killing it at 160 paces

I was still doubtful that this animal was responsible for killing the lamb, and was proved right as several more lambs were killed over the next two weeks. Then the slaughtering stopped overnight and Catherine's enquiries revealed that the killer was almost certainly a dog belonging to holidaymakers renting a cottage about half a mile away. The attacks on her ducks stopped right after I shot the vixen, so at least my efforts had not been in vain.

TIPS & TRICKS

Foxes have prospered in this country because they are clever creatures. They are just as capable of working out how best to approach a potential food source as you are. Expect them to exploit the wind as well as nearby natural cover at every opportunity.

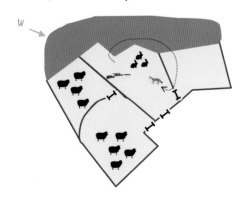

FREE RANGE FOX

DATE:	15 May 2011	**RIFLE:**	Sauer 202
PLACE:	Mervyn's Farm	**CALIBRE:**	.22-250
TIME:	22:00	**AMMO:**	55gr Nosler BT
SUNSET:	20:57	**RANGE:**	170yd
STATE OF MOON:	Waxing gibbous	**CALL TRACK:**	Fox cub distress
WEATHER:	Dry with full cloud cover	**OPTICS:**	D480 GenIII NV riflescope
WIND DIRECTION:	North-westerly		

Mervyn – a farmer friend – called to say that he'd seen a fox near the chicken sheds, and that he'd be very grateful if I could go over and attend to it. Since I always put anyone with livestock concerns to the top of my list, I said I'd drive over that evening to see if I could find it. Like most of the landscape in this part of the world, his place is far from easy to work over, as the way it rises and falls makes it very difficult to see very far. Unsurprisingly, the field the foxes seem to favour as their main transit route from the main area of cover across to the next has huge amounts of dead ground in it. This gives them a degree of security, so although I have shot a few there, I try to avoid it.

On the other side of the hedge is a large flat field, and this is sometimes used to house the chicken sheds. Moved around regularly to minimise the risk of disease, wherever they get placed the foxes are never far behind. My job is to make sure that I get to them before they get to the chickens. I took on the shooting just after they'd had an attack when they lost about 175 birds in less than an hour. If you think what a free-range organic chicken costs, and then multiply it by 175, it's easy to see that the result is going to be a loss of at least a thousand pounds to the farmer.

Not many businesses can afford to take a hit like that on a regular basis, so it's vital that my predator control activities are successful. In spite of the huge investment I've made in equipment and time, I still don't charge for what I do. Some people find this hard to understand, but I get recompense in other ways. Some people give me sacks of home-grown teddies (Devonian for potatoes), others the occasional chicken, sometimes it's a leg of lamb, or maybe I'll be handed a nice big bag of juicy pork sausages. A few tell me that while I'm dealing with the foxes, I can take as many deer as I like. Another

advantage of keeping money out of the equation is that I can decide where I go, and when. I only shoot for people I like – anyone who doesn't appreciate me being there doesn't get a second visit.

I arrived just as it was getting dark. Parking up in the yard, my first mission was to have a chat with Mervyn to establish as much as I could about the known movements of my appointed adversary. That done, I got myself all kitted out and started by scanning the field in front of the farmhouse. This is the one with the difficult terrain, so I wasn't unduly surprised to find that there was nothing visible. At least there was no moon to contend with – the only decent vantage points have absolutely no cover near them, so if there's any light at all, there is no way to remain unseen.

Moving on to where the chicken sheds were, I tried again, giving the whole area a thorough scanning with the NV spotter: nothing of interest. It was clearly time to get the caller out, so I paced out about 80 steps and placed it facing out towards the nearby stretch of cover. This is made up of an extended line of light scrub that grows on either side of the stream that borders that side of the farm. Immediately next to this is a narrow field, which is separated from the one I was looking over by a thick hedge, which is also a popular hiding place for all manner of animals. Returning to some slightly higher ground, I set my sticks up and got ready to start the caller.

First, I had to choose which sound to use though. I didn't want to play any of the prey distress tracks that I normally use there, in case the fox had learned to

> **TIPS & TRICKS**
> When a prey distress call doesn't work, it is always worth trying one of the many fox calls instead. This may catch the attention of an otherwise uninterested individual.

associate them with danger. Since it was the right time of year for the adults to be anxious about their young, I decided it might pay off to begin with a series of distressed fox cub calls. Some five minutes or so went by without response, but then I spotted a set of eyes over in the far corner, some 300yd out. By the way they were moving it was clearly a fox, and by their brightness, probably a male. It was obviously a very experienced animal, as it kept itself well down into the dead ground, only raising its head far enough to see across the field. It continued to move along the base of the far hedge without stopping, but wouldn't come any closer. When it reached the large dung pile that straddles the end of the field, it ducked in behind and disappeared from view. I was hopeful that by the time it reached the other end it would be curious enough to stop for a good look, so I got everything prepared – I adjusted the focus to get a crisp picture, ensured the brightness of the laser illuminator was just right, and moved my feet to get the best possible stance. I settled my breathing and readied myself. Just as I did so, the fox appeared and, as I hoped, it paused to look out towards the caller. I placed the reticle high on its chest and released a shot. It tumbled forwards and out of sight into the long grass. I counted out the number of paces, and reckoned it had been about 170 yards from me. Mervyn was delighted to hear that I'd got to grips with what could potentially have been a major problem so quickly, and as FERA wanted carcasses for their trichinella testing study, I passed on his contact details to them.

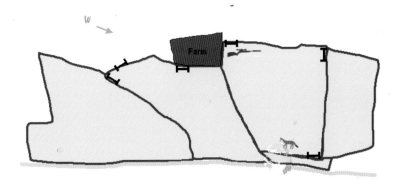

LEFT: The fox first appeared amongst the trees seen on the left – at this stage it was just a set of eyes glowing in the dark. It then made its way to the right using the dead ground on this side of the hedge. When it reached the dung heap – (the pale mound on the right), it circled round behind it and then came forward just far enough to see what all the noise was about. It fell where it was shot.

A GOOD START

DATE:	21 May 2011	RIFLE:	Two x Sauer 202
PLACE:	John's Farm	CALIBRE:	.22-250 & .308
TIME:	23:30	AMMO:	55gr Nosler BT
SUNSET:	21:05	RANGE:	45yd
STATE OF MOON:	Waning gibbous	CALL TRACK:	None
WEATHER:	Dry with full cloud cover	OPTICS:	D480 GenIII NV riflescope
WIND DIRECTION:	South-westerly		

The Devon County Show is an enormous affair that takes place over three days in May. I was doing my bit, helping out as a volunteer on the British Deer Society stand, when a friend passed on a message that my foxing capabilities were needed on a farm that bordered one of my existing permissions.

The following morning I called John, the owner of the farm. I agreed that I'd go over the next day so that he could show me around. As I'd previously been told, his property lies alongside one of the big farms that I look after, so it was great to be able to push the boundaries out a bit further and get into some of the places that had looked so promising from afar. I arrived about an hour before dark, and we started out by walking up the hill in brilliant sunshine to where the chicken sheds were sited. John was talking away ten to the dozen when all of a sudden we saw that there was a fox right next to the chickens. Luckily, it was on the right side of the electric fence, but it would doubtless have been through before very long, had we not appeared. Seeing a fox just a couple of minutes after arriving was so unex-

TIPS & TRICKS

Chicken sheds can be a real draw for hungry foxes, so it is a good idea to check around them especially just after dark.

pected that I wasn't ready, and it had run off through the nearby hedge before I could even unsling my .308.

Not wanting to let it get away, I rushed around to the field beyond, but there was no sign of it. By the time we'd done a bit more of a walk around it was getting dark, so we returned to the farmyard. There, after concluding our chat, I jumped into the Disco, stuck it in low ratio and drove up the steep track to revisit the chicken sheds. Parking up in a relatively hidden spot, I unlocked the firearms cabinet and swapped the .308 stalking rifle for the .22-250 NV rig. I did a tour of the various vantage points I'd seen earlier, then looped around on the breeze to come back towards the chickens from downwind.

Creeping up to the end shed, I had a quick scan and immediately spotted a fox nosing around inside the area that was supposedly secured by the electric fence. It was very close, so I had to get my sticks up very carefully – that done, the rifle was on them in moments, and seconds later the fox lay dead. I estimated the range at about 45yd, and on inspection found that it was a young vixen, almost certainly one from the previous year. I later sent FERA an email, telling them where the carcass was so that they could collect it for their trichinella study.

After that little success, I tried a quick session with the vixen on heat call, but as nothing came in, I called it a night and went home. On my way down the farm lane a cub ran across in front of me, so it was clear that I still had plenty of work to do there. Still, for a first visit, I hadn't done at all badly, and as it was such a lovely place, I was keen to return for more action!

LAST LIGHT DOG

DATE:	27 May 2011	**WIND DIRECTION:**	North-westerly
PLACE:	Jim's farm	**RIFLE:**	Sauer 202
TIME:	20:45	**CALIBRE:**	.308
SUNSET:	21:13	**AMMO:**	165gr Sierra GameKing SP
STATE OF MOON:	Daylight (morning crescent)	**RANGE:**	Around 85yd
		CALL TRACK:	Young rat distress call
WEATHER:	Dry	**OPTICS:**	D480 GenIII NV riflescope

A chap called Rhys had contacted me to see if I'd be willing to take him shooting as he was just getting into hunting, having previously done a lot of target work. He now wanted to gain some more experience, hence his request. I was happy to take him out, and decided to start by shooting on a piece of ground where one of the farmers was having bunny problems. We arrived a couple of hours before dark and began working our way around the property. I was pleased to see that Rhys could not only shoot pieces of paper, but also live quarry, soon accounting for four bunnies and a pigeon.

Since the farmer had also experienced fox problems there too, I was keen to tackle them as well. About 20 minutes before it got dark, we set the caller out near a pond, using the remains of the pigeon as bait. Rhys, who had never witnessed a caller in action, was amazed when, within about a minute, two foxes came steaming in at great speed. Most stop to sniff the air before approaching, but these didn't, and the moment they got to the caller they scented me and immediately turned and ran. One of them made it to a hedge, whereupon it paused briefly. I was tracking it all the way, and it had barely stopped moving when one of my 165gr GameKing soft points hit it in the chest. It went down like a sack of spuds – unsurprisingly really, as I developed these rounds to knock down a fully-grown red deer stag.

The other fox didn't make that mistake, and ran on right through the rough ground and out of the other side into the field above. There it stopped for a moment, but I didn't get a chance of a shot. We tried some other calls, but it had clearly been spooked and there wasn't any response. By then it was getting dark so we called it a day and packed up.

TIPS & TRICKS

If you use a remote control electronic caller, it is vital that you do not walk across any likely fox approach routes while you're placing it. Any wary foxes will smell your scent trail straight away, and will usually immediately turn and run. Likewise, if they get close to the actual caller, the same thing will happen, so it's best to mute the device the moment you see a fox. This way, it will stop to see where the creature it was running in on has gone – giving you the ideal opportunity to take a shot.

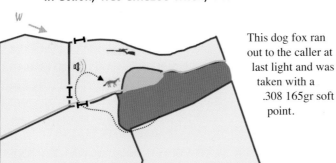

This dog fox ran out to the caller at last light and was taken with a .308 165gr soft point.

NEST RAIDER

DATE:	28 May 2011	CALIBRE:	.22-250, .308 & .17HMR
PLACE:	John's Farm	AMMO:	.22-250: 55gr Nosler BT;
TIME:	19:15		.308: 110gr Hornady V-Max BT;
SUNSET:	21:14		17HMR: 17gr Remington BT
STATE OF MOON:	Daylight, waning gibbous	RANGE:	Fox 60yd; Roe 150yd
WEATHER:	Dry	CALL TRACK:	None
WIND DIRECTION:	Westerly	OPTICS:	D480 GenIII NV riflescope
RIFLE:	Two x Sauer 202 &		(.22-250) & Swarovski Z6
	CZ American		2.5-15x56 (.308)

A few days after my encounter with the young vixen, I went back to John's for a second visit. Having seen a cub in the lane the night before, I knew there was a chance I'd see it again, so I pulled over as soon as I reached the start of his property, and got the HMR all loaded up and ready. There were about two hours of daylight left, and I was hoping that I'd get a chance to drop a few bunnies for pet food. I'd only gone a short way, however, when a cub appeared about 60yd ahead of me. I stopped the truck, lowered the window and got the HMR in position, but by then it had disappeared back into the foliage. I started to edge the Disco forward and a few seconds later it came out again briefly. Luckily, I was ready, and I managed to shoot it before it dived back into the verge. I drove over to where it had fallen and then got out to inspect it. The bloody thing had clearly just raided a songbird's nest, however, as in its death throes it had regurgitated a nestling. I was annoyed that I hadn't caught

up with it a few minutes earlier before it had managed to kill the defenceless little chick.

John was pleased to hear about the two foxes I'd shot, and after a chat, I went back down the lane on foot with the HMR to see if there were any more cubs about. I didn't see any, but I did creep up and shoot three bunnies. Having established that there was nothing to see at that end of the farm, I then drove back up to the chicken sheds where the cub's carcass was placed alongside the one from the previous night. Since I'd now shot enough rabbits to keep the dog fed for a couple of days, I swapped the HMR for the .308 and went walkabout. Cresting one bit of high ground, I saw there were several bunnies scuttling about in amongst all the gorse bushes below. I was more interested in seeing if there were any roe deer in the new plantation opposite me though.

Settling myself down just above an area of burned scrub, I waited to see if anything would show. After about 15 minutes, a roe doe came out into the young saplings from the left boundary. I was hopeful that she would be accompanied by a buck, so bided my time. About five minutes later, my hopes were rewarded when a buck came out from the same place. I'd already got the rifle in position – something that was not easy, given the fact that I was lying on the side of a very steep hill, and my intended quarry was more or less level with me on the other side of the valley. Before going any further, I checked the distance with the Swarovski rangefinder. It showed me that it was 150yd out – as my rifle was zeroed for 110yd, this was fine. When I was happy that everything was right, I steadied my breathing and squeezed off a shot. I was using some 110gr ballistic tip ammunition I'd developed as a lightweight round for when I used the NV add-on for foxing. The cartridge also proved to be perfect for roe though, as the buck just collapsed on the spot.

Rather than attempt to drag the carcass up a hill that resembled a cliff, I drove back through the yard and then down into a field that ran along the edge of the stream. The buck was lying where it had been hit – the bullet had gone straight through its chest; so the elevation was spot-on. It had small antlers with four large points, one small one and signs of a sixth having been there. I dragged it back to the truck and hung it

TIPS & TRICKS

Young foxes usually start hunting on their own at much the same time as fledgling birds leave their nests. This makes the baby birds extremely vulnerable, and countless thousands are killed before they're even able to learn to fly properly

from the lifting frame while I gralloched it. Just as I was finishing, a much larger buck came out of the woods and started barking at me from about 75yd away. I managed to grab the binos and briefly saw the beast, which had a very nice set of antlers. I quickly slid under the back door and grabbed the rifle, setting it up on the bonnet. Sadly, I took about two seconds too long, and the buck was out of sight.

I drove back to the farm to tell John about my success, but there was no one about. I continued on up the track back to the chicken sheds, and tried the caller in the valley field on the other side of the hill. After about 15 minutes I gave up as there was nothing moving. In the stillness of the night, I could hear some cubs squabbling down by the stream below the plantation, but at that distance, I couldn't tell if they were coming from foxes or badgers. On getting nearer, I managed to work out where they were: a deep mass of bushes to one side of the stream. A few moments after I'd identified the spot, a badger came running out, so I packed up and left them to it. On my way back to the truck, I could see that there were rabbits all over the place but, alas, there was no further sign of foxes. Until I got back to the truck, that is, when I spotted a set of eyes moving towards the chickens. I set the three-leg sticks out, and shot a small, but quite old, dog fox. It had terrible teeth and a large bald patch, presumably mange, on its back. I put the carcass with the other two and emailed FERA to let them know.

While this cub may look innocent, it had just killed a young songbird nestling and would undoubtedly have taken many more.

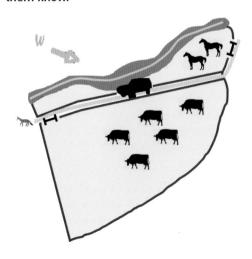

WOODPECKER KILLER

DATE:	29 May 2011	WIND DIRECTION:	North-westerly
PLACE:	John's Farm	RIFLE:	Sauer 202
TIME:	17:00	CALIBRE:	.308
SUNSET:	21:15	AMMO:	165gr Sierra GameKing SP
STATE OF MOON:	Daylight (morning crescent)	RANGE:	100yd
		CALL TRACK:	None
WEATHER:	Dry	OPTICS:	Swarovski Z6 2.5-15x56

A week after my first trip to John's farm, I returned for a late afternoon walk around. You simply cannot beat knowing your ground, and there's no better way to learn it than to visit it frequently. I'd chosen to take my Sauer .308, as there was always the chance that I'd encounter a roe buck or spot a fox. It was a beautiful sunny day, and although the steep hills made for hard going, it was still a great pleasure to be there. A few bunnies thumped their feet and tore off into the hedges as I wandered around. There are so many secluded spots on this farm that you just never know what you're going to find. Both John and his brother Tim, do their best to avoid using chemicals unnecessarily, and as a result the wildlife thrives. One excellent indicator of soil quality is the number and variety of fungi that sprout in amongst the pastures. I've found several species there that I've never seen anywhere else.

As I continued, I kept checking around with my stalking binoculars, but it seemed that all the bigger creatures were sleeping the day away. I could, however, just about hear a woodpecker's alarm call, somewhere way off in the distance. My first thought was that it might have been protesting at some fox cubs playing in the sun, so I started hiking in that direction. As I got closer, the shrieks got louder and louder, until I was able to see the small black and white bird in the upper branches of an old ash tree, sited at the top of

TIPS & TRICKS

The more you learn about nature, the easier you will find it to blend into the countryside around you. And the better you do this, the better a hunter you will be. It is a good idea to find out all you can about everything from plants and trees, to insects and amphibians. That way, when you see the relevant evidence you will have a much better idea as to what animals are on your ground, as well as what they have been doing.

a steep incline. This dived off to my left, eventually reaching a stream a couple of hundred feet below. I kept scanning the hedges below the tree, but couldn't see anything moving. Just then, I spotted the remains of a small bird that had recently been killed. Not recognising the feathers, which were mostly black with four white spots on them, I picked a couple up and put them in my pocket.

Since the woodpecker seemed to be a bit of a false alarm, I turned to head back towards the farm, whereupon I immediately saw that a fox was trotting away from me, and was nearly at the cover on the other side of the field. It was quite obvious that it had just passed me, but due to the

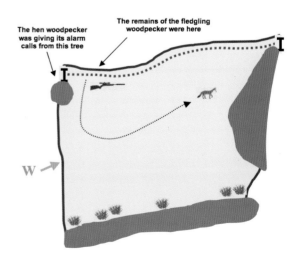

The hen woodpecker was giving its alarm calls from this tree

The remains of the fledgling woodpecker were here

severity of the slope, neither of us had realised that the other was there. It was also clear that this was what all the alarms calls had been about. I had the sticks out in moments, and in no time I was settling the .308's reticle on the fox's rear end. Now I'm not a fan of taking what is sometimes referred to as a 'Texas heart shot', however, the 165gr soft point bullets I was using wouldn't care which end they hit. Either way, they'd make a serious mess. I gently squeezed off a round, and the fox went straight down like a lead balloon. At the sound of the shot, the woodpecker took off and flew over my head and directly across the valley into the safety of the large woods there, shrieking all the way. On examination, I found the carcass was that of a large dog fox. The bullet had made a bit of a mess of him, but at least his finish was instant.

The rest of my armed ramble was less eventful, and I returned home satisfied that I'd not only done my homework on a new permission, but that I'd successfully dropped another candidate chicken killer. The follow-up to this story is that I later showed the feathers to an expert ornithologist friend, and he instantly identified them as being those of a fledgling Lesser-Spotted Woodpecker. No wonder I didn't know what they were. Anyway – it would seem that the fox

Nature at work. This large dog fox had just killed a baby Lesser-Spotted Woodpecker. Its mother's alarm cries brought me in, and I shot it, preventing any more fledglings falling to its powerful jaws.

had only just killed it, and in response the mother bird then gave her alarm calls, which brought me in, and I in turn, killed her nestling's murderer. It's sad to know that once again, I'd arrived just too late, but at least I had the comfort of knowing that the culprit would never do it again.

JUNE

June is characterised by emerald greens, often seemingly impossibly vivid, on the verdant trees and lush undergrowth. The rapidly growing grasses are just what the rabbits and deer want, however, they can make life very difficult indeed for the foxer. Likewise, the long evenings and short nights are unsuitable for the use of NV equipment – at least they are to those with any kind of a domestic life. Anyone who tries to creep in to the house long after midnight without disturbing anyone will know what I mean. On the brighter side, many of the grass fields will have been cut for hay, haylage or silage, and it is worth visiting them on the same day they have been mown as foxes will often be there too, sniffing about for any animals that got caught up in the machinery.

Talking of rabbits, this is a good time of year to get out and shoot them. Those which are not fit for your own consumption or dog food are ideal for use as drag bait. Simply tie a length of cord around the back legs and then tow the remains around the area into which you want to bring your foxes. This can be done by hand , better, from the back of a vehicle thus avoiding a human scent trail. It's a great way of dealing with early cubs: ideally, the caller

June brings the start of summer – although the warm temperatures are welcome, the late sunset and long grass can make life extremely difficult for the NV foxer. Instead, it is much better to spend the sunny evenings patrolling for the new batch of cubs.

gets them into position, and the smell of bunny holds them there long enough for a shot. It's always difficult to know how to time these sessions though. If the cubs are too young, they will be too nervous to break out from cover, and you risk educating them that a caller can mean danger. Leave it too late, and you will have missed your opportunity. The best method is probably to spend some time watching the area, and when you've satisfied yourself that they are the right age, go into action.

One of the great advantages of hunting regularly is that you get to see so much more in the way of wildlife than the ordinary person. This is especially true for those who use good quality NV gear: I have often likened it to having your own personal natural history documentary. As the sun settles behind the horizon, and twilight falls – what we call 'dimpsy' in Devon – all manner of creatures come to life. It's a great pleasure, for example, to hear

THE FARMER'S MONTH
Sheep shearing.
Irrigate crops.
Silaging and hay making.
Ragwort removal.
Muck spreading

the high-pitched squeals and chattering sounds from bats as well as the calls from barn, tawny and little owls. One of my favourite sights of June is the well-named Ghost Swift moths clambering up the grass stalks and then fluttering around just above ground level. The males have crisp white wings, and these stand out well against the dark surroundings. Less welcome are the legions of mosquitoes, midges and gnats. Some people use repellents, I find a good face veil helps deter them, and I rarely get troubled.

In the warmer chalk and limestone areas you might be lucky enough to see glow-worms. In spite of the name, they are actually beetles. At night these otherwise unremarkable brown insects produce a spectacular bioluminescent green light to signal to one another. Their larvae feed on slugs and snails, so they are not only delightful to see, but useful too! Flying a few feet above them you may sometimes spot night-jars. These beautiful birds nest on the ground, but have such good camouflage that it is almost impossible to see them unless you know they are there. On the wing they hunt flying creatures like moths and crane flies. Sadly, their numbers are falling, partly due to habitat loss, but mainly because of predation by foxes and badgers. We can do little about the latter, but controlling the vulpine populations benefits these and many other ground-nesting creatures.

At this time of year the farmer is, once again, beholden to the weather. In an ideal world, the second cut of grass – be that hay, haylage or silage – is taken. If the ground is too wet, however, everything has to wait, and if things don't dry out the nutritional value is soon lost. In some years the fields are so wet that cattle have to be taken indoors. When this happens it is a nightmare for the farmer, as he's already busy enough. Worse than that is that he has to start using up food supplies that were earmarked for winter feeding, and if he doesn't get enough grass cut later in the year, it can mean significant financial hardship. He either has to buy in expensive replacements – at a time when many other farmers need it too, so the prices are high – or he has to sell his livestock when, the prices are low because lots of others have to sell their animals too.

In the meantime, the sheep are ready to be sheared in most places, so are usually moved near to the farmyard in readiness. When it's been hot, they are pleased to have their fleeces removed as it leaves them both lighter and cooler. The shepherd also gets a good chance to worm them and give them a general check over. Their feet get particular attention in order to stop the development of footrot and other maladies. Once the grass has been brought in, the next job is to feed the ground to improve the chances of getting a third cut. Manure is usually the preferred choice, but artificial fertiliser can give faster results. It's also important to pull up any ragwort plants as they are toxic to all livestock. Anyone who does this needs to make sure they wear gloves as the sap can cause nasty skin conditions. Nature lends a hand as the larvae of the cinnabar moth – those little orange and black striped caterpillars we know so well – are extremely efficient at stripping the foliage back.

BELOW: This bee swarm revealed itself as a large white object through the thermal imager, but as it was halfway up a hedge, it was unlikely to be a rabbit or a fox. Closer inspection revealed the truth!

BOTTOM: It is not unusual to hear, or sometimes even see, otters when out foxing at night. They do occasionally show themselves in daylight, but with few exceptions where they have got used to human presence, usually only in very secluded places.

CUB CLEAR-UP

DATE:	1 (and 23 June 2010)	**RIFLE:**	CZ American (Sauer 202)
PLACE:	Roger's Farm	**CALIBRE:**	.17HMR (.308)
TIME:	17:15 (20:30)	**AMMO:**	17gr Remington BT
SUNSET:	21:19 (21:32)		(180gr Norma BT)
STATE OF MOON:	Daylight, waning gibbous	**RANGE:**	50yd (65yd)
	(Daylight, waxing gibbous)	**CALL TRACK:**	None (High-pitched
WEATHER:	Dry (both times)		Snowshoe Hare)
WIND DIRECTION:	South-westerly (north-westerly)	**OPTICS:**	Swift 8–32x50 (Swarovski Z6 2.5-15x56)

Late one sunny afternoon, my mate Andy and I went over to one of the farms I shoot on regularly in order to do some range work. This involved setting a target out and checking how a variety of different home loads performed in my Sauer .308. I'd also taken my .17HMR, as I hoped to shoot some rabbits. We'd set the target up, but hadn't got as far as unloading the rifles from their cases – so we were somewhat frustrated to see a vixen run out of the bushes and almost up to the target. Had she appeared about two minutes later, it is highly unlikely that she'd have made it back to

TIPS & TRICKS

If you are faced with clearing up some cubs and you don't get a chance to shoot the adults first, the likelihood is that the mother vixen will move the remaining litter to another location as soon as she feels it's safe to do so. If this happens, the best way to find them is to wait a couple of days, and then listen in the late evening. The odds are that you will be able to identify the new earth from the sounds of the cubs squealing.

safety. As our guns were still locked away there was nothing we could do about it. As soon as she got wind of us, she did an emergency stop and ran back off in the direction she'd come from.

Annoyed by the bad timing, we set about testing the new loads. These were composed of 165gr Sierra GameKing soft-points over N140 Vihtavuori powder. Andy also had some factory PPU ammo that didn't work at well in his rifle, so we also checked that. We must have fired about 30 or so rounds when we noticed that across the valley there were six fox cubs running

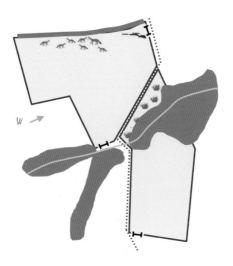

While it may seem a pity to shoot foxes as young as this, within just a few weeks they would have been killing all manner of livestock and wildlife.

about, some 350yd away. Andy is a long-range specialist, so he could easily have made short work of them, but unfortunately the neighbouring farm lay directly behind, so there was no way that we could shoot directly at them.

I couldn't leave them, as the farmer had chickens nearby as did several of the neighbours, so I set off down into the valley with the intention of circling around and coming in from downwind. Because it was so hot I wasn't keen to carry anything heavier than necessary, so I took the HMR rather than the .308. While I was doing it, Andy sat on top of his pickup truck and watched through the spotting scope. I made it across and up to the gate into the field where they'd been, but at that stage I didn't know if the cubs were still there. I started creeping along the hedge towards where they'd been, but I hadn't gone very far when a pair of crows began shouting to the world about my presence. One would have to assume that the cubs must have got used to hearing such alarm calls, as I found they were still there when I stuck my head around a large bush to look over the relevant area.

I wasted no time in getting the HMR up on the sticks, and in short order shot two of the cubs. The other four immediately dived into the hedge and disappeared from sight. It was obvious that the mother would soon move them somewhere else, but culling two of the brood was clearly a good start.

*   *   *   *

For about three weeks (23 June) I didn't see a sign of the cubs, so I had no idea where they'd been moved to, but then late one evening when I was out shooting rabbits I heard the unmistakable sound of young foxes squabbling. They were on the edge of some deep cover at the top of a hill. The vixen clearly thought this was the safest place to locate them, as it has excellent all-round vision. Now that I knew where they were, however, it was down to me to try and outwit her. The next evening I went back over, and started out by shooting a bunny for bait. I carried it over to my chosen ambush field.

Once there, I tied a piece of cord around its back legs and dragged it around in a series of loops that ended at the point where I'd decided to site the caller.

I then returned to the cover of a hedge and set my sticks up. I switched the caller on with the high-pitched Snowshoe hare track and waited. Within a minute, a young fox ran out, but before it got to the bait, it turned and ran back towards the hedge. It was clearly uncomfortable being out in the open. I tried to track it through the scope, but it kept stopping and turning, jumping from side to side as it did so. I then raised my head and saw that there was already another fox almost on the bait. It, too, stopped briefly, at which point I knocked it down with a 180gr ballistic-tip round from my .308 Sauer. It was a bit of overkill, I have to admit, but I knew the rounds were accurate, and they were taking up space in my ammo cabinet. At the sound of the shot, the first fox ran for cover. About a minute later another one appeared – this also nearly made it to the bait, but it was dropped before it got there. Another minute or so later and a third fox appeared – this one was much more wary, and came right around on the wind, stopping and darting back and forth. Eventually it stopped long enough for me to take a shot and it went down a few yards from the other two. All three were taken at about 65yd.

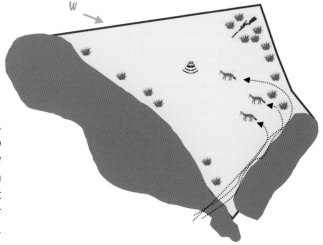

95

PIMP MY STICKS

DATE:	15 June 2012	**RIFLE:**	Kimber Montana
PLACE:	Jim's Farm	**CALIBRE:**	.204 Ruger
TIME:	20:30	**AMMO:**	32gr V-Max
SUNSET:	21:30	**RANGE:**	100yd
STATE OF MOON:	Daylight, morning crescent	**CALL TRACK:**	Young rabbit distress
WEATHER:	Dry	**OPTICS:**	Swarovski Z6 3-18x50
WIND DIRECTION:	North-westerly		

It was nearly my 52nd birthday, and in the run-up to the big day, the matter of what my Good Lady was going to give me raised its head. Since she's been going through chemotherapy and then radiotherapy since the start of the year, she's understandably not been at her best. It was my job, therefore, to sort out my main present. Right up until the last minute, I was intending to buy some lightweight stalking boots. Just before I went off to buy them, however, I discovered that the ones I was interested in were likely to fall to pieces in no time at all. This, together with their high price and the company's reputation for poor after-sales service, dissuaded me from going down that route.

A bit of head-scratching resulted in a visit to Blue Fox Target Sports – my local gun shop (and the best in the area by far) – to check out a set of shooting sticks that I'd seen on my last visit. I knew they were expensive, but I also realised that if I didn't find a suitable present, it was entirely possible I'd end up with something I really didn't want. Since most of my shooting is off sticks, I'm very fussy indeed about them. I've tried all the usual DIY methods – two bits of plastic cane held together with a pair of nun's knickers, that sort of thing. After many trials, I settled on a pair of telescopic walking sticks, pivoted with a stainless steel bolt and Nyloc nuts. A year or two later, I added a third leg. Much to my surprise, I found it was a distinct improvement. I'd shied away from doing so previously, as I was concerned about the time it'd take to set them up, but the reality was that – with a bit of practice – they were fine.

One of my pet hates when I'm out either NV foxing or deerstalking is kit that makes any kind of

noise, be it a slight rattle, a propensity to clang into other objects or anything else that might give me away to a nervous animal. I also hate equipment that can let me down – such as sticks that lose a lower section, usually in the dark and just before you need to take a shot. Consequently, I'd ended up covering my set with a mix of cloth tape and strategically placed lumps of foam. That way, the tape stopped the sections from coming loose or rattling, and the padding prevented the legs from banging into each other. Although they worked very well, they were not perfect. If I was hunting over steep ground – something we have a lot of around here – I was always struggling to get them to sit at the right height. I know I could have removed the tape to make them adjustable again, but I hate the 'twist to lock' system.

During the winter it's possible to use a bipod as well as sticks – if you like lying in thick mud, but in the middle of June, the grass is so long that bipods are next to useless unless you're lucky enough to have something like a trailer to shoot off. I've tried

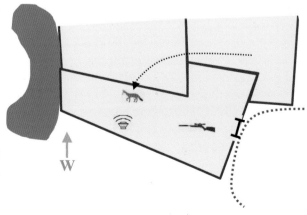

the versions with really long legs, but have never had much success with them. I was, therefore, keen to discover if the Vanguard tripod sticks that James had in the shop would pass my critical eye. When I got there, he had several customers queuing for attention – no change there, his helpful attitude attracts people from miles away. It was good for me, though, as it provided an excellent opportunity to give the sticks a really close examination.

One of the first areas I looked at was the U-shaped yoke on the top. It had the ability to rotate through 360 degrees, and I decided that would be a very good thing. Although we all know the rule book says that foxes will always approach from downwind, the problem is that Charlie doesn't much care for such commandments, and will do whatever he feels like. Many is the time that I've hurriedly attempted to reposition my sticks when a bright set of eyes has appeared from completely the wrong direction.

The next feature to come under the microscope was the locking system on the legs. These were simple over-centre levers that when pushed into place clamped the sections together – just like the ones you often see on camera tripods. They felt a bit flimsy, but looked as though they should work well enough. The range of adjustment was fine, going from very low to high enough for standing shots. Although the blurb advertised that by unscrewing the rear leg the sticks could also be used as a bipod or a monopod, I wasn't at all interested in that. I was, however, pleased to see that the rear leg was mounted so that it could swivel almost up to the horizontal. That would mean I'd be able to sit at the base of a bank with the rear leg passing under my armpit. Another good thing. Before long, it was my turn for service, so I handed over my debit card and did the necessaries. On returning home, my wife promptly confiscated them, saying it wasn't my birthday yet...

Come the morning of my big day, and I was able to repossess them. A brief foray that evening was soon ended by torrential rain, but in the few minutes

TIPS & TRICKS

Some people have the luxury of flat ground to shoot on where bipods or shooting bags can work well. The rest of us have hilly landscapes to contend with. To be really effective, your rifle needs to be steady enough to shoot with total confidence. A set of adjustable shooting sticks will allow you to sit on the side of a steep bank and still have a rock solid aim.

I'd been able to use the sticks, I'd found that they were far more clattery than I'd expected. The next morning saw me set to with the camo tape and sheets of foam. After a few false starts, I ended up with something I was happy with. The upper sections of all three legs were covered in camo tape, while the middle sections of the front legs were taped in place. The lower portions were, however, left free to slide up and down. A lump of foam was added to each of the 'knees' to stop the legs banging into one another. The rear leg was left more or less unmolested. The adjustment clamps each had a thin strip of cloth tape positioned over the cam to add a little more clamp pressure. This gave them a more confidence-inspiring feel. The last part of the pimping program was to cut a narrow length of tape to go around the bright orange collar that sits under the top yoke. Why anyone would choose to use such a garish colour on a hunting product is beyond me!

All that remained was to test the customised sticks out in anger. The weather though, was doing its best to make this a no-go. High winds and the threat of rain made it look an unlikely evening for a shoot. After checking the Met Office's radar map and having a bit of a ponder, I came up with a cunning plan. I noticed that if I were to go to a farm that lies in the foothills near the small market town of Crediton, I might find some shelter as the wind would be hitting the small valleys sideways on. A quick phone call to the farmer confirmed that I'd be welcome to go over, so I got everything together before stopping to change into my hunting gear and to have a quick meal, after which I loaded the truck and set off.

Some 15 minutes later, I arrived on site, and checked in with the farmer. He was kind enough to sign off a letter giving permission for me to take an assistant who needed mentoring. This was an FAC condition imposed by our local constabulary, and without it, the poor bloke would be stuffed. Anyway, took the opportunity to catch up on all the gossip – where the foxes had been seen, and so on. The farmer had to walk over a couple of fields to check his new calves, so I slung the .204 Kimber over my shoulder, grabbed my pimped sticks, and accompanied him. A brief inspection showed that both the cows and their three two day-old calves were all in tip-top condition. A fourth was due – possibly that night – to a grumpy Charolais that kept snorting at our presence, but as all was well, the farmer headed back while I set off to see if any foxes were about.

I had about an hour of daylight left, so decided to try a mix of baiting and calling. I had the FOXPRO Scorpion in my pocket, so now I needed some bunny. A few rabbits had scampered away as I'd walked down the track, but they'd all been too small and too near to be worthy of a shot. A little further on, however, I spotted a couple of decent-sized ones on the other side of the field. A dab on the Leica's

rangefinder button told me that they were a touch under 100yd out, so I set the sticks up and tried the rifle for fit. I immediately found that the Harris bipod was too wide to sit in the yoke, so to remedy this I had to slide the gun further forwards until it cleared. I wasn't happy about it, as it compromised the balance point; nevertheless, I got a good aim and gently squeezed off a round. The bunny almost exploded – it was a gory end for it, but certainly a humane one.

The sound disturbed another nicely sized individual, and although it hid for a few seconds, it couldn't resist sitting up to see what was going on. By then I was ready, having reloaded and pocketed the empty case. Once again, the bunny went down with a massive 'whump'. The .204 never fails to impress, I must say, despite my being more used to larger centrefire calibres. The sticks had now accounted for two bunnies, and as no more were in sight, I climbed over the wire fence and walked out to recover my bait. When I got closer, there was no doubting my

This fox fell to my new adjustable shooting sticks which allowed me to set up an ambush in a position that would have been nigh-on impossible without them.

opinion that the bunnies had been hit hard. They were both a real mess. I thought to myself that it was a good job that they were only intended for fox bait, as I'd hate to have to skin and paunch them in that state.

While I was thinking this, a slight movement caught my eye in the narrow gap between a large dung heap and the nearby woods. Another couple of bunnies had appeared out of the brambles and were sitting looking in my direction. I dropped one, but when I went for the second bunny, I misjudged the position of a large lump of dung and ended up shooting that instead. The rabbit didn't flinch, so I cycled a fresh round into place and lined up for another try. Just as I was doing so, however, the bunny ran back a few paces. It made the mistake of stopping for a last glimpse over its shoulder and that was, indeed, its last look at anything.

With four very bloody rabbits in hand, I carefully approached a large field that slopes down towards a small stream. At the far end is some cover where a pair of magpies had been kicking off about something they didn't like for the last five minutes. It could have just been a roe deer, but I was hoping it was one or more foxes. A good look around with the thermal imager failed to spot anything other than livestock though, so I climbed a short length of wooden fence next to the gate and slowly made my way onto a small rise that looked out over the whole field. Again, I checked with both the binos and the thermal, but as all was clear, I walked out towards my chosen killing zone. I set the bunnies some 20yd apart, in a line that sat across the wind – that way, I hoped to create the widest possible scent trail. Each bunny was given a thorough squishing with my foot before being chucked a few feet – they were thrown so that I'd leave the minimum amount of scent. Once I was happy with their positioning, I switched the FOXPRO on, and placed it nearby – some 100yd out.

Looking back to where I was going to be shooting from, I checked the backdrop to make sure there was no chance of me being skylined. Nope – there was a nice big oak tree, beyond which there were plenty of gorse bushes and other scrub. Perfect! Once I was in position, I brought the sticks into play. Standing was out of the question, as I had no cover at all, so I had to find a lower stance. The ground was too damp

for me to want to lie or sit on it for very long, so I decided to kneel instead. I knew I wouldn't be able to do that for very long, but it gave a decent amount of height whilst keeping me low enough to minimise the risk of being seen. I always use a face veil – even in the dark, as there's nothing like a bright white face to give you away. Dark clouds were racing not far above my head, and as a result the light was already poor. I was hoping that this would work in my favour though. The sticks quickly adjusted to my chosen height, and I was ready. Before going any further I removed the bipod to improve the way the rifle would sit in the yoke.

I gave the area a once-over with the thermal, then switched the caller on. I started with the screaming adult rat, but in spite of this making the magpies chatter angrily again, nothing showed. After five or so minutes of that, I changed to the young bunny distress call. Every now and then I'd pause the caller to let the peace settle before starting it afresh. All the time I was scanning continuously, but without luck. Just as my knees were beginning to set, I spotted a white shape in the next field through the thermal. It looked like a fox, but by the time I'd got the bins up, it'd disappeared. Damn, had it seen me, I wondered? Another check with the thermal showed something coming out of the hedge, immediately downwind of the caller. I was on the rifle in moments, and sure enough, found myself looking at a fox, warily sniffing the wind. The bait had done its job, holding the Charlie there for long enough for me to slip the safety off and get a good aim. The round hit it incredibly hard, bowling it over in no uncertain terms. Result!

The fox proved to be a small vixen. She was too big to be considered a cub, but too small to have been last year's progeny. I can only surmise that she was the result of a very early brood, which would make her some five months old. I'd shot another one of a similar size on a farm some 10 miles away the previous week, so it's quite clear that she was not unique. As no other foxes showed, I called it a day and set off back. The farmer was delighted, so my Brownie points tally was notched up a bit further!

A FOURHEAD PROBLEM

DATE:	24 June 2012	RIFLE:	Kimber Montana
PLACE:	John's Farm	CALIBRE:	.204 Ruger
TIME:	20:30	AMMO:	32gr V-Max
SUNSET:	21:32	RANGE:	100yd
STATE OF MOON:	Daylight, evening crescent	CALL TRACK:	None
WEATHER:	Dry	OPTICS:	Swarovski Z6 3-18x50
WIND DIRECTION:	North-westerly		

John's farm is a few miles from here – to the north-west of Exeter – and is set in the most beautiful countryside. It can be a bit of a swine to hunt over, though, as it's made up of lots of small valleys with steep sides. These are interspersed with myriad woods that provide almost impenetrable cover for all manner of wildlife. The unforgiving terrain and innumerable hiding places can make it nigh on impossible to see your target until you're more or less on top of it.

Most of the land is rented out to a neighbour, who I also shoot for, but one area is reserved for about a thousand free range organic chickens. When I first started shooting there, the place was crawling with foxes, and I had quite a job getting matters under control. Within a couple of months his losses to predation had plummeted though, and I was able to spend more time elsewhere. We agreed that he would call me if he saw any foxes about, and I left him to it – only calling back now and then to shoot some bunnies.

One weekend I decided to drop in and see how things were going – if nothing else, I figured it wouldn't hurt to cull a few more bunnies to top up the supply of dog food. It was mid-evening when I pulled into his yard, and as I did so he wandered out from his mother's house. The family had just finished a large meal, and he'd obviously been enjoying a copious amount of vino collapso. 'Ah, I've been meaning to call you,' he said as he swayed slowly from side to side. 'There's been a bloody fox coming in and taking my chickens in broad daylight.'

On asking for further details, it seemed that there were probably two or more animals involved, as he'd seen foxes approaching from completely opposite directions. We then exchanged a few pleasantries, during which time I agreed to lock the birds away for him. I certainly didn't want him staggering around up there while I was shooting, and it was quite clear that he knew he wasn't in a state to do it. He was very grateful and obviously relieved, so I left him to return to his wine glass and drove on up the hill towards the chicken arcs.

The track is, like most things on the farm, badly in need of some attention, having been extensively washed-out by the numerous cloudbursts that seem to hit the valley. It not only climbs at an alarming angle, but the last bit looks more like a section from a trials course, with large rocks just where you need to make a sharp turn to the left. Still, the Disco manages it well enough if you give it enough welly. Having negotiated this, I began tackling the main part of the track – here the slope is much more gentle, but the problem you face is that the tractors have carved such deep ruts that you need to take great care to avoid the wheels getting caught. This is made more difficult by the thick coating of ultra-slippery mud. It's not bad in daylight, but can be rather treacherous after dark.

TIPS & TRICKS

One of the pleasures of summer hunting is that sitting quietly in the evening sun can be a most effective way of spotting foxes. By choosing a position with a good view of a small valley, the edge of some woodland, or over some rough ground, you can often spot your quarry well before it even knows you are there.

Once you're clear of the worst bit near the top of the hill, the hedge on your right stops abruptly for no apparent reason, and the field of chicken arks suddenly opens out before you. A movement caught my eye. A fox was running away from the birds. It stopped for a moment to look at me, then it was gone, hidden by the thick vegetation which grows profusely along the base of the far hedge. It had been quite small, with dark colouring.

I parked up on the far side of the huts and got my kit on: Leica binos on a chest harness, mini TI around my neck and Kimber .204 over my shoulder. This was all set off by a full face veil, gloves and tripod shooting sticks. I slipped the FOXPRO Scorpion caller into my camo fleece, and I was ready. The first thing to do was check the birds. Had the fox got past the fence and killed any, I wondered? I got my answer in seconds. A few feet inside the compound there was a bird with no head. I picked it up – it was still hot, so could only have been killed in the last few minutes. And there was another. Again, it was still hot, and its head was missing. It was hard to see how many birds had been taken as the grass was so long, but I found four in total – all with their heads bitten cleanly off. Three were inside the fence, while the fourth was on the outside.

I locked the live birds up, then gathered the dead ones together and placed them in a pile about 50yd down from the far hedge. I hoped the wind would take their scent and distribute it across the field, so that if the fox returned it would soon encounter the smell. I then hung the FOXPRO on a

This fox was taken with the .204 Kimber Montana in the late summer evening. It was heading straight for the chicken houses, so there is little doubt that it was one that had to be dealt with.

metal stake and retired to the depths of an empty chicken ark. From there, I could see the entire hedgeline as well as most of the field. After letting things settle for a few minutes, I started the caller on a distress call. Although it was labelled pheasant, it actually sounded very similar to the alarmed squawks the chickens made whenever they were picked up. I kept checking the area with the thermal, but as nothing showed after about half an hour, I decided to leave it for a bit and take a wander around instead.

I unlocked the far door of the ark and quietly positioned it so that I could get back in without making any noise. I also realised that if I was careful when I returned I'd be able to stay out of sight by remaining behind the arcs. I slipped between the nearby barley crop and the hedge, and in seconds I was lost from view. There is a small but very steep valley at the far end of the field, and as I approached it, I took great care to remain unseen. After scanning the area with both the binos and the thermal, I then broke my cover and scaled the barbed wire fence. That accomplished without incident, I settled myself in under a blackthorn bush and began a methodical search of the valley below.

The ground there drops away sharply – it's heavily grazed by rabbits, so the grass has that characteristic sparse look to it. There used to be a thick stand of gorse bushes over the warren, but the

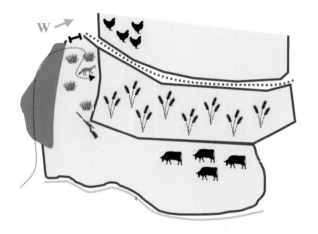

farmer burnt these back, and now all that remains is an assembly of black twisted stumps, seemingly writhing about in the last throws of agony. At the bottom the grass thickens up, and then gives way to a small stream which wends its way between a thin line of small trees. These are mostly hazel and ash; under them grows all manner of thick vegetation, from low yellow trefoils to white-flowered cow parsleys which tower to head height.

On the far side of the stream is a plantation, established by some well meaning city type. Not long ago it was a field, but he spent huge amounts of money planting various kinds of trees. He told all the local farmers that they were to stay well away from it, as he'd started it as a wildlife reservation for his grandchildren. After a couple of years though, he received a bit of a reality check when he finally accepted that his precious arboretum was being hammered by the roe deer.

While I was scanning around, a bit of a commotion broke out – a buzzard was being harassed by some crows. They weren't getting it all their way though, for the big bird finally lost its patience and turned on them. The crows then made off to the far woods shouting in protest. A few minutes later some blackbirds started chinking away in alarm at something down by the stream, some 150yd out. Two rabbits that I'd been watching then sat up on their haunches and began looking in the same direction. Could there be a fox down there, I wondered? I was ready for action whatever appeared. I'd set my sticks so that they were at the perfect height for a seated shot. This was partly because the ground was far too steep for them to allow a standing shot, and partly because it kept my profile low. The scope was also focused at the appropriate range, and I'd set the mag to give me a good blend of field of view and image size. Five minutes passed, and nothing had changed – the blackbirds were still going like hell, but no matter how hard I looked, there was nothing to be seen. Patience is key, I thought to myself. Another 10 minutes went by without incident.

Finally, after about 20 minutes, I realised that my bones were beginning to set on the damp ground and decided that the birds must have simply been spooked by the buzzard. I stood up and reset the sticks to the right height for a standing shot, and made ready to go back to check the chickens. Just as I did so, a fox wandered out from the very spot I'd been watching all that time. I couldn't believe it! I sank to my knees and did my best to get the sticks set, but by the time I'd done so, it had gone out of sight behind a large oak tree that stood at the end of a small wood. Now, I knew it had two choices: one was to go up the hill on the far side of the trees, the other was to come through and into the pasture to its right, which would place it somewhere in front of me.

This field is actually composed of a very short valley. It's only some 100yd long, but its steep sides are very popular with the bunnies. I figured the fox was probably making its way to the chickens, but that it would want to check the area first. I got myself ready and began watching with the thermal. Seconds later, the fox appeared out of the trees. It was covering the ground very quickly – nose down, and continuously darting left and right. At first I thought it was going to go through the far gate, which would have put it completely out of sight, but instead it came around and began coming straight towards me. The problem was that it was constantly disappearing behind large thistles or clumps of tall grass, so I couldn't get a clear shot. It then suddenly turned left and ran towards the hedge that bordered the barley field. Had it made it, there's no way I would have found it again. In turning sideways on, however, it presented me with my one chance. I didn't waste it, and a loud 'whump' told me that my round had hit home in a very convincing manner. The fox fell without a twitch.

I had a quick scan around, but as there was nothing else to be seen, I walked over to check my kill. It was a young dog fox – not much body size, but with a very good weight. Clearly, the poultry diet had been to its liking. Nearby, I found the remains of a chicken that looked as though it'd been devoured about a week previously. I took a couple of photos and carried the carcass back to the track by the chicken arks where I left it for the farmer to dispose of since he always likes to see what's been killing his birds. It was definitely not the one I'd seen earlier on, but it shared the same dark coloration, so could well have been one of its siblings.

The light was now going, so I fitted the NV add-on to the rifle and swapped my binos for the NV spotter. I then set myself up in the disused ark and after a few minutes began the caller. At first nothing showed, but then I caught sight of a heat source in the hedge with the thermal. It was clearly a fox, as I could see it leaping up and over the vegetation. I had not realised just how long the grass had become, and I quickly lost sight of it. Unfortunately, the fox continued on until it was downwind of me – I caught a brief glimpse of it, – and then it was gone. I guess that's the price of shooting at this time of year. Still, I'd dropped one of the two that were known to be there, so I was happy that I'd made a good start. On my way home I pondered over how long it would take me to get to grips with the other one.

Three evenings later (on 24 June) I went back to see if I could catch up with the other one. I'd checked the Met Office's wind map, however, and discovered that it was blowing in the worst possible direction – directly from the farm towards the chicken arks. I came up with a plan and called John to check that no one was going to disturb the area before I got there. In essence, I was going to park below the farm and then circle round to the chickens by way of a deep valley. That way, my scent should not cause a problem. As I was going to have a fair distance to cover along with a lot of steep hills, I was travelling light. My FOXPRO caller, spare torch, second fleece, and various other stuff got left behind.

My plan worked well until I got to the first gate where, a long way above and looking down on me, was a herd of young bullocks. Bullocks wasn't the word I had in mind when I saw them, but I had little choice but to go in with them. I was taught as a lad that you should never allow cattle to get uphill of you as they are curious creatures and will run down to look

Magpies

> **TIPS & TRICKS**
> Many animals will give audible warnings when foxes are present. These include birds such as jays, magpies, crows, rooks, jackdaws, blackbirds, thrushes and woodpeckers, as well as mammals like squirrels. Learning to identify these calls is really important if you want to become a successful hunter.

at you. If you're unlucky, they won't be able to stop in time to prevent you getting trampled. With that in mind, I decided that the only course of action was to march directly towards them, knowing this would spook them into running away. I also knew they wouldn't run very far, and that being the stupid animals they are, they'd soon come back for a second look. This meant that I couldn't waste a moment in making it to the high ground, and I was breathing heavily by the time I got up there. After a bit of to-ing and fro-ing, the cattle charged off up the valley and didn't bother me again.

I don't know if it was the sound of all the hooves, but there were no foxes to be seen when I got to the chickens. There was, however, a buzzard in with them – it saw me poke my head around one of the arks and tried to fly off with something, but dropped it. Not wanting to give up on its meal, it landed again and continued feeding. While it was doing so, I gave the area a thorough scan with the thermal imager. As there was no sign of Charlie, I decided to go and see what the buzzard had been eating – by then it had flown off. I've seen them in with chickens before, but have never witnessed one

killing any. This individual had been eating a dead pullet, but it was impossible to say whether it had died of natural causes, been killed by a fox or if the raptor itself was responsible. I know there's a lot of talk about relaxing the restrictions on shooting them due to their predation on pheasant poults, but as I think they're lovely birds, I for one don't want to see the day when I'm asked to do so.

There was no other evidence of foxes having been around, mostly because the farmer had spent the afternoon pressure-washing the disused arks. I was hoping that the peace and quiet would encourage the fox to come back, so I shortened my sticks and sat below the adjoining barley crop to watch over the area. I wasn't happy with my position though – the wind was blowing from my left to my right, and both the chicken arks and the hedge I was covering were directly ahead. My problem was that I could only really see the area to the right of the arcs, where the birds were out feeding. By then I'd decided that if the fox came back, it would probably approach from downwind – that is, from the left, where I wouldn't be able to see it. So I decided to come up with a new plan. I'd circle around on the wind and set myself up to observe

DATE:	27 June 2012	RIFLE:	Kimber Montana
PLACE:	John's Farm	CALIBRE:	.204 Ruger
TIME:	20:30	AMMO:	32gr V-Max
SUNSET:	21:32	RANGE:	100yd
STATE OF MOON:	Daylight (first quarter)	CALL TRACK:	None
WEATHER:	Dry	OPTICS:	Swarovski Z6 3-18x50
WIND DIRECTION:	North-westerly		

the far side of the hedge where I expected the fox to come from. This would involve a hike of about half a mile. I had to scale two gates before I could get into the first field, but once there I started making my way through the long grass. I'd only gone 100yd or so, when some magpies started kicking up a fuss on the other side of the valley, off to my left. They may well have been ragging a fox, but I couldn't see any sign of it, even after keeping close watch for five minutes or more. As this was a distraction – the area I was interested in was off to my right, I carried on. At the next gate I could see there were a couple of rabbits grazing away, but nothing else was around.

The moment I moved off, the little bunnies scampered into the safety of the undergrowth, and I was on my own again. As I neared the top of some woodland, a roe doe suddenly jumped up and tore away into the trees. She must have been couched up in the ditch, as I'd not see any clue that she was there. Since she may well have had a fawn nearby, I diverted my path to avoid the immediate area. When I made it to the far side, I stopped for yet another scan. Most of the hedge I was interested in was still hidden behind the brow of the hill – that was just fine with me, as I wanted to go a bit further yet. The ground I wanted to watch was a small patch at the far end of the field, which separated a large woods from the hedge that ran down to the chickens.

A few steps before I got to my chosen observation point, however, two magpies suddenly started shouting in protest at something. I knew it wasn't me, as I was still out of their sight, so I shrank back into the foliage of the adjacent hedge, and got the rifle mounted. My feet were in the proper stance, but there was a small rock under my right foot. I looked down briefly and kicked it out of the way. As I glanced up, I saw a fox had broken cover from the hedge about 120yd off, and was now out into the field. It must have spotted my movement, though, because it turned and looked directly at me. Before it could run off – something it was clearly about to do – the .204 barked and my target fell on the spot. The magpies didn't know it was dead and carried on shouting at it. When it was clear that no other foxes were going to show, I went over and examined my kill. It was a small vixen – as it was the same size and had a similar dark coloration, it was almost certainly the one I'd seen that had killed the four chickens. And like the other one I'd shot, it was incredibly heavy for its size. By the time I'd dragged it back my arms were aching. The farmer was well pleased, though!

JULY

By July most of the cubs are starting to explore the big world around them – unfortunately, this often puts them in direct conflict with people. While some get hit by cars, others manage to find their way into chicken runs where they can wreak complete havoc. From the foxer's perspective, it is a good time to get to grips with the year's new progeny, as they have yet to learn exactly what is dangerous and what is not. Calling both in daylight and after dark with screaming rat or squealing bunny sounds can be extremely effective, however, the long vegetation can make this very difficult to put into practice. It is not uncommon to see or hear fights underway as the young foxes begin to establish their group hierarchy.

The high temperatures of summer are a welcome change from those of the winter, however, they can complicate things for anyone who uses a thermal imager. This is because there is little contrast between the heat radiated from the ground and that coming from living creatures. Consequently, it can be very hard to see anything smaller than a cow, especially in the first few hours of darkness. Instead

July sees the start of the first harvests – although most farm equipment is built to make huge round bales these days, there is still a call for the old-fashioned methods to be used, as can be seen here with these hand-stacked stooks of thatching straw.

of being a stark white, for example, rabbits may appear a dull grey colour. If the skies are clear though, the landscape soon cools down, and then it is much easier to what is what.

July is the peak month for moths, and as the light goes they start to warm their flight muscles by vibrating their wings. This isn't really noticeable with the smaller species, but the louder ones can sound a bit like hornets. Since these insects are loaded with fat, they make tasty snacks for hungry predators and it is common to see foxes snuffling about and snatching at them in long grass or along hedgerows. Every now and then you may well also hear large flying beetles zooming around – occasionally, they may even crash into you. There's nothing to worry about though – although their jaws can be quite powerful, they will only bite if provoked. Other insects are not so

THE FARMER'S MONTH
Second grass cut of hay, haylage or silage.
Irrigate crops.
Cereals cut with combine harvesters.
Worming treatments and fly repellents applied to livestock.
Sheep shearing.
Fields 'topped' to control weeds.

accommodating – horseflies, for instance, can be a real problem on hot days. If I spot one buzzing around me, I put my back to a wall, bush or hedge. This prevents them from flying behind me – I then stay still and wait for my would-be tormentor to land on me, whereupon I swat it. Another method is to keep a lookout for one of the larger dragonflies – these usually establish a small territory and then patrol it regularly. If you stand in the right place they will swoop down and capture any flies that are troubling you. At night you can do the same thing with bats, but you have to move slowly so that you don't spook them.

If the weather has been good, the landscape will soon reverberate with the whirring and clanking of combine harvesters and silage foragers. This is a welcome sound to both farmers and foxers. To the former it means and end to worry about whether rain will prevent the crops being brought in. To the latter, it means lovely open fields with lots of visibility. As ever, it is always worth checking the fields that have been cut as foxes will often be found nuzzling through the stubble for dead rodents or those which are darting about eating fallen grain. If the ground is dry there will be few worms about, and since these can be a major food source for hungry foxes, it forces them to look elsewhere.

Conversely, if it rains heavily the cattle may have to be brought indoors. This uses up large stocks of fodder that would otherwise have been kept for winter. The farmers will also be struggling to keep the sheds clear of slurry. Whenever the ground is damp it can be a good idea to check out any fields or pastures where earthworms are likely to be lying on the surface. It's only in the last 20 years or so that scientists realised that foxes ate so many of them, and this was only achieved by observers watching them with NV systems. Once they suspected what they were witnessing, the biologists concerned began analysing fox dung at the microscopic level where they found countless thousands of setae. Since these are the tiny bristles that worms use to help move themselves around, they provided conclusive proof that foxes eat earthworms. It just goes to show that there is still much to learn about the biology of many of the creatures we often take for granted.

Elsewhere, there will be many young and vulnerable animals around – at the larger end of the scale these range from red, sika and fallow calves through to roe and muntjac fawns. The smaller examples include all manner of species of fledgling birds, as well as leverets (baby hares) and, of course, bunnies. It would be a brave fox that tried to attack a red deer calf, for its mother would be very protective and more than capable of killing any such aggressors. The fawns of the smaller deer, however, regularly fall victim to both foxes and badgers. Similarly, both of these predators will actively seek out and kill adult and young hedgehogs, which is, sadly, the main reason why there are so few of them around these days. The tree-huggers would have us believe that the world is just like the cast of *Wind In The Willows* – the reality, of course, is as Tennyson observed: 'Nature, red in tooth and claw'.

BELOW: There is little to match the splendour of a freshly emerged Peacock butterfly, with its vivid colours and striking eye spots.

BOTTOM: Magpies are a scourge on the countryside, and should be controlled whenever the opportunity presents. They not only actively seek out and kill the eggs and nestlings of all manner of small birds, but will also not hesitate to peck out the eyes and tongues of infant lambs as well as any other defenceless animals they find.

FIGHTING FOXES

DATE:	4 July 2011	**RIFLE:**	Sauer 202
PLACE:	Gerald's Farm	**CALIBRE:**	.308
TIME:	20:30	**AMMO:**	165gr Sierra GameKing SP
SUNSET:	21:30	**RANGE:**	220yd
STATE OF MOON:	Daylight, evening crescent	**CALL TRACK:**	None
WEATHER:	Dry	**OPTICS:**	Swarovski Z6 2.5-15x56
WIND DIRECTION:	North-westerly		

One Friday evening at the beginning of July I decided to head off to a local farm to see if there were any roe bucks about. It had been a lovely day, and there was about an hour and a half of daylight left. Eventually, I emerged from the tunnel of overhanging oak and ash trees onto a dirt track, at the end of which is a traditional five-bar gate. Fixed to the middle of it, is a brand new 'Beware of the bull' sign. They're not kidding: one of the farmer's sons was recently knocked down by it. I was not pleased to see that the area beyond the gate was jammed solid with cattle. I was faced with a dilemma. Do I leave the truck and proceed on foot, or do I open the gate, and try to fight my way through?

Since I was carrying two rifles in the truck, I wasn't going to leave it out of sight in spite of the fact that I have a gun safe mounted in it. Then I was a bit taken aback to see another 4x4 coming the other way. It turned out that the driver was in charge of this year's batch of pheasants, these being raised in some pens in the woods I was heading towards. We had a quick chat. He was pleased to hear that I was taking care of the Charlies, as my name had come up on the local rumour mill as a bit of a foxing specialist. Just as he headed off, I made the mistake of saying words to the effect of 'You won't be seeing many foxes around here...' I said this with every confidence, as I'd only seen one over the last year, and that took a .22-250 round. The foxhounds had also been through without finding signs.

A few minutes later, having got the truck through the now disinterested herd of cattle, I parked up and snuck into the adjacent copse. On the far side of this there is a spot that gives me a great view of the margins of the large wood opposite. This is composed of various broadleaf species – mostly oak, ash, beech and sycamore, and is home to all manner of wildlife, including red and roe deer.

I set my tripod sticks up and began scanning the area with my Nikon HGL binos. In front of me and to the left there's a field that is typical of the uplands around here. It's mostly coarse grass interspersed with reed tussocks and tall thistles: 'dashels' in the local parlance. On my right, the wood reaches to within 75yd or so at its closest point, and then runs away at a slight angle towards a small river. Along its edge there is a narrow strip of low scrub – mostly brambles and gorse: 'fuzz' as the locals call it, which is doubtless a corruption of 'furze'. The deer tend to use this as a refuge while they make their last checks before moving out into the open, so it's worth taking the time to study it carefully.

The bushes I was hiding in were a mix of hawthorn and blackthorn (sloe), with a few small

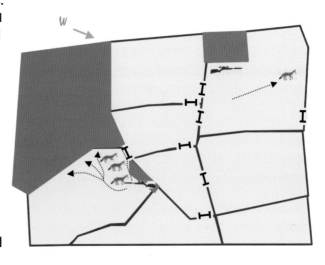

elder and alder trees sheltering under some bigger ash and oak trees. Being a late summer evening, there were large numbers of small mosquito-like insects swirling to and fro in energetic mating swarms. They didn't trouble me though, so I was happy to watch them wheeling in their ghostly dances. Deep in the woods there was a load crash, much like a red deer knocking a dead tree over.

A minute or so later, a hare came gambolling out of the brambles to my right. It must have been laid up a few feet away, but as the wind was blowing from it to me, it didn't know I was there. After a bit of lolloping about, it disappeared into the long grass and was lost from sight. After little while, I heard another crash, this time a little closer. 'Are the deer on the move?' I wondered to myself. As it was early July, the reds were strictly off the menu, but should a roe buck appear, it would be fair game. Doing my best not to be distracted, I scanned across the field again, but nothing was moving. Just then, the crashing started again – this time it was close, to my right, and coming much closer. I got the rifle up on the sticks, hoping it was two bucks in a territorial contest.

The sound was so loud, however, that I thought it was more likely to be several red deer coming through together. Imagine my surprise then, when two small creatures – at first sight looking much like muntjacs – came barrelling around the corner straight towards me, at what appeared to be about 40mph. They were young foxes; the one in the lead was yelping and clearly running for its life. The one about a foot behind it had a determined 'I'm going to kill

you' look about it. Both had their ears flat against their heads – hence why they looked like muntjac, and a few feet behind them was a third fox, which was also looking seriously aggressive.

The first of the three jumped the small ditch and continued to run directly at me – very closely followed by the others. They passed within about a yard of my feet, whereupon they were suddenly downwind of me. They immediately stopped for the briefest of moments, clearly confused by the sudden presence of human scent. At this stage I was desperately trying to get a bead on one of them that had paused about 12ft away, but in what seemed like a millisecond, they scattered at great speed in different directions, leaving me not the slightest chance of a shot. I tried using the mouth caller to bring them back, but they were long gone.

I waited until the light had fallen too far to shoot with my Swaro scope, then climbed back over the fence and walked over to the truck. I swapped the binos for my NV monocular, and the .308 Sauer for the .22-250 Sauer NV rig. The FOXPRO Scorpion caller went in the left pocket of my DPM fleece, and the remote control in the right pocket. I was now ready, and moved upwind to the end of a long hedge.

Although it was still too light to use the NV properly, a stirring in the long grass about 50yd ahead saw me reach for the mono. I fumbled with the gain control – this allows the sensitivity to be turned right down – and quickly scanned the area. Sure enough, there was a fox moving through the long grass. I switched the device off and lifted the rifle – which was sitting on its bipod at my feet, onto the sticks. Again, I turned the gain right down, but I couldn't see where the fox had gone. In desperation, I turned the IR laser on to its lowest setting, but it wasn't enough. I clicked the rotary switch around to give it more and more power, until I was satisfied that there was sufficient IR to get eye reflection. A moment or two later, I picked out two fox eyes, then they disappeared again, only to reappear briefly before being lost once more in the thick vegetation.

By this stage I was thoroughly disoriented – due to the light levels, the sight picture was unlike anything I'm used to. I was not at all sure just how far away the fox was. When I spotted it again, I guessed that it was quite close, so due to the scope height above the barrel, I allowed some hold-over and fired. It was clearly further away than I thought, as the bullet went straight over its head. D'oh! It nervously darted from side to side – not knowing which way to run, before diving through a hedge and out of sight.

I was hoping that I might be able to call it back, so found myself a spot to prop the FOXPRO Scorpion about 50 paces out and set the thing going – but nothing came to investigate, in spite of trying all manner of calls, from injured hare to distressed fox pup. In the end I had to give up and go home. Frustration wasn't the word – how the hell was I going to deal with these bloody foxes? If I didn't get to grips with them soon, the pheasants would have a very hard time, and we couldn't be having that...

Saturday night saw me some 15 miles in the opposite direction on an organic chicken farm where I took a load of bunnies with the HMR: 14 for 16 shots wasn't too shabby, but as ever, the two misses haunted me for several days. Still, at least the ones I'd got helped top up the freezer so that we'd have something to feed the dog with over winter. On Monday I decided that I'd head off back to the site of the fighting foxes to see if I could get a crack at them.

TIPS & TRICKS

Foxes fight to establish their social position from a very early age. They continue to do this all their lives, and it is not at all uncommon to hear shrill screams from fighting foxes. Injuries – sometimes severe, can occur. Sometimes, one of those involved will decide it's had enough and will run for safety – when this happens they may be almost completely oblivious to what is going on around them. I've even heard of fleeing foxes accidentally running over cliff edges in their desperation to escape.

That evening, I was in pensive mood as I drove over. A track by Rainbow was playing on the radio, the late evening sun was shining across the beautiful countryside, and in the greater scheme of things all was well with the world. My failure on the Friday had been bugging me all weekend, though, and I was anxious to level the score. Having said that, if the foxes wouldn't come to the caller, how was I ever going to find the damn things in the long grass? The obvious answer would be to start baiting them into a shootable position, but that would take several days to set up. I wanted blood tonight.

I met two vehicles on my journey over – positively busy for around here, but both times I managed to find a spot in the hedge for my Disco so that they could get past without either of us having to back up. When I arrived at the end of the track I was mightily relieved to see that the cattle had been moved to another part of the farm. Even better than that was the fact that apart from the main gate, all the others had been left open. Not only did this mean that there would be no livestock where I was heading, but it meant I wouldn't have to jump in and out of the truck every time I went from one field to another. Result!

My intended starting point was on the far side of the farm. From there I would be working into the wind, maximising my chances of bouncing Charlie before he knew I was there. As I drove along, I kept a careful watch – at least as careful as I could, bearing in mind the way the Landy was jumping up and down over the rough terrain. The modern tractors that farmers use these days weigh so much that they make a mess of the soft ground, leaving deep ruts and potholes. Eventually, I reached the area I was aiming for and just before I parked up I was delighted to see that the grass in one of the big fields nearby had been cut.

Choosing where to begin was a no-brainer, and it took me moments to get kitted up. I was travelling light this time – just my rifle, sticks and binos. I locked up and moved off, pulling my face veil and gloves on as I did so. A quick check at the gateway showed that all was clear, and I snuck in under the cover of the hedge in order to help hide my profile. I was listening out for early warning signs – magpies scolding, jays screeching or crows complaining, but there was nothing more than the song from a lone skylark and the occasional mewling buzzard call drifting across the landscape.

A small copse lies at the end of the first hedge, and as this sits on a north–south axis, it casts a useful amount of shadow in the late evening. I was glad to make full use of this, but before I'd gone more than a few steps, a flash of movement caught my eye. I raised the binos and immediately saw that a fox was running from one side of the field to the other. It was about 200yd away, and had about another 100yd to go before it would be in the safety of cover. There was, however, also a small rise that created some dead ground that it could easily run into if it sussed I was there.

Luckily, the low sun was right behind me, and I reasoned that the fox would struggle to see me. I still crouched down low, folding the bipod's legs out as I did so. Although I had my sticks with me, if I was going to get a chance of a shot, it was going to be a long one, and I needed the best possible rest. At one point the fox went out of sight over the rise, but as I figured he'd come out again in a few seconds, I took the opportunity to scuttle forwards a few yards. While I was doing so, I cranked the Swaro to the maximum x15 magnification and set the focus to just over 200yd. This done I threw myself on the ground and got behind the scope. My binos were digging into my solar plexus, but I didn't have time to deal with that.

By now the fox was closing in on the hedge, but just before it got there, it paused and looked into the bushes ahead of it – presumably it must have seen a rabbit or something. As it did so, I squeezed off a round. Luckily, I'd done some range checking with the rifle only a week before while setting up my Unique Alpine. I knew the windage was smack on at 209yd – which happened to be the distance between the flat-bed farm trailer and the backstop that I was using as my range – and that the drop was five inches. As my current target was facing away from me and looking up, I chose to aim at the top of its head, since this was approximately five inches above the centre of body mass. The 165gr .308 soft point hit it hard, slamming it over and rolling it onto the ground in no uncertain manner.

As I walked over to where it lay, I counted my steps: it worked out at 230 paces, so about 220yd all in. It proved to be a dog fox, and almost certainly one of the youngsters I'd seen fighting, so I was very pleased. The first thing I did was turn my mobile on and send a text to the chap with the pheasants. I then photographed the carcass before hanging it on the barbed wire fence for the farmer to dispose of. I spent the last half hour or so of daylight checking various other parts of the farm, but with no luck.

I was hiding in these bushes waiting for deer to appear when the foxes nearly ran into me

I LOVE IT WHEN A PLAN COMES TOGETHER

DATE:	16 July 2011	**RIFLE:**	Sauer 202
PLACE:	Roy's Farm	**CALIBRE:**	.22-250
TIME:	22:30	**AMMO:**	55gr Nosler BT
SUNSET:	21:22	**RANGE:**	200yd
STATE OF MOON:	Waning gibbous	**CALL TRACK:**	None
WEATHER:	Dry with clear skies	**OPTICS:**	D480 GenIII NV riflescope
WIND DIRECTION:	Westerly		

As part of my routine patrolling of Roy's farm, I set out one night to do a quick tour around the lanes behind my village in the Land Rover, stopping at all the gates where I have permission to check for foxes with the NV monocular. Apart from a couple of horses and a few sheep, however, I saw nothing at all. This was probably because the moon was both high and very bright. By the last field I'd more or less given up, so when I pulled into the adjacent lay-by I was feeling a bit hacked-off. After I'd climbed out, I closed the door as far as the first click, and left it there – I didn't want to make any more noise than I had to, and I was only going about 10ft for a quick check around.

Trying to avoid the crunchy gravel underfoot as well as the long tendrils of aggressive bramble, I made it to the gateway. Once there, I lifted the mono to my eye and turned it on – and straight away I saw there was a fox about 75yd out and seemingly hunting for worms. Damn! Once again, I'd not bothered to unload the rifle from the truck as I didn't think there'd be anything around.

Doing my best to make it back across the lane without being heard, I retrieved the gun from its case, slipped a magazine in, and slid the sticks out from between the seats, desperately trying to ensure I didn't clang them on anything metallic. Something must have given me away, though, for by the time I'd made it back, the fox was heading off over the brow of the hill.

Oh, how jolly dashed annoying. Or words to that effect...

So, the next night I planned to revisit the scene. The field the fox was in had been the scene of several lamb attacks earlier in the year. As far as I knew, I'd already dealt with the culprits, but Roy would not be impressed if I missed the opportunity to go after this one too. Although the moon was going to be full, it was rising late, so I figured I'd get half an hour or so of darkness before it made an appearance. A quick check of the Met Office's website showed me the wind hadn't changed in the last couple of hours. It was still very much in the west, which was just where I wanted it, since the most direct approach would be from the east. The other factor that I hoped was going to be in my favour was that it had rained earlier in the day. Consequently, the ground would be nice and wet – ideal for the worms that a hungry fox might choose to start its night's foraging with.

Unfortunately, although the sun set on time, the light just didn't seem to want to go and when I pulled away from the house at 10:15, it was still twilight. Still, I couldn't afford to sit around as the moon wouldn't wait for any man. The journey only takes about a minute, so the engine was barely warm as I coasted into the lay-by which sits at the bottom of a steep hill. A narrow stream runs close by, wending its way along the base of the valley for about half a mile before meeting the area's main river. Fields lie on either side of the stream, with those on the left quickly giving way to thick woodland. The area I was interested in on this occasion was the steep meadow on the right. This rises in a moderate incline for about 100ft, before levelling off at a big 'Devon bank'. The rich soil and lush grass there must make the worms especially tasty, for it is a veritable magnet for foxes.

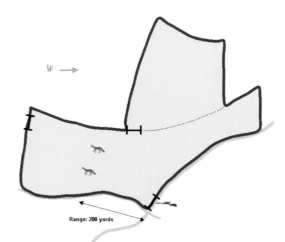

As I killed the lights and applied the handbrake, I switched into hunter-killer mode. I'd already got the NV mono around my neck, and my attire was soon completed with my gloves and face veil being pulled on in moments. Fortunately, the rifle slid out of its bag without catching on anything in the dark (the Disco's interior lights are taped over), and sticks followed suit without making a sound.

In seconds, I was in the gateway and scanning the ground before me. The first thing I saw was a herd of cattle about 200yd out, just uphill of the stream which ran past a few feet to my left. Blast! They weren't there last time... About 50yd or so on the other side of them, however, was a familiar shape. Yes, a fox was nose down in the grass, worming. As I watched, it looked up – its eyes glaring brightly in the glow from my laser. The

moment this happened, I raised the NV – there was a chance that this individual had seen my laser before, so I didn't want to risk it sussing me out. Once I'd switched the illuminator off, I turned the tube's gain up (making it brighter) and went back to observing it. When I was happy that it was no longer looking in my direction, I scaled the gate then stopped to formulate a plan.

Foxes are past masters at the art of disappearing into the undergrowth. Moments after this photo was taken, the fox was nowhere to be seen.

For some unknown reason, this field is a magnet to foxes. Countless numbers have fallen to the rifle here.

I was now faced with a dilemma. If I tried to approach the fox along the line of the stream, there was a distinct chance that the cattle would get spooked. If this happened, all hell would break loose as they charged madly around the field. If I went to my right to approach from uphill, I'd risk being seen. There was also a large bog in the way. Cars were driving by every few minutes, and each time they did so, the high ground was lit up by their headlights. I had to gamble that the fox would come further up the field – there was every hope that it would do so, as it had been much closer to the road when I'd seen it the previous night.

In the end, I decided to try and make it to the cover of some brushwood that was stacked just above the stream. I reasoned that from there I should have a good field of fire, albeit that I'd be shooting uphill. My plan slowly started to come together. I gradually picked my way through the potholes and reed tussocks, stopping every 10ft or so to check where the fox was. Sure enough, it was heading my way, heavily preoccupied with snuffling through the long grass. I finally made it to my chosen spot without falling flat on my face or giving my position away. Once there, I inched the tripod sticks out – doing my best to get them stable

enough to stay upright when I took my hands away. This done, I had another quick scan before unslinging the rifle. The fox had gone! I couldn't believe it. I'd been really careful to avoid making any noise or sudden movements.

It was clearly time to stop and take stock of the situation. I had a really good look around with the NV. Then another. Apart from the cattle, there was nothing moving. Where had it gone? A bit of head scratching later saw me switch the laser back on – and there was my answer. A long dark shadow revealed that there was a slight rise ahead of me, which created a stretch of dead ground. The fox must have simply walked a few feet forwards and gone out of my sight. This is the main reason why I use a laser – with a GenIII tube, you don't need the extra illumination, but you do need to see low-lying shadows if you want to fully understand the shape of the terrain.

Once I'd realised this, I went back on full alert. There was every chance that the fox was now very close to me. Luckily, there was a large patch of dashels (thistles) above me, and I figured the fox would probably do everything it could to avoid them. I couldn't see past them though, so I slid my thumb up between the legs of the tripod and lifted it – still in the open position, and set it down again a few feet further forwards. In this way, I slowly moved in amongst the spiky plants until I could see beyond them. And there was my intended target. It was still nose down, but was moving quite quickly. If I didn't act fast, it would soon be down-wind of me. I slid the rifle off my shoulder as smoothly as I could, and got it up onto the sticks. From here on I went into auto-pilot: feet positioned for maximum stability, NV switched on and refocused, tube gain up slightly, laser on, left arm locked, safety off, reticle on target – slightly high to allow for the close range – and 'bang'. It was all over. The fox simply fell on the spot without a twitch.

I reloaded, retrieving the empty case into my hand rather than have to search for it in the thistles, reapplied the safety and slung the rifle back onto my shoulder. I made a quick check with the mono to give myself a bearing on the carcass, and – much to my surprise – saw another pair of eyes shining back at me from the top of the hill. In moments I

was set up again, but when I switched the rifle-scope on, there was nothing there. I spent some time searching for it, but without success. On retrieval, the carcass proved to be that of quite a large dog fox. Since it had been worming I was half expecting it to be a vixen, but I guess it's a case of 'beggars can't be choosers'. The area was very badly hit by mixy a few years ago, and the rabbit population still hasn't recovered. The pheasant shoots are only just putting their birds down, and most of the nestling song birds have fledged. None of the fruit is ripe yet – especially the blackberries that foxes seem to love so much. There don't seem to be many rodents around either, and as a result, there's not much else for a hungry Charlie to eat around here. Except lead, of course!

TIPS & TRICKS

As well as all the better-known things, foxes will also spend a lot of time hunting and eating worms. Damp summer evenings are guaranteed to bring these slippery creatures to the surface, where they stretch out on the ground – both searching for dead leaves as well as potential mates. When compared to the amount of energy used, they provide a good nutritional return. A fox that hunts worms one night may well be killing chickens the next though, so it is still viable and justifiable quarry.

This fox skirted around a thistle patch in order to dodge the sharp prickles. It wasn't able to avoid being seen by the NV, though.

AURAL SIX

DATE:	23 July 2012	**RIFLE:**	Kimber Montana
PLACE:	Jim's Farm	**CALIBRE:**	.204 Ruger
TIME:	From about 19:30 to 23:00	**AMMO:**	32gr V-Max
SUNSET:	21:13	**RANGE:**	80–120yd
STATE OF MOON:	Evening crescent	**CALL TRACK:**	Various
WEATHER:	Dry, cold	**OPTICS:**	Swarovski Z6 3-18x50
WIND DIRECTION:	North-westerly		with GenIII NV add-on

While at the Exeter boot fair, I stopped for a quick chat with my mate Paul, who runs a large tool stall there every now and then. Although he's been a very keen shooter all his life, he was mostly a shotgun man until he used my HMR a few times. After shooting a good number of bunnies though, he was sold on the idea of getting a rifle or two. Like so many people, he'd put it off applying for his FAC for ages, but finally got around to it. Several months on, it eventually arrived, and he rushed out to Blue Fox and bought himself a nice Browning T-Bolt in .17HMR.

He was like an excited kid once he'd got his new toy in his sweaty hands, and was really keen to get out and use it in anger. Since he has about 50 acres of his own, he'd got it all zeroed and put plenty of practice rounds through it by the time I took him out. Shooting is his first love, so in the run-up to his FAC being approved, he'd joined me on several of my foxing sessions. We agreed I'd pick him up that evening, and I left him to his customers.

With my day's jobs done, I put the batteries for the thermal imagers and fox caller on charge then hit the sack for a couple of hours. When I reappeared, my Good Lady presented me with a big plate of scrumptious food – once that was scoffed, I loaded up and headed off to collect Paul. I'd already arranged to go over and see Jim – one of the farmers I do a lot of shooting for. He has a huge number of sheep and cattle, and not only owns a vast amount of land, but rents masses of other ground too.

One of these areas is centred on a beautiful Tudor manor that is owned by a retired banker. The scenery is as stunning as the house, and teems with rabbits – and where there are bunnies, there are usually lots of foxes too. Jim has had a lot of trouble with Charlie there during the lambing season, and he was keen for me to get ahead of the problem by hitting the cubs now. Paul and I dropped in so that I could confirm the land boundaries, as I'd only been there a couple of times before, and would be working a part that I didn't know. While we were discussing it, Jim also mentioned that he'd seen a fox near the old scramble track on his own farm, and that he'd like me to see if I could catch up with it. All that done, we drove over and had a good session. We saw two foxes in daylight, of which I managed to call in and shoot one. After it got dark, we called in another two, both of which fell to the .204.

Jim was very pleased when I gave him the news the next morning, and even more so when I said that we were going to come over again that evening to try and find the scramble track fox. I duly collected Paul at the appointed hour, and we set off with some really stinky bait in the back. This comprised some venison trimmings that had been vac-packed and then frozen. I'd taken it out of the freezer about a week before, and for most of this time it'd been left in the sun to get really ripe. A couple of quick sniffs convinced me that it would be a very bad thing if either of the bags split in the truck, so I folded them

over and stuck them through the vac-packer again, just to be sure. Once on site, we slowly drove up the long track, doing our best to avoid the worst of the tank traps caused by the weeks of incessant rain. These had now dried out, and were as hard as rock. On the way we kept an eye out for bunnies, but for some unknown reason, there were very few about. We eventually reached the far end of the farm, and parked out of sight of the disused scramble track.

With our face veils on, rifles over our shoulders, and sticks in hand, we cautiously approached our chosen killing zone. Paul was using my Nikon HGL binoculars, while I had both my mini-thermal and Leica range-finding binos. Neither of us could see anything of note, so we looked around to identify the best spot to set up. The most obvious choice was a stretch of old trackway, which would have given us a commanding view of the natural bowl formed by the ground in front of us, but unfortunately this was about two inches deep in stagnant water. Just below it were some narrow steps cut into the side of the hill by the passing of innumerable sheep. These proved to be ideal, so we adjusted the sticks to suit, and Paul set off down the hill to position the FOXPRO.

To our left was a small area of woodland on the side of a steep hill. This cover was mostly made up of a mix of ash and oak trees, with a dense understory of blackthorn and bramble bushes below. To our right was another steep hill, but it was clad with a thick stand of gorse bushes. I've seen foxes in there

many times before so was hopeful that we were in the right place. The two hills are only about 100yd apart, and lying between them is a small pond. I'm not sure when the scramble track was last used, but it was before Jim bought the place some 15 years ago. In spite of this, the wheel ruts are still prominent and there is no doubt where the bikes ran. It must have been a magnificent and fearsome place to ride. These days it is a scene of utter serenity, with wrens chattering away in the bushes, young buzzards calling from further down the valley, and all manner of songbirds twittering here and there in the branches.

When we first arrived, we'd also heard some magpies giving their distinctive alarm calls, but these had stopped a few minutes earlier. Still, it held promise that there could be foxes about. There was about an hour of daylight left, and when I was happy that the area had settled back down after our disturbance, and that everything else was ready – rifles focused at the right ranges, set to the optimal magnification, etc., I started the caller. I began with a rabbit distress call as this carries well over distance – after a few seconds at full volume, I cranked it down so as not to spook any foxes that approached. After about a minute, a small fox ran in from downwind – I immediately hit the mute button so that it'd have to stop and look for the source of the sound. The moment it did so, a .204 round dropped it.

About five minutes later, I saw a large bunny run out of the gorse. It's not unusual for a rabbit or a hare to do this, so I laughed and whispered to Paul, 'Look at that daft bloody bunny!' As I said it, I suddenly realised that it wasn't any kind of lagomorph, but was instead another small fox. I told Paul that he could shoot it with his HMR – it was only about 75yd out, and having seen him drop bunnies at 175yd, was confident that both he and the rifle were more than up to the job. His sticks were pointing in the wrong direction though, and by the time he'd moved them the fox had reached the caller and sniffed human. It immediately ran back to the gorse, but

> ### TIPS & TRICKS
> Young foxes are both very curious and remorseless killers – they will often run in to a distress call without giving a thought to the wind direction. Daylight calling sessions can therefore be very effective, however, because of the unpredictable nature, it is really important to watch every possible access route closely.

paused for a final look before diving back into cover. As Paul was still fumbling with his sticks, I whispered, 'Sorry – I'm going to have to shoot it,' and squeezed off a shot. There was a loud 'thump', and my second fox of the evening was down.

We tried calling for another 10 minutes or so, but when nothing came, we retrieved the caller, and moved on to try another location just over the hill. This was unsuccessful, but at one point the magpies kicked off big time in the next stretch of woods, so something had obviously upset them – whether it was foxes or a roe deer we'll never know. As the light was now starting to go, I suggested that we head back to the truck and change the kit around ready for when it got dark. One good thing about the steep terrain around here is that it gives you a good workout. It's nothing like the mountainous country seen in places further north, but all the hiking up and down certainly helps to keep one healthy!

Back at the Disco, we swapped the binos for NV monos, and I set Paul up with a large thermal imager so that he could act as my spotter. We only had to go a few yards to reach a huge field – fortunately, this had been home to a large flock of sheep until a few days before, so the grass was nice and short. We

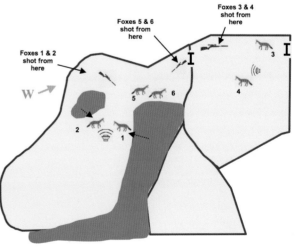

chose an ambush point under the cover of a tall hedge. But now I had a problem – there was no wind to speak of, so I had not the slightest chance of working out the likeliest fox approach routes. I took one of the bags of stinky bait and placed it about 80 paces out, and then put the caller nearby.

With all that done, I started with the rabbit distress call. When that didn't work, I tried another labelled 'The Kiss of Death'. This is a synthetic call that sounds like an electronic simulation of a crazy rat fighting a piece of polystyrene. Looking around with the mini-thermal, I saw a white shape that appeared to be a rabbit looking out into the field from the hedge, only about 50yd from us. I whispered to Paul that there was a bunny watching the proceedings, but then realised that I might have been getting a false size perspective. This is easily done with a thermal, as you get so little landscape detail. I therefore carefully swivelled the rifle around and double-checked through the NV. I found myself looking straight at a fox – which by now had spotted me and was facing directly towards us, its eyes lit up by the laser. I had the safety off in a millisecond, and my third fox dropped with a convincing thud.

I let things settle again, then started the first of a series of distress calls, but these didn't bring anything in, so I tried the fox squalls. These are basically screams that foxes use to tell other members of their group where they are. You can often get other foxes answering you, if you play things properly. After that, I moved on to the vixen mating call, but that didn't result in anything either. I then decided to try a cub in distress call, in the hope that it might bring a concerned vixen in. A minute or so later a rabbit appeared about a 150yd out. I double-checked that my ID was correct with the NV mono, and then moved back to the thermal. A few seconds later, a large white shape appeared between us and the rabbit. It was clearly a fox, but my sticks were pointing in the wrong direction, so I hastily repositioned them and got myself on it. It must have sussed us, as it was heading away from us at some speed. At one point it paused sideways on, and went down to a V-Max from the .204. That was number four.

Something told me to go and have a quick look back by the scramble track, so I picked the sticks up and tiptoed my way back through the gate. My first

check with the thermal revealed what looked like two bunnies directly below me. I couldn't see them properly though, as they were on the other side of a rise in the round. I'm not getting caught out like that I again, I thought, and moved forwards to get a better look. Sure enough, it was another two small foxes. The first one dropped on the spot, but the second moved just as I fired, and I missed – it ran a few yards and stopped to try and work out which way it should go. By then I'd reloaded and my sixth fox of the night fell on the spot. All were of a similar age and weight, with there being a mix of males and females. I've not spoken to the farmer yet, but I know he'll be delighted. That makes it 14 foxes in the last nine days. I know that's nothing to anyone who lamps from a vehicle, but it's not bad for someone shooting on foot!

Land Rovers and other 4x4s are indispensable to the serious shooter.

AUGUST

On farms across the whole country, August continues the theme started in July – whenever the weather is suitable, combine harvesters, foragers and associated machinery will be out cutting and baling the crops. Slowly, the barns will fill up with bales and the clamps with silage. If the bales – which are generally wrapped in plastic these days – are left out in the open they may be damaged by crows pecking through them. This allows the rain in and spoils the contents. Most farmers will be very pleased if the numbers of these destructive birds are controlled by keen shooters – it's important not to put any bullet holes in the bales though, or you'll be just as unpopular as the corvids!

If the sun has been kind, most of the fields will be clear by the end of the month, leaving masses of stubble for foxers to shoot over. It's always worth discussing the plans for these fields with the farmer though, as some will go under the plough almost straight away, putting them out of bounds to vehicles. Those that are left though will be a magnet to anything that likes to eat fallen grain. This includes rodents like rats, mice and voles, as well birds like pigeons, rooks and magpies. Before long, vast

August is a good time for the shooter – not only is the ground usually dry and the air warm, but with the crops being cut it's once again possible to see the foxes, rabbits and deer where before they would remain hidden.

numbers of green shoots appear between the stubble, and these are considered highly desirable by many herbivores, especially rabbits and roe deer. With so many prey species about, it's no surprise that foxes won't be far behind, especially if it's too dry for worms to be near the surface.

If nothing else, at least August sees night falling at a more reasonable time – by the end of the month it's getting dark by about 8:30 p.m. As a result, those of us who like to shoot with night vision or the lamp get more of a chance to get out without having to worry about divorce proceedings being issued. It's important to keep an eye on the state of the moon though, as if the skies are clear you will really struggle to move around without being seen. Town foxes are more used to the extra light, but most of those from the countryside hate it, and will generally sticks to the shadows. Sometimes the area's dominant

> ### THE FARMER'S MONTH
> Lambs weaned.
> Second or even third silage cut.
> Cereals harvested.
> Ploughing for next year's crops;
> autumn and winter crops planted.
> Pasture topping.
> Dung spreading.

animals will be more relaxed about it, as the main worry for them is fights with other foxes.

Some cattle produce calves during August. Where this is the case, it's well worth keeping a watch over the afterbirth – the best time is just after it gets dark. The local foxes will know it's there, and will be anxious to be the first to start eating it. Once it's either been cleared up by the farmer or consumed by animals, the next thing to check is the calves. Their droppings will be much richer than usual, and the milky taste will be popular with both foxes and farm dogs. Elsewhere, there will be lots of other food sources available, so callers may not work very well. If the usual prey distress sounds don't bring anything in, it's worth trying some fox squalls – these are communication calls, and are usually heard in the first hour or so after dark. In most instances they can be loosely translated as 'I'm over here, where are you?'. These sounds should be used sparingly, though, or there is the risk they will act as repellents. Skilled use of the caller can see a sort of conversation being established between yourself and a fox, where it calls a couple of times, and you reply in like manner. If you do it properly, the respondent will move in to see who he or she has been 'talking' to. If you've set yourself up properly, you should be able to get a shot in before long. Once again, patience is the key.

Most gamekeepers will be close to putting their pheasant poults out, and those that do will be extremely anxious that they don't get killed by foxes before they learn how to roost safely. Partridges are even more vulnerable, as they seem to lack any sense of danger, be that from a hungry predator or even an approaching car. Most shooting estates will have been doing a lot of predator control work in the run up to releasing the poults, however, there are always more about, especially when one of the so-called 'charities' has been dumping their unwanted foxes in the locality. Consequently, this is not a time to relax – it is, however, vital that any shooting activities are agreed in advance not only with the landowner, but with the keeper too. He will not be impressed if you fire shots too close to his birds and they are spooked into flying into dangerous spots.

As ever, the farmers will be busy. This month they will not only be frantically trying to get all the combining finished and the hay/straw/silage stored,

but they will have to get the fields ready – that is fertilised and ploughed ready for the next crops to go in. These include such things as Swiss chard, spring cabbage, winter cabbage and kale. These need to get properly established before the frosts start, or they will be ruined. Other tasks include running mowers around to cut the weeds down – this is known as 'topping'. It's mainly intended to control docks and thistles as these quickly get out of control if not managed properly.

BELOW: The larva of the Elephant Hawk Moth uses eye spots to intimidate would-be predators. It is, however, completely harmless and is one of nature's treasures.

BOTTOM: The male stag beetle bears an impressive set of pincers in order to fight off any rivals.

RAIN STOPS PLAY

DATE:	4 August 2012	**RIFLES:**	Kimber Montana &
PLACE:	Jim's Farm		Sauer 202
TIME:	19:45–22:00	**CALIBRES:**	.204 & .22-250
SUNSET:	20:55	**AMMO:**	32gr V-Max & 55gr Nosler BT
STATE OF MOON:	Waning gibbous	**RANGE:**	150yd
WEATHER:	Dry, cold	**CALL TRACK:**	Distressed rabbit
WIND DIRECTION:	North-westerly	**OPTICS:**	D480 GenIII NV riflescope

I've been accompanied on several of my recent sessions by my good mate Paul, but he wasn't able to join me last night, so I set off on my own. When I got to the farmyard, I was pleased to see that the gates to the higher track were all open, which saved an awful lot of faffing about, so I carried on without stopping. I had to go carefully though, as the surface is deeply rutted, and the rainstorm we'd had earlier in the day had left it extremely slippery. The mud terrain tyres on the Disco coped admirably though, and by keeping my thumbs well clear of the steering wheel I made it to the top without any injuries. On reaching the end of the track, I performed a multi-point turn so that the truck would be facing the right way when it was time to leave. I hate manoeuvring in such tight spots in the dark, it's a sure fire way to smash a tail light or dent a body panel.

One of the things I've disciplined myself to do is to get everything ready before I go peering over any gates or hedges. Many is the time that I've wandered a few feet from the truck and peeked into a field only to find a fox looking straight back at me – with the rifle still nestling in its slip and the ammo all tucked up in the pouch! Not wanting to go there again, I got everything together – face veil, binos, mini TI and gloves, then loaded five rounds of 32gr V-Max into the Kimber Montana .204. With that slung over my shoulder, I grabbed my sticks and I was ready to see what was around.

I'd chosen to park at that spot because the nearest gateway provides an excellent vantage point over the surrounding countryside. At this stage the sun was getting low in the sky, and there was about an hour of daylight remaining. Its rays were illuminating the landscape with a beautiful glow, and I was confident that any foxes in the area would take advantage of this to dry off after the showers we'd had. I therefore took particular care to scrutinise all the hedges in case Charlie was lying up somewhere sunning himself. I systematically scanned every likely feature, starting with those closest to me, and working my way out. There were loads of sheep and cattle out there, with a few flocks of rooks dotted about searching the soft soil for worms and grubs.

There was no sign of either roe deer or foxes though, so I broadened my search to include the next farm, where I also shoot frequently. Moments later, I caught sight of a familiar shape at the top of a very steep goyle (small valley). A few tweaks of the focus wheel on my Leica bins resulted in me looking at a large fox – from his build, he was almost certainly a dog. The white hair on his chest shone brightly in the August sun, and when he turned sideways on, the commensurate white tip on his tail stood out prominently. He was snuffling through the long grass as he went, clearly searching for any opportunistic prey. I immediately knew where he was going though, for a few yards further on were several hundred tasty free-range chickens. The rangefinder on my bins only goes out to 1,200yd, and they wouldn't lock on to where he was. I eventually got a reading some 300yd short of his position, so he must have been nearly a mile away. It was obviously too late to do anything about it now, but there was little doubt where I'd be shooting next time out.

By now the sun was even closer to the horizon, and the area above it was lit with vivid patches of red and orange. Elsewhere, the sky was a beautiful clear

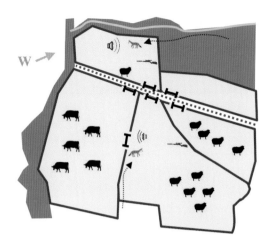

blue, interspersed with steel grey clouds. Some of these looked a little threatening as they sped from one horizon towards the other. Down at my level the wind was brisk, but dropping – black clouds in the far distance gave a portent of bad things to come though.

I figured I'd spent enough time doing my homework, and as I'd only seen a few rabbits during my last few sweeps of the area, I moved on. Before locking the truck I packed my NV mono, NV add-on and FOXPRO caller into a small ex-military shoulder bag originally intended for PVS-7 NV goggles. This way I'd be able to continue shooting into the dark without having to return to swap my kit around. Since there were flocks of sheep and a few cattle in all but one of the fields near me, I had little choice in where to begin. Fortunately, this field was where I'd originally intended to start with the caller – it dives from the track down a steep hill towards a narrow stream which burbles its way through a thicket of small trees. On the right hand side is an extensive wood, from where I hoped to call in a fox or two.

I was a little surprised to see a solitary sheep just beyond the gateway. It looked very sorry for itself, and it didn't really seem right that it was there on its own. Its black ears, which identified it as a Gloucester – as opposed to the white-headed Dorsets – drooped forlornly as it watched me approach. I didn't know if it'd accidentally been left behind when the others were moved, or if it'd escaped from another field and now couldn't get back. The other possibility was that it'd been deliberately separated due to some kind of

medical issue – I resolved to remember to check with the farmer on my way home.

Climbing over the gate, I did my best to avoid spooking it – it was clearly feeling sorry for itself, and the last thing it needed was me frightening it unnecessarily. I therefore circled quietly around it before slowly making my way down the edge of the woods. Every few paces I stopped and checked the hedges at the bottom and far side of the field with the binos. Satisfied that I wasn't missing anything, I got to a spot that I felt would give me the best blend of height, vision and cover. From there, I reviewed the wind direction and selected a position for the caller. Counting out my steps, I made it 97 paces to the clump of grass I'd chosen as my marker. There was a convenient gap in the vegetation just beside it, so that was where I put the FOXPRO. It looked nice and stable, which is a good thing as I didn't want the caller to fall over. This not only reduces the sound but can also mask the control signal, which is deeply frustrating if you're frantically trying to mute the call as a fox comes tearing in.

Returning to my ambush point, I set my sticks out so that they sat well on the steep ground. The rear leg was up under my right armpit, with the front two settled into the grass below me. This allowed me to support my right elbow with my left hand, giving a really stable aim point. Any foxes that came in from downwind would now be well away from my own scent trail, but at the same time still covered by the rifle. As the approach routes were all under 100yd, I chose to use a reasonably low magnification so that I'd have a good field of view through the scope. This is always a good thing when the action gets really fast-paced. Remembering that I was meant to collect my stepson from work, I checked my mobile phone – luckily, I found I was getting a full-strength signal, so no worries there. After a quick check to make sure the focus on the scope was how I wanted it, I started the caller. I began with the baby rabbit distress call as this carries well over distance – using full volume at first, then gradually reducing it so that any foxes that came in wouldn't be put off by the sound level.

Within about 20 seconds, a magpie began chattering its alarm call down in the woods. Right where I'd have expected a fox to come from. I kept a close watch, and sure enough, about a minute later a small

This fox's approach was heralded by a magpie alarm call. When it ran out towards my caller, I was ready and waiting.

Once there, I removed my binos and replaced them with the NV mono – there was no need to carry kit I wasn't going to use. I also fitted the NV add-on to the rifle and was therefore able to leave the bag behind too. Having done all that, I now had to select another calling zone. Although there was a large flock of sheep in the field overlooked by the vantage point, they were all at the bottom end sheltering from the weather. Since what was left of the wind was blowing up the hill diagonally away from them, I expected any foxes to come in from the top, so was happy that it would be a good spot for an after dark ambush. The only possible fly in the ointment was that a massive black cloud had appeared on the horizon: was it coming my way, I wondered?

Before setting the caller out I decided to have a thorough look around with the thermal – I didn't want to go waltzing across the field if there was already a fox close by. To this end, I slowly made my way down the hedgeline, scanning as I went. The cattle in the next field showed up as really strong hot-spots, as did the sheep. There was a large dip in the ground between my position and the sheep, however. I realised that I'd have to be careful to ensure that I could see into this when I started the caller as well as along the top hedgerow. There was nothing else apparent though, so I made my way back to the top of the hill as quietly as I could. Before I got there, I heard a few rain drops hit the ground around me. Then some more. Since the cloud I'd seen earlier had looked angry, I didn't waste a moment and luckily made it to the safety of my truck just as the storm hit.

fox ran out into the field. I immediately hit the mute button, and it stopped straight away to sniff the air. As it did so, I started the caller again, and it ran forwards. When it was where I wanted it, I hit mute again. The fox stopped for a second time, then turned to look back into the woods. As it did so, my V-Max bowled it over without so much as a twitch. The sound of the shot echoed around the small valley, and then all was quiet once more. I gave it a couple of minutes for everything to settle down, then tried again. Nothing showed, however, in spite of me experimenting with several other calls.

In the end I decided that, as the light was going, I should move on and get myself set up in another position. Before doing so, I had to photograph the fox and move its carcass to somewhere the farmer could collect it for proper disposal. When I got to it I found it was a sub-adult vixen. The round had hit it centre chest, and the opposite side was completely blown out. No suffering there, which is how I like it. The caller retrieved, I looked back up the hill. The wind had died completely, and the air now seemed to be brooding – definitely a calm before the storm moment. I zigzagged my way up the hill, past the sorry-looking sheep, and back to the truck.

Wondering how to occupy my time while the cloud passed, I spotted a notepad tucked down the side of my seat, so as there was nothing else to do, I wrote up the first part of the evening's events. I was nearly at the point of recounting the kill when the rain stopped. Not wanting to leave it there, I carried on scribbling away for a minute or two and it was a good job I did, for the heavens suddenly opened for a second time. Had I been out there, I'd have been soaked. Deciding that discretion was the better part of valour, I waited until I could see that the sky had lightened, indicating the cloud had, indeed, passed. As I'd already worked out the lay of the land, it only took me a couple of minutes to get the caller in place. This time, the sticks were set to their full height so that I'd get the best possible view.

Although it was only a day or so past full moon, the thick clouds ensured that the night was really dark. I was stood with my back to a hedge, and was clad from head to toe in camo, with all my kit wrapped in camo tape. In fact, Paul had commented only a couple of days previously just how effective my set up was, as even in daylight I was really only visible when I moved. I am definitely not one of those who like their kit to be pristine and sparkly. That's OK on the range, but it has no place in proper hunting. I know that I look like some kind of military tramp, but it works for me. I was therefore confident that even though I was going to be standing up, little would see me. As there was a tall hedge about 100yd in front of me, I turned the NV's tube brightness down to suit the short distance. Satisfied that all was ready, I started the FOXPRO with the distressed bunny call.

I already had the rifle up on the sticks, and I was using my left hand to scan with the thermal. Almost immediately, I spotted a white shape half way down the field, looking up towards the caller. It certainly looked fox-like, so I let the thermal hang free and got on the rifle. As it was about double the distance I'd set the scope for, the image was quite dark, so I could not be completely sure what I was looking at. As the laser was switched on I could see bright eye reflections, but that wasn't good enough – I didn't want to shoot a tawny owl by mistake. Before I could reach the gain control to turn the tube up, it jumped up and turned to go. Now there was no mistaking things: it was clearly a fox, and a large one at that. It was also very obviously spooked by the laser – it ran about 10ft, and then just before it disappeared, it turned for a last look. As my round hit it, the fox flipped over, then rolled out of sight. Result!

TIPS & TRICKS

Once a fox has managed to associate the light from a lamp with danger, it can become a very difficult individual to get to grips with. This may come about because someone has shot at it and missed, or because someone has shot at another fox nearby and hit. Either way, it makes no difference whether the light comes from a white lamp, one with a coloured filter, or simply the red glow from a laser illuminator. Once it has made the connection, it will run at the slightest hint of light. That is why it is best to use the minimum possible amount of illumination – a thermal imager can be a great asset here, however, they are extremely costly and therefore out of the reach of most foxers!

Since time was pressing on, I thought it would be best to collect the carcass straight away, rather than wait and risk getting my taxi call before I'd had a chance to do so. I therefore checked that all was clear with the thermal, then set off down the hill. I knew I might have a problem locating the fox's body – with a lot of thick vegetation around, it's only too easy to lose one. As an illustration of this, the other night Paul and I spent the best part of an hour looking for a carcass without success. We'd even criss-crossed the field in my Land Rover with me climbing up onto the roof on several occasions to search with the thermal. In the end we gave up and went home.

We returned the next morning for a search in daylight – but even then we couldn't find it in spite of it being an open field. Just as we were giving up and Paul was starting to rag me about not being able to count it in my tally, I found it. It was lying there in full view with a set of tyre tracks within two feet of it... Anyway, on this occasion, it only took me a few minutes to find the carcass – it was stretched out in some long grass. I was delighted to discover it was a large dog fox – given its location, it was almost certainly one that I'd seen several times, but not been able to get my rifle onto.

With all the usual stuff attended to – photos, carcass removal, and so on – I ascended the hill, retrieved the caller and packed everything away. My timing was perfect, so I drove back down to the farmyard where I had a brief word with the farmer's wife, who relayed messages to her husband from an upstairs window, as he was enjoying a nice soak in the bath. Apparently, the sorry-looking sheep was meant to be on its own – I didn't gather why, but assume it was so that the vet could get to it easily. I was given a sincere thanks for dealing with the foxes, and was on my way. I returned home to end what had turned out to be an excellent evening. That made it 29 foxes in 20 days!

CRANE FLY CATCHERS

DATE:	6 August 2011	**RIFLE:**	Sauer 202
PLACE:	Roy's Farm	**CALIBRE:**	.22-250
TIME:	21:30	**AMMO:**	55gr Sierra GameKing HP
SUNSET:	20:53	**RANGE:**	200yd
STATE OF MOON:	First quarter	**CALL TRACK:**	None
WEATHER:	Dry, cold	**OPTICS:**	D480 GenIII NV riflescope
WIND DIRECTION:	North-westerly		

Roy, who I've mentioned several times already, raises a lot of sheep and so is very keen for me to keep the foxes in the area under control. We expect one or two new ones to appear over the course of a year, but in the summer of 2011, there was a large influx of 'foreign' foxes – that is, they didn't seem to fit into the countryside, and a few had signs of possible human medical intervention – treated mange, and so on. We can only assume that they had been released by a supposed animal charity. Not only is this probably illegal, but it is morally wrong too. Dumping a load of town foxes into an area thick with free-range chickens and young sheep is economic vandalism. It is also cruel to the creatures themselves, as the resident foxes will at best chase them off, and at worst severely injure or kill them. As a consequence of this, the outsiders are run from pillar to post until they find an area that is unoccupied. At first it must seem to them as though they've struck lucky when they find such places, but the reason they have no vulpine occupants is that they've almost always got very efficient keepers or pest controllers.

The first of the influx got lucky, as I was having dreadful problems with my NV riflescope. To cut a long story short, the unit had not been built properly, as a vital securing bolt was missing from the forward support leg mounting for the for the objective lens. The rifle had held a perfect zero for a long time – well

TIPS & TRICKS

The first time I saw foxes snuffling around in long grass, and then suddenly leaping up into the air and snatching at something, it took me some time to work out what was going on. Whatever they were eating, it was quickly consumed, and they'd then start snuffling around again only to repeat the procedure. Having watched this going on for a while, it eventually dawned on me – they were catching crane flies shortly after they emerged from their pupae as adults (as photo at right).

over a year of being used four or five times a week. But when the recoil finally shook the front lens off its axis, I suddenly found that I couldn't hit a thing. It took me ages to work out the cause of the problem. It's not that the bolt had dropped out or was 'forgotten' – when I eventually stripped the whole thing down, I found that the holes didn't even come close to lining up, and so it could never have been fitted. What was really frustrating is that putting another hole in the proper place was a very straightforward task, and so it could easily have been done by the supplier.

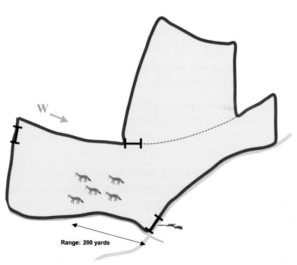

Range: 200 yards

Anyway – what it meant was that every time I took the rifle out, I found that the point of impact had moved a couple of inches. This resulted in me missing the first two foxes that suddenly appeared in Roy's lower meadow. Once I'd sorted the matter out, however, I returned and consigned both foxes to history. When I first saw them, I couldn't work out what they were doing – they were snuffling in the grass and then leaping up in the air and snatching at something a couple of feet off the ground. I'd never seen this behaviour before, and it wasn't something that I'd ever read about in any of the scientific works. In the end, I decided that they were probably catching crane flies. Over the coming months and years it was something that I was to get used to seeing, as it is, in fact, a commonplace thing around here.

Four days after shooting the two foxes, I went back to check that all was clear, but to my surprise, there was another one out in the field. I shot it off sticks at 140 paces, and when I went out to retrieve the carcass, I found it was a big dog fox. Wondering where all these adult foxes were coming from – you could understand it if they were cubs, I went back again after leaving it a further eight days. Once again, I parked up in the lay-by and climbed out for a quick look – I was only passing by on my way to another farm, so I was really only going through the motions. The last thing I expected to see was another fox, but lo and behold, that's exactly what I saw. A shot from sticks made it drop on the spot – this time it was a medium-sized vixen, which I measured at 130 paces.

I was busy elsewhere for a while, so the next time I stopped by was five days later, on my way back from a fruitless trip to a local farm. Again, it was more of a formality than with the expectation that anything would be there, but I was amazed to see there was yet another fox scratching around in the field. This time it was a bit further out, and it must have seen the truck pull up as it was clearly nervous. It was looking across the field towards me, and by the way it kept turning and checking its escape route, I was expecting it to run at any moment. Rather than risk it seeing the movement involved in setting the sticks up, I carefully rested the rifle on the second highest bar of the gate. This put me in a nice solid kneeling position, so I had a really stable aim-point. I waited until my intended quarry turned sideways-on, and gently squeezed off

a shot. There was the sound of a solid hit, and it simply crumpled where it stood. I counted it out at 170 paces. Again, it was a large adult: this time a good-sized dog fox.

BELOW: Crane flies – known to many as 'Daddy Long-Legs', can occur in huge numbers when they emerge from their underground pupal stage. They then become an important food source for all manner of animals, including hungry foxes.

BOTTOM: The first of two foxes that night and of five that were shot in Roy's lower meadow in just over two weeks. Through the night vision I could see that they were snuffling in the grass, and then leaping a couple of feet into the air to catch something. In the end, I realised they were catching crane-flies. I'd never seen or read about this behaviour before, but I now know it's very common around here.

HEAVY LOAD

DATE:	13 August 2009	**SHOTGUN:**	Benelli M2
PLACE:	Gerald's Farm	**CALIBRE:**	12 bore
TIME:	20:00	**AMMO:**	50gm 3in Magnum BB
SUNSET:	20:39	**RANGE:**	30yd
STATE OF MOON:	Last quarter	**CALL TRACK:**	Screaming rat
WEATHER:	Dry and cold	**OPTICS:**	None
WIND DIRECTION:	South-westerly		

Having done a lot of foxing with a rifle, I was intrigued to see how well a shotgun would perform when used for close-range calling. I didn't have anything suitable though, so after looking around at what was available, I settled on a Benelli M2 semi-automatic. This had a three-inch chamber and was proofed for magnum loads, so it would take pretty well any cartridge I could find. There were several reasons for my choice – but top of the list was reliability. Checking it over in the gun shop, I was interested to see that it had dovetail scope mounts. These are primarily intended for what is known as 'practical shotgun' (PSG) – a form of competition where the shooter walks down a range while various targets spin around or pop up. I, however, was looking at them – not surprisingly – with an eye to the possibility of fitting some kind of NV scope.

That evening I tried it out on a pattern plate (where you shoot at a metal target) to see what the spread was at the sort of ranges I was likely to use it at. The results showed me that I should stick to the recommended 30yd, which I was happy with. Since I'd just been asked to do a few predator patrols around a large pheasant pen on a nearby farm, I decided that it'd be an ideal place to take the M2 for its maiden outing. Although I was intending to see if I could call anything in just before dark, I'd also been told the red deer had been trashing the feed bins, and that it'd be

appreciated if I could keep an eye out for them too. I set off a bit earlier with the .308 slung over my shoulder. I'd been given a quick tour around the area in question the previous night by the keeper, but I hadn't done any actual shooting yet – consequently, I was hoping my trip would prove fruitful.

The ground was dry enough to allow me to drive almost all the way across the fields, meaning that I was able to park up a few yards from the woods I was intending to work around. I'd only gone about 200yd when I spotted a pair of red deer ears above some brambles. I'd just reached the edge of the cover, whereas the animal they belonged to was still inside. In order to avoid being seen, I settled down onto one knee and got ready to let the safety catch off. The wind was in my favour, so I was in no hurry. A few minutes later it moved forwards, but even though I now had what was quite clearly a big red deer in my sights – and a clear kill zone shot at that – I couldn't tell if it was male or female. It was only about 35ft from me, but as it had its head in amongst some thick branches, and there were no other distinguishing features visible, I had to hold back. At more or less the same moment it moved forwards and spotted me – without pausing for thought, it went charging off into deep cover, barking all the way. I was fine with that, as I'd now seen that it had been a hind, and so out of season.

TIPS & TRICKS

If you are using a shotgun to shoot foxes:
a) Keep the range below 30yd
b) Only use heavy shot – everyone has their own ideas, but you won't go far wrong with BB
c) Before you start, set a board up at your expected target distance and see what sort of pattern you get. Don't shoot unless you're confident that you can hit the kill zone reliably
d) Empty your pockets of spent cases – that way there's a better chance that you'll only chamber a live round!

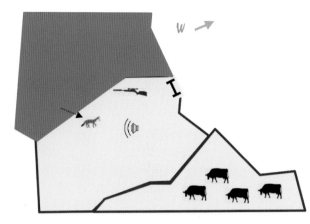

I left it about 15 minutes and started to creep into the woods to see if I could work out where she'd gone, but almost immediately a grey squirrel spotted me. Instead of doing the sensible thing and keeping quiet, it jumped around in the top of a big oak tree shrieking its head off. Now the whole world knew I was there, so there was clearly little point in my continuing into the woods. I decided to wind the squirrel up by staying under a large branch where it couldn't see me. When I didn't move, it made the mistake of coming down to see where I'd gone. I watched it creeping lower and lower, and willed it to come below the level of a large

muddy bank a few yards further on, as this would provide a nice safe back-stop (about a million tons of Devon hill). Its curiosity was getting the better of it, and I could see that before long I'd get my wish. I therefore put my sticks up, rested the rifle on them, and when the tree rat was in the appropriate position, I gave it a .308 ballistic tip from about 25ft... Kabooom...

Since the day's rifle shooting was now at an end, I went back to the truck and swapped the Sauer for the Benelli M2. I loaded it up with three-inch magnum cartridges – two in the magazine and one in the chamber. Since these were carrying 50 grams of BB shot, they were going to make a mess of anything they hit. Returning to the edge of the woods, I set the FOXPRO Scorpion up and then settled myself onto a convenient tree stump. This position gave me plenty of background cover, so I was confident that I was unlikely to be seen by anything coming to the caller. After about 10 minutes on the screaming rat call, a young male fox suddenly broke cover and ran out to what it clearly thought was going to be an easy meal. Two quick blasts (the second shot simply because I could) had it rolling over like it'd been hit by a freight train. Any doubts the M2 would be a useful addition to my cabinet were now thoroughly dispelled!

BELOW: **This Benelli M2 semi-automatic shotgun has a magnum-proofed three inch chamber, and so can safely be loaded with 50gm BB cartridges, which are excellent for shooting foxes at close range.**

AFTERBIRTH AND THE AFTERLIFE

DATE:	24 August 2012		**RIFLE:**	Sauer 202
PLACE:	Robert's Farm		**CALIBRE:**	.22-250
TIME:	21:30		**AMMO:**	55gr Nosler BT
SUNSET:	20:17		**RANGE:**	80yd
STATE OF MOON:	First quarter		**CALL TRACK:**	None
WEATHER:	Dry and cold		**OPTICS:**	D480 GenIII NV riflescope
WIND DIRECTION:	North-westerly			

One evening someone left a message on my answerphone saying that Robert, a farmer friend of mine, had given them my number. They went on to say that they could do with my help in dealing with some problem foxes. They didn't leave their name and I was none the wiser as to who it was who needed my assistance. I wasn't too worried as I'd been out pretty well every night on the foxes, and even then I was only just keeping up with all the land I had. A couple of weeks later, however, I thought I should check back with Robert as I'd not seen him for a while, and it would give me a good opportunity to find out who the mystery caller was.

One has to be a little careful when trying to catch up with farmers in August: if the weather is good most are harvesting, and if it isn't, they can be a little tetchy. Still, as Robert mainly farms cattle, that wasn't an issue. When I raised the subject of the unknown caller, however, the only person he could think of was one of his neighbours. This chap had recently had some pheasant poults killed by foxes, and as a result he was keen to speak to me. Robert also said that he'd been meaning to call me for a couple of weeks as his cattle had been calving, and he knew that some foxes had been in eating the afterbirth. He'd been so busy, that he hadn't had a chance. As he was speaking, I recalled how the previous year I'd crept up to the nursery paddock and shot two foxes in amongst the calves. I was keen to see if I could pull off the same stunt again, so arranged to go over later that evening. The weather had been extremely variable – it had been chucking it down for most of the day. The Met Office's radar map was showing that there should be a few breaks in the clouds though, so if luck was with me, I'd get enough time for a short session. I'd already been through my kit, charging up the batteries on my mini-thermal and fox caller and refilling the ammo pouches.

Before going any further, I called the neighbour and was given a cordial invite to shoot over two large pieces of land. It was agreed that I should go over at some stage and sort out a proper boundary map. I'm always pleased to take on ground that lies next to areas that I already shoot, especially where it makes the access options better. Still, that could all wait for another day: right now my priority was to get my immediate plans sorted out.

Since it had been raining heavily for much of the evening, my intention was to wait until it was properly dark before going out. This left me with a dilemma: should I take the Kimber Montana in .204 Ruger with the NV add-on, or the Sauer 202 in .22-250 with the dedicated NV riflescope? The former is really light and a joy to use, while the latter is heavier but its optics are so good that in the end there was really no choice: the .22-250 it was to be. When I decided it was dark enough, I loaded the truck and set off. Rather than head directly to Robert's, I made a brief deviation to check some bait in a small valley behind the village. I've written several accounts about shooting foxes in this field, but when I checked I was disappointed to find there was nothing about. Oh well, nothing ventured, nothing gained. I continued on my way.

I pulled into Robert's yard a few minutes later and parked up near the pony stalls. A couple of inquisitive heads peered over the gates and watched me as I got everything ready. First, the shooting sticks came out; then a battery was fitted in the thermal – this was then hung around my neck. After that, I slipped the harness for the NV mono over my shoulders. A magazine was snapped into in the rifle and rain covers fitted over the scope and laser. Then all I had to do was pull the face veil and gloves on. Since I was going to be shooting over bait in the form of afterbirth, the FOXPRO caller could be left behind. That and the remote are surprisingly bulky, so I was pleased to be travelling light. Just I was doing my final checks, I heard heavy rain drops hitting the ground, and within seconds the heavens opened. Hacked off with how the evening had started, I climbed back into the truck and waited for the shower to pass.

separated from the yard by an enormous Leylandii hedge which has a massive arch cut through with a wide gate underneath. Although I was annoyed to find it closed, I was thankful for all the overhead cover as the rain started again. I took the opportunity to use the thermal and the NV mono to take a look over the nearby fields – as these were in pasture, the grass was short enough to see if anything of interest was around. The rain had driven most of the wildlife away though, and all I could see was a solitary rabbit.

Gradually the shower moved off, and I was good to go. The nursery paddock is only about 100yd down a stony track, so I didn't have far to travel. Although the pebbles have a habit of crunching underfoot, the rain dripping off the trees was making so much noise

It was the best part of quarter of an hour before the pitter-patter on the roof subsided sufficiently for me to risk setting off. Locking the truck, I surveyed the blackness ahead of me. One of the things I hate about farmyards is security lights. They always seem to come on just when you don't want them to. I knew that there was one I couldn't avoid. It not only illuminates the whole area, but also stays on for ages. Sure enough, it came on within a few paces, and my shadow was projected over the sides of the buildings. I kept to the edge of the track to minimise the disturbance over the nearest fields,

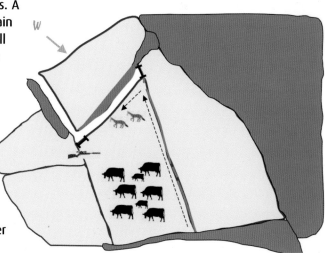

that I didn't have to worry that much. All the same, I tiptoed the last few feet until I was in sight of the cows. At that very moment, the moon chose to come out from behind a dark rain cloud – just my luck. A quick check with the NV, however, showed that there were no foxes in the vicinity, so I quickly got myself set up underneath a big hedge where its shadow would give me some cover.

I was hoping that if Charlie was around, he'd taken refuge during the deluge and that he'd reappear at any moment. My feet were in a couple of inches of water, so I knew I couldn't move them in a hurry without the sound giving away my location. I took great care to ensure that I was in a good shooting stance before anything showed up. My next job was to remove the rain covers from the NV riflescope and get it focused at the appropriate range. I also needed to check that the laser was working and that there weren't any watermarks or dust spots on the lens.

As I mentioned above, for the last few months I've been taking advantage of the long summer evenings by carrying the super-lightweight .204 Kimber. This allows me to cover long distances in daylight, and then when it gets dark I just slip the NV add-on in place. While this works nicely, it was lovely to be looking through the Sauer's high-end GenIII NV riflescope again – the field of view and quality of image are just stunning in comparison. Happy that everything was ready from a technical perspective, I began scanning around with the NV mono. The foxes always seem to come from far side of the field where there is some dead ground. This can hide most of a fully-grown fox, there's usually enough of its back showing for me to get a heat signature with the thermal imager. Once I've got some warning that something is there, I switch to the NV and try to get a glimpse of eye-shine.

Last night it didn't go quite like that as I spotted a set of eyes with the mono before I'd got as far as trying the thermal. The fox was coming along the base of the hedge on the far side, and circling around so that it would be able to approach the cows from downwind. At one point it disappeared from view behind a rise, and I'd lost it – the thermal came to the rescue though, and revealed that it had come onto the track and was now heading straight for me. From its size and caution, it appeared to be a mature animal

This was one of two foxes that had been feeding on the afterbirth that resulted from Robert's cows calving.

that was wise to the ways of the world – this would be a good fox to take out. When it was about 80 yards from me it paused to look into the field and sniff the wind. At that point, a 55gr ballistic-tip hit it in the chest with a convincing 'whop'. It dropped without a twitch. At the sound of the shot the cows all started in surprise, but within a couple of seconds were back grazing away again, the disturbance forgotten.

My next issue was whether my time would be better spent waiting to see if any more foxes would show, or whether it'd make more sense to drive back and sit watching the bait back in the valley behind the village. I decided to do both, so began a series of sweeps alternating between the NV and the thermal. About five minutes later I saw a white heat source in amongst the cows and calves. It hadn't been there the last time I'd looked, and if my calculations were correct, it could well be the top half of a fox way off at the far side of the field. By the time I'd switched the thermal off and got the NV mono on, it'd moved in behind the cows, so I was still none the wiser. I kept looking though, and half a minute later I got a positive ID on a large dog fox. He was moving at speed, nose

to the ground and appeared to be following the scent of the one I'd just shot. When he was clear of the cows, I moved onto the riflescope and picked him up as he circled back around on the wind. I kept the laser off until the last few moment to avoid spooking him. As he moved to go in towards the calves from downwind, he turned sideways on to me, and at that point I switched the illuminator on. His eyes shone brightly as he briefly looked in my direction, but before he could do anything more another ballistic-tip was sent on its way. A solid 'boof' indicated a good hit, and he crumpled on the spot in a tangle of legs and tail. This time the cows barely lifted their heads. I left it another quarter of an hour or so, but when nothing else showed, it was time to clear up and move on.

The first fox was a mature vixen – with big teeth, a solid neck, and a good body weight. The second one was out in the field not far from the cattle. As I'd suspected, it was a big dog fox – probably weighing around the 20lb mark, or just over. His teeth were bigger still. I hauled the two of them back to the gate where they could be taken away for disposal. Unfortunately, the bait field proved to be devoid of foxes.

SEPTEMBER

Back in medieval times, 24 September signalled the start of the harvest. These days, however, it begins much earlier. Indeed, the month is perhaps best characterised by the sight of all the stubble fields. These are the result of the cereal crops being cut, although they are generally not ploughed in for a month or so, depending on the farmer's priorities. Anyone who has done it will tell you that trying to move through stubble on foot quietly is a nightmare. The myriads of short, dry stalks will crunch and snap at the merest hint of movement, although you can sometimes reduce the noise by following the tyre tracks of the combine – if you can find them. Where the bales have been left out, you will find that they are excellent things to hide behind, making for superb improvised ambush points.

The low height and colour of stubble means that foxes can usually be seen from a long way out – they will often be found preying on the many rodents which descend on cereal fields after the harvest. Spotting them from afar can give you an excellent opportunity to get close to them without being scented. Prey distress calls may or may not work

By September, the nights are beginning to draw in and most of the crops have been harvested. This gives the foxer a better choice of places to shoot as well as more time to go about his activities under the cover of darkness.

– that will depend on the amount of other food available, however, territorial sounds might well bring in any individuals that are anxious to chase off unwanted interlopers.

Bait can work extremely well, however, and nothing works better than natural sources. This is why it's always a good idea to stay in close contact with your farmers – the afterbirth from calving, for instance, can attract foxes from miles away. In most cases these hungry animals will want to be on site as soon as it gets dark – any later and they risk losing their easy and nutrient-rich meals to other foxes. Any cattle in the area are likely to be unimpressed at having predators near their calves though, and so may well be very aggressive to them. If you are thinking of staking out such fields in the hope of shooting the foxes, it's a good idea to find out in advance whether the cows and any attendant bulls

THE FARMER'S MONTH
Finish combining.
Silage in the clamp.
Straw in the barn.
Preparation for sheep sales.
Ploughing
Potatoes harvested.
Plant winter wheat, oilseed rape and barley.

might also be a risk to you. If so, then it's best to ensure there's a fence between you and them. It's also a good idea to keep a close eye on the wind direction as it's a good bet that any approaching foxes will come from downwind. This is because the scent will tell them what hazards they may be about to face – including other individuals of their own species that might well want to fight.

One of the crops that every foxer and deer stalker quickly learns to hate is cattle maize. This grows to a considerable height – typically 6–8ft – and is so thick that it can easily hide entire herds of deer. Foxes will often lie up in it or move through it, making them impossible to see. From the farmer's perspective, the main issue is trying to prevent the maize from being destroyed by wild animals. The main culprits for this are badgers and deer, both of which can cause massive amounts of damage.

As the evenings start drawing in, it begins to get colder once the sun goes down. This is a good time for those who use thermal imaging equipment, as it is much easier to see living creatures when there is a reasonable temperature contrast between them and the ground. It's generally still warm enough for a wide variety of invertebrates to flourish though, and foxes will often spend hours hunting such things as earthworms, slugs, snails, crane flies and moths, all of which have high nutritional values, albeit in very small packages. Blackberries and similar soft fruit are always favoured, as are more traditional things like rabbits – especially young ones that haven't learned the hard ways of the world and thus easier to catch. Several times I've observed foxes casually walking past a group of alarmed bunnies, only to see them reach a point that is downwind whereupon they curl up and go to sleep. By the time the fox wakes up, the rabbits have forgotten all about it. A short crawl later, and one of them will have become its meal.

By September, most keepers will have put their pheasants out full time. They will, however, still be spending an inordinate amount of time looking after their poults – endlessly refilling feeders and checking that watering points are working properly. While doing so, they will also be constantly on the lookout for signs of predators. The partridge season also opens on 1 September, so those who keep these delightful (but stupid) birds will be even busier. Game cover crops, which are farmed areas of plants put out for pheasants and partridges to feed and hide in, also need to be looked after if they are to be in a suitable condition for the birds. A wide variety of different species are used for this purpose, including millet, sorghum, kale, maize, quinoa, artichokes, buckwheat and various grasses or grains. These not only give game birds places to feed and hide, but massively increase the biodiversity, providing sanctuary for all manner of small birds, insects and other creatures .

Grey squirrels seem to be everywhere at this time of year. When these tree rats were let loose in this country it was the start of an environmental disaster. They not only do huge amounts of damage to trees, stripping bark and chewing new growth, but are also really bad news for any late fledglings. Anyone attempting to creep up on foxes or stalk deer during the daylight hours runs the risk of being revealed by one or more squirrels suddenly giving their shrill alarm calls and flicking their tails. This can, however, work two ways as sometimes their cries will tell you that something is coming your way, giving you early warning to get ready for a shot.

BELOW: A full moon can seriously hamper any attempts at getting close to foxes, so a bit of cloud cover can be a relief.

BOTTOM: Foxes will eat more or less anything they can catch – including juicy frogs like this which make a welcome addition to a night's menu. It is therefore a good idea to keep an eye on any ponds in the area, in case they are being checked over by a hungry Reynard.

KEEPING IT REAL

DATE:	15 and 28 September 2010	**WIND DIRECTION:**	North-westerly (both)
PLACE:	Critter's Shoot	**RIFLE:**	Sauer 202 (both)
TIME:	20:50 (10:30)	**CALIBRE:**	.22-250 (both)
SUNSET:	19:30 (19:00)	**AMMO:**	55gr PPU SP (both)
STATE OF MOON:	First quarter (waning gibbous)	**RANGE:**	around 80yd (100yd)
WEATHER:	Dry and cold, with full cloud cover (both)	**CALL TRACK:**	None (both)
		OPTICS:	D480 GenIII NV riflescope (both)

My friend Critter was having problems with a fox that had been taking his pheasants. I had tried to once, but even though I managed to call it in on one occasion, it came from an unexpected direction and ran off before I could shoot. I decided that it would be better if I went stalking for it, rather than try another calling session. Thus one mid-September evening, I drove over and outlined my plans to him. He was happy to leave it all to me, and as he wasn't feeling well, I set out on my own. I left his cabin – a temporary measure while his more permanent accommodation was being sorted out – and walked down the track and over the cattle grid. This has to be treated with great care in the dark, as it'd be a sure-fire recipe for a broken ankle. From there I had a quick scan around the edges of the large pond, but as there was nothing to be seen apart from ducks and geese, I headed towards the sheep pens at the top of the valley.

Critter had found a sickly roe the day before which needed putting down – the poor thing could barely stand and was clearly in a very bad way. After doing the kindest thing he cut it open for a quick examination. There was little wonder that it was so ill, as it had huge abscesses throughout its visceral cavity. Although he intended to burn it, he'd not had time to do so, and had left its carcass out as bait in the meantime. I was intending to circle around on the wind to see if there was anything feeding on it, but more or less as soon as I'd gone far enough to see into the field, I spotted a fox about three-quarters of the way up the hill. This put it about 70 or 80yd from me – it was making its way along a well-trodden sheep path, heading away from me. I set the sticks up and managed to get focused in on it, but as I did so it realised that I was there. It clearly hadn't worked out what I was though, for it only ran a short distance before sitting down to watch me. This provided an ideal

opportunity to get a good shot placement, and my round hit it high in the chest. When I went over to check it out, I found it was a large vixen cub. Critter was very pleased when I got back, and the next day he called to say that he'd discovered a dead pheasant nearby.

Although I'd managed to shoot one of the foxes that had been taking Critter's pheasants, he was still finding dead birds every morning. I went over for another session a couple of weeks later (on 28 September). I arrived just after dark and started working my way along the field above the main track. A few owls were screeching, but unusually, I heard no foxes calling, so overall it was very quiet. I did, however, hear something disturbing the pheasants in the woods around the pens across the valley. I couldn't be sure if it was a roe deer or a fox, but suspected the latter. The moon had been very bright the previous week, but on this occasion it was very dark indeed with almost no wind at all. I reached the far end of the first big field, then made my way down to the driveway. I could see that the strip of pasture by the stream was a potential ambush point since it looked as though it was a likely movement corridor. I set myself up under the trees and began watching. I could hear the pheasants were being disturbed again, and before long a set of fox eyes appeared amongst the trees, heading towards the stream. It then disappeared for a minute or so, then reappeared about 50yd upstream. It then started chasing something in the bushes – I couldn't

The shoot that Critter manages is located in one of the most beautiful valleys in the country. It is, however, an extremely difficult place to control foxes due to the nature of the terrain.

see what it was, but then a pheasant suddenly began screaming before giving a final dying gasp. The fox then moved about behind some large trees for a few minutes – presumably burying the unfortunate bird. It then jumped the stream without warning and came onto the open ground at speed. As it did so it turned to go up the valley – I fired a shot and it went down heavily.

Critter was very pleased at the news, and as his bird losses dropped dramatically over the next few weeks, I'd clearly got one of the main culprits.

FOXING IN THE MOONLIT NIGHT

DATE:	15 September 2011	RIFLE:	Sauer 202
PLACE:	Pat's Farm	CALIBRE:	.22-250
TIME:	21:30	AMMO:	55gr Nosler BT
SUNSET:	19:30	RANGE:	About 100yd
STATE OF MOON:	Waning gibbous	CALL TRACK:	None
WEATHER:	Dry and cold	OPTICS:	D480 GenIII NV riflescope
WIND DIRECTION:	North-westerly		

I'd had a long day, juggling the pressures of trying to run a company with no money, keeping the stone mason who was working on my house on track, and ensuring that everything had been properly attended to after having a new roof put on the place. I'd got away with ignoring the decrepit state of the slates since I'd bought the old house 11 years ago, but the ever-increasing amount of rain that was coming through meant I couldn't put it off any longer. The great forest of scaffolding was due to come down, but before it did I still had to sort out various things, like reposition the TV aerial, add an attachment point for the telephone cable, and repaint the bits where the new soffits didn't quite match up to the old render. Putting the cream Dulux Weathershield on wouldn't have been so bad, but due to the positioning of the scaffold lifts, I had to more or less stand on my head for about an hour while I applied it.

By late afternoon I was dead on my feet, but all the same I was still determined to get out for a foxing session. I therefore tried to relax for the couple of hours before darkness fell. Some chance, my Good

Lady had various important tasks that needed sorting out, after which she served me up a delicious roe venison stir-fry. This had been a bit of an experiment – the day before I'd butchered a couple of roe haunches, most of which we'd eaten that night as pan-fried steaks, and very nice they were too. But as there was enough left over for another meal, I carefully cut the remains into thin strips and then made up a marinade using olive oil, balsamic vinegar, honey, coarse ground black pepper, and soy sauce. The meat and marinade were then transferred to a plastic bag and vacuum-sealed. I figured that this would help the meat to absorb all the flavours. Luckily, I was right – the stir-fry was delicious!

By the time we'd polished away this fine repast, it had already been dark for about half an hour – and that meant I'd missed the opportunity to get out before the moon rose. 'Oh well', I thought, 'Let's hope there's plenty of cloud cover.' I quickly checked the Met Office website to see which way the wind was blowing, and discovered that it would be coming in quite gently from the south-south-east. This meant

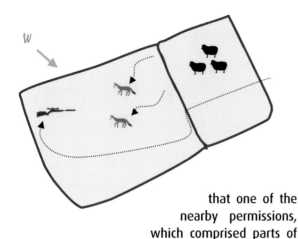

do was lift the locking mechanism and give it a nudge and it swung open – completely silently! The ground before me sloped uphill for about 30yd, so there was nothing much to see except long grass. Away to my left it fell away down to a narrow stream bordered by boggy ground. On the other side – and belonging to a farm where I did not have permission to shoot, were a couple of fields populated with cattle. It was hard to see whether they held any foxes though, due to the row of tall beech trees that towered over the boundary.

In an attempt to remain unseen and unheard, I more or less tiptoed my way to the top of the rise, using the hedge to my right as cover. The moon, however, had other ideas and as I got to the brow it decided to ruin my efforts by coming out from behind the clouds, lighting the landscape up for miles around. Since foxes are very good at spotting movement, I thought it'd be best to stay still and scan with the mono until the moon was obscured again. I could see that the field held a large flock of sheep – all of whom were looking directly at me. So much for my covert approach...

A minute or two later, and the world went dark again. A second gate opened and closed with the tiniest of sounds, and I was clear of the livestock. Now all I had to do was make my way over two grass pastures and I would be at the large field I was aiming for. Every few yards I stopped and checked for foxes. Nothing seen, I arrived at the small wooden hunting gate which sits on the boundary with the next farm. This had been installed many years before to enable the fox hounds to cross what would otherwise have been a more or less insurmountable obstacle. A full height Devon bank topped off with thick bushes of vicious blackthorn and hawthorn, all interspersed with sprawling tentacles of sharp bramble is enough to put the keenest hunter off. Although the gate was only used very occasionally and its hinges were very stiff indeed, they didn't make a sound as I made my way through.

Beyond the gate though, I had a problem. The ground was not only littered with a thick layer of dry twigs and crunchy leaves, but there was a significant drop into a ditch, followed by a sharp climb back up into the field. To complicate things further, the moon had come out again, and if I wasn't very

that one of the nearby permissions, which comprised parts of three different farms, would be my best choice. Although I'd shot over one of them many times, I'd only recently been given the go ahead to hunt the ground I had in mind. I'd seen quite a few foxes in the nearby fields, but as the main area had been covered in standing corn until about a week before, it had been a no-go zone. As this had now been cut, however, I decided it should be just right for finding Charlie.

I quickly gathered my things together, sent the farmer a text, and set off. It only takes a couple of minutes to drive there, so the engine was barely warm when I arrived in the farmyard. I already had the NV monocular around my neck and as it only took moments to pull on my face veil, grab my sticks and sling the Sauer .22-250 over my shoulder, I was on my way down the track in no time. I was relieved to see that the gate into the first field I had to pass was open. This meant there were no livestock in there, which in turn meant that I didn't have to worry about loads of spooked sheep charging about all over the place. I took the opportunity to scan the field with the mono, but all was quiet. On the opposite side of the track there's a small orchard which is used as a recuperation area for any sick or injured animals. As I approached I could see there were two large sheep lying close to the fence, but luckily they didn't appear to be too concerned as I crept past a few feet away.

My next obstacle was a metal gate that marks the end of the track. Although this had the potential to screech and clang loud enough to scare everything for miles around, it was actually that most rare of things on a Devon farm – a properly hung gate. All I had to

This was a difficult session – not only was the dry stubble a nightmare to cross due to the amount of noise it made, but the bright moon lit the landscape up making it almost impossible to move without being seen. In my favour though, was the recently spread pig slurry which helped mask the scent of human.

careful, I'd be dreadfully exposed. I therefore decided that I'd better check there was nothing close by before make any attempt to cross onto firm ground. Within moments of turning the NV mono on, however, I was faced with a pair of eyes blazing back at me in the reflected IR from my laser illuminator. A large Charlie was about 50yd away to my left, and staring straight at me, and judging by the brightness of its eyes, it was a dog fox. I had no choice though – a shot was out of the question as there was simply no room to open the sticks, and there was nothing else to hand that I could rest the rifle on.

I did my best to minimise the noise I made, but by the time I was through and into the large shadow cast by the tree above, the fox was nowhere to be seen. Cursing my misfortune, I checked the rest of the field. About 200yd away to my right was another fox. This one was smaller and had much duller eyes; probably a vixen. Luck was against me once again: it was directly downwind of me, and had its nose up sniffing the air. Moments later it disappeared over the brow and out of sight. I tried using the mouth caller to bring it back, but without success.

I pondered my situation for a bit and decided that the best thing I could do would be to wait for the darkness that would result from a large cloud which was heading across the sky towards the moon. I figured it would give me a couple of minutes to cross the field – once there I could hide under the cover of the far hedge and then make my way around to where the fox had last been seen. By then I would be downwind of it, maximising my chances of getting a shot in. While I was waiting for my chance to move, I scanned the field again. An eye shone back at me from the opposite side of the field, about 300yd away. I watched it for a bit and although it first appeared to be a rabbit, I eventually confirmed it was a hare.

As the cloud moved in front of the moon, the light fell once again. I'd already identified a convenient set of tractor wheel tracks from where they'd been spraying manure. These ran exactly where I needed to go, so I found my way to them and set off. This was significant as the rest of the field was covered in high stubble. Any attempt to walk across it would result in loud crunching sounds that would give my position away to all and sundry. The downside of using the wheel tracks was that they were filled with pig slurry, and it stank as I walked through. Still, it wasn't all bad as it would help mask the scent of human!

I stopped and scanned around a couple of times before making it to the other side, but kept it brief as I couldn't hang around since the clouds were starting to thin out. Once I was in the cover of the hedge I checked again. I could see that the hare had run out into the middle of the field, but I still couldn't see over the brow into the area where the fox had been. Another set of tractor tracks led towards the main gate, however, and as this overlooked the hidden ground, I followed them. The contrast of the moonlit stubble and the dark tractor lines intersecting at perpendicular angles reminded me of the film *Tron*. As I switched from line to line, I thought back to when I'd seen the film when it first came out in 1982. I was a mere 22 years old then, a young an impetuous chap who spent all his time chasing loose women and riding fast motorcycles. Ah well, I reflected – at least I hadn't wasted my time!

I stopped a few yards short of the gate – no need to skyline myself when the hedge was high enough to hide me. A quick scan revealed there was a fox

> **TIPS & TRICKS**
>
> Trying to hunt foxes when the moon is bright can be exceptionally difficult. Although they do not have very good shape recognition skills, when there is sufficient light they are extremely good at spotting movement, even over several hundred yards. Few experienced foxes will even leave the shadows, so they tend to move within the cover of undergrowth, making it even harder to spot them. To stay undetected, you will have to do much the same and stick in close to hedges and trees where the moonlight cannot reveal you.

coming up another set of *Tron* lines towards me. It was about 100yd out, but was clearly very nervous. I set the sticks up and mounted the rifle on them. I got the scope switched on and focused in one movement, then raised my index finger to release the safety catch. On the Sauer, this is mounted just in front of the trigger. There was just enough moonlight for the fox to see me, but it couldn't decide what I was. As it turned sideways to move off in a different direction, I squeezed off a shot. There was a loud 'pop', and it fell on the spot. I love those Gameking hollow-points!

I marked the fox's position, but before setting off to retrieve it, I had another scan around with the mono. Although the riflescope gives me twice the magnification, the limited field of view means it's far too easy to miss seeing something important. Sure enough, straight away I saw two sets of eyes. The first set belonged to the hare, which was now sitting upright to see what was going on. It was about 150yd out, the second set though was at least another 100yd beyond it, but was twice as bright. There was little doubt this was a dog fox, and probably the one I'd seen earlier. It had also been spooked by the shot, and was Tronning it straight towards me – presumably, it had heard the echoes and figured that I was in my usual place on the other farm. It made good speed, covering about the ground in bursts of 40–50yd, then stopping to survey the scene before continuing. Whether it could smell the fox I'd just shot, or whether it spotted me, I don't know. Either way, it suddenly decided to turn and head away. As it did so, I loosed off a second hollow-point and there was another loud 'pop'. Game over for him.

The first fox turned out to be a medium-sized vixen, and the second a large dog. Both were left by the gate where the farmer could easily find them. I had another quick look around before heading off for home. 'Well, you can rest a bit easier tonight,' I thought to myself as I watched the hare hop off towards the woods. And with that, I was on my way.

NATURAL WARNINGS

DATE:	24 September 2009	**WIND DIRECTION:**	North-westerly
PLACE:	Mervyn's Farm	**RIFLE:**	Sauer 202
TIME:	18:30	**CALIBRE:**	.308
SUNSET:	19:09	**AMMO:**	165gr Sierra GameKing SP
STATE OF MOON:	Daylight, evening crescent	**RANGE:**	65yd
		CALL TRACK:	None
WEATHER:	Dry and cold	**OPTICS:**	Zeiss Conquest

I'd had a frantic week, so was keen to get out, not having picked a rifle up for three days. Around six-ish that evening I was all loaded up and on my way to the chicken farm where I'd been trying to knock over the remnants of a litter of fox cubs. As I drove over, I reflected on my last visit. I'd had a shot at the only remaining adult from the family group. At first I thought I'd missed. I'd set a camouflage net up in the top corner of a field, and then dragged a couple of bunnies that I'd split open across my 'killing zone' to leave a nice smelly scent trail. I then sat in wait with my NV set-up. Just as the fox came in two things

Late one summer evening, this fox jumped out of cover whilst attempting to catch a rabbit. It was only there for a brief moment, and under normal circumstances it wouldn't have been possible to shoot it. Its presence had been betrayed well in advance, however, by various magpies, squirrels and blackbirds. Consequently, there was already a .308 round in the air as it paused before returning to the safety of the undergrowth.

suddenly worked against me. First, the wind shifted around behind me; and then, to make matters worse, the full moon came out from behind some dark rain clouds and lit up my position as though I was on stage. I had to crouch down in the long grass to avoid being seen. The fox came in to about 60yd – on the crest of a small rise – but just stood there looking straight at me. It was clearly very nervous, and I realised that I would only have the briefest of chances to get a shot in. I balanced the rifle on my knee and took what I thought was an excellent shot, with a convincing 'thwump' at the other end. But the fox rolled over and disappeared in the adjoining undergrowth, and I managed to convince myself that I'd messed the shot up. Back then I didn't have the luxury of a thermal imager to help find missing carcasses. Fortunately, the horrible smell that began emanating from the dense scrub over the next few days told me that my aim had, indeed, been true.

When I arrived, the farmer and one of his contractors were in the process of loading up the muck spreader. I checked where they were going to be working, and figured that with the wind being in the north west, my best chances would be if I were to work up the 'goyle'. This is a Devonian word that means very small valley. The one I was headed up has a narrow stream that's covered in dense vegetation, mostly small hazel and birch trees, with the odd medium-sized ash and oak growing here and there. Underneath there is a more or less impenetrable mix of brambles and nettles – impenetrable, that is, to humans: for everything else it is a veritable motorway, being particularly popular with roe deer, foxes, and bunnies. On the far side there is a young plantation which is bounded by a tall deer fence. The side I was on has a recently cut meadow, so my plan was to work slowly along the edge, watching out for both foxes and roe deer. Over my shoulder I had my trusty .308 Sauer 202 Outback topped off with a Zeiss Conquest scope. In my right hand I was carrying my shooting sticks, and looped around my neck were my Nikon HGL binos. Clad head-to-toe in ex-military DPM. I was also wearing a full head veil.

Within moments of reaching the goyle, I heard clear 'de-dum, de-dum' hoof footfall sounds coming from the undergrowth, followed by a loud crack as a large animal trod on a stick. As this coincided with the muck spreader starting, I couldn't decide if the roe deer – for that is what it certainly was – had been spooked by me or by the farmer. I waited a few minutes, but as the sun was going down I realised that I could not afford to waste any time. To confuse matters, two jays started kicking off about 300yd behind me. They were shrieking at something they didn't like, and I considered changing tack to see if it was a fox. The wind would be against me though, so I stuck to Plan A.

A few moments later – about 200yd ahead of me in a dense area of woodland – a hell of a row developed. It started with a squirrel's 'vut, vut, vut' alarm call, which was then was joined by two or three magpies. Something had upset them badly, and I had to try and work out if it was the deer I'd heard a few minutes before, or if it was a fox going about its business. I decided it was probably the latter, so carefully made my way to within about 150yd of the far hedge and then got myself in under the overhanging hazel branches, trying to look like I belonged there.

In the past, I'd seen foxes making an early evening patrol of the furthest side of the field, but with the muckspreader banging away over the hedge, I figured it was far more likely that they'd come down towards me instead. After a

TIPS & TRICKS
The animals around us can often see, hear and smell things a lot better than we can, many having senses that are highly specialised. If you inspect a deer skull, for example, you will see that much of its volume is dedicated to the olfactory system, i.e., the sense of smell. Some creatures will also have the advantage of looking down on the world either from the wing, or from the tops of trees. It is therefore extremely useful to be able to interpret their communications – such as being able to distinguish territorial calls from alarm cries, for instance.

few minutes, a sixth sense told me that whatever had caused all the fuss was coming my way. Several blackbirds were behaving oddly – flying in and out of the trees and making distressed alarm calls. A squirrel high up in the oak tree just in front of me started screeching, and the magpies in the woods had gone quiet. Just then, a bunny appeared out of a hole and sat in the short grass surveying the world. It hadn't seen me, so I thought it would make a convenient sentry. Thirty seconds or so later, another bunny joined it. By then, I'd set the sticks up and had the rifle ready for action. A few moments went by, and another bunny suddenly went barrelling past them both in no uncertain manner – they didn't hang around to see what the problem was, and were gone in an instant. A few milliseconds later a fox appeared right where they had been sitting. I slipped the safety catch off and BANG! The fox – a young vixen, went down like the proverbial sack of manure, and it was game over.

The farmer was well pleased – for two reasons. Firstly, there was one less predator to attack his large flock of free range organic chickens. Secondly, as I'd agreed to shut his birds away for the night, he and his good lady wife were able to go to the pub for a rare evening out – more Brownie points for me, and a good result for all concerned. Except, of course, for the fox...

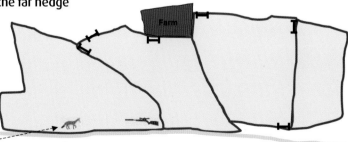

A REALLY TOUGH MISSION

DATE:	29 September 2012	**WIND DIRECTION:**	Westerly
PLACE:	Ian's Shoot	**RIFLE:**	Sauer 202
TIME:	21:00	**CALIBRE:**	.22-250
SUNSET:	18:57	**AMMO:**	55gr Nosler BT
STATE OF MOON:	Waxing gibbous and very bright	**RANGE:**	Around 200yd
		CALL TRACK:	Young rat distress call
WEATHER:	Dry and cold	**OPTICS:**	D480 GenIII NV riflescope

One of my friends, Rob, an electrician, keeps an ear open on my behalf, and as the result of him doing a wiring job on a 5,500-acre estate on the south-western fringes of Exmoor, I got an introduction to the new gamekeeper. The previous incumbent had let things slip badly, and there had been no shoot for two years. Consequently, the foxes had got rather out of control. Ian, the new keeper, did an excellent job of getting to grips with the situation, taking some really good numbers on innumerable nights out lamping with an assistant. The problem with such methods, of course, is that while you can cull all the inexperienced animals easily enough, you're left with wise ones that are inevitably lamp-shy. And they are the ones that do most of the killing. After a long chat on the phone, I was asked to go and show him what I could do with my NV and thermal imaging equipment.

The first time I went over was in early May: we drove around with me standing on the back of his pick-up in the manner traditional of lampers. We didn't see much as he and his team had shot pretty well everything that was stupid enough to show itself. I did manage to knock down an old dog fox, however. I spotted it as we pulled up at the base of a steep rabbit-infested hill, but the moment we stopped it ran over the brow and out of sight. It had obviously worked out that the Ford Ranger signalled danger, so we left it for a few minutes and then I started making rabbit distress noises with the BestFoxCall mouth caller. About 30 seconds later, the fox returned, and I carefully tracked it through the NV as it made its way down between the gorse bushes. At one point it paused to sniff the air, and as it did so, I sent a killing round on its way. I was particularly pleased, as it was

A full moon can make life very difficult for the nocturnal hunter – not only are the foxes much more wary, but the extra light means that they can see movement from a long way off.

a very difficult shot – a long way above us on a steep incline, and the best part of 200yd out.

In spite of our success, Ian realised that his way is more suited to lampers, so the second time I went over we did it my way. We drove to specific trouble spots and then walked in to place the caller in my tried and tested manner. We managed to bring four to the rifle that night, and from there on Ian and I worked to optimise our respective skills. He would carry on lamping as usual, but whenever he spotted a lamp-shy animal, he'd tell me where it was. I'd then go in a few nights later, find it, and shoot it. This proved to be really successful, although I started out going over on my own, I later took my mate Paul with me. Between us, we did really well. By late September we'd taken every single animal we'd been tasked with shooting.

I'd had a bad week though, and when I was told of my latest mission I was worried that I was going to tarnish my unblemished record. I'd had the dreaded man-flu for at least ten days, and as a result was well below par. I'd had no choice but to cry off from several of Ian's invites to go over as I simply wasn't well enough. I couldn't put it off any longer though: a dog fox was taking four to five partridges a night on a part of the estate I'd never been to before, and he was desperate to stop the slaughter. The animal in question had been seen when it was driven from some cover the day before, on what was the estate's first shoot day of the new season, but unfortunately, no one had been close enough to take it down.

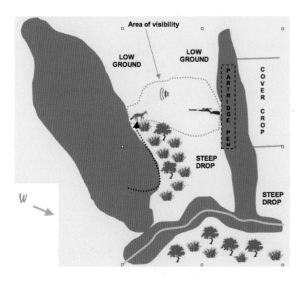

Paul and I drove over that evening with about an hour of daylight remaining. I was keen to get there early as I was hoping to get some photos before it got dark. We were a little delayed – on the way we saw a fox at the side of one of the narrow lanes. It was nuzzling at a discarded burger box when we came around the corner, but it dived into the hedge as soon as it saw us. There was a small lay-by about 100yd further on, however, so I pulled over and got my camera out. More or less as soon as the car behind us had passed, the fox jumped out into the road again. Unfortunately, the sun was shining straight into my face, so although I got photos of it, the quality of the images wasn't really up to scratch. All the same, it was good to snap a series of a fox going about its business.

We'd arranged to meet up with Ian at the big hill where I'd shot the first dog fox. However, unknown to us, he was having problems with pheasants wandering too far. Consequently, he was at least half an hour late by the time he'd driven them back towards the pens. It gave me the opportunity to take some more photos, while Paul used the time to scan around the area with both the binos and the thermal.

Eventually, Ian arrived and we wasted little time in following him over to the problem area. This took us down a narrow winding lane. After a mile or so of climbs and drops, with both of us trying to avoid running over young partridges, he pulled over and opened a gate into a steep pasture. We drove up the grassy hill and past a cover crop to the top of the hill where he had a partridge pen. Ian then drove in a loop and parked up. Jumping out of his pickup, he told us that this was where the killings were taking place. He pointed down below to some woodland hidden in a deep goyle (steep-sided valley); apparently, that was where the fox had been flushed from the day before. I looked around in dismay. The ground dived off steeply in every direction, and as a result there was almost nowhere that you could see more than 50yd. Down in the dips the trees were so thickly packed and lined with gorse there wasn't a cat in hell's chance of seeing anything moving.

Walking over the brow of the hill, I hoped that I'd find somewhere more suitable for the task, but it was even worse – I found myself looking straight at a large collection of farm buildings. There was no way that I'd be able to shoot in that direction. To make matters much worse, the moon was full and almost up to the top of the trees and it was completely clear with not a cloud in sight. Scratching my head, I told the keeper that he'd really handed us a tough one. Apologising again, he said he knew it was a difficult ask, but he had no other way of dealing with the problem. They're not allowed to use traps on the estate, so one way or another, it had to be sorted with a rifle. I told him to leave us to it, but that if we failed, the best thing would be to bait the one bit of ground that we could see from our position. Having agreed that, he wished us luck and drove off.

Paul counted out 110 paces and placed the FOXPRO caller in our agreed location – in front of the one area where we could see right down to the cover. When he got back, having walked in a loop to avoid leaving a scent trail near any likely fox approach routes, he began scanning with the thermal. Not long after, well before it was properly dark, he told me that something had just come up the rise and then turned and run away. He thought it was a fox, but I wasn't convinced: it is only too easy to mistake a hare for a fox when using a thermal. However, if it had been a fox, it would probably go around on the wind to try and come up behind us, so I suggested he go and stake out that side of the hill. He thought it a good idea, so set himself up in the cover of the trees behind me.

While he was sorting himself out, I started the caller on a young rat distress to see if there really was a fox on the prowl. Within a minute or so, just as I was scanning the area in front of me and without any warning, two large white shapes suddenly came flying past me just a few yards away. With my heart trying to leap out of my throat, I caught up with them in the viewer ... panic over! It was just two hares coming in to see what the screaming was all about. Breathing deeply to calm my pulse rate, I quartered the area again. One of the hares settled almost right in front of me, its body heat glaring strongly in the thermal. Beyond that, about 100yd out, I could see a faint white heat signature. That was just the caller. The

warmer parts of the trees in the wood stood out, as did the many fenceposts, but the most obvious objects were the sheep in a field some half a mile or so off. As the air temperature fell, the disparity between the cold ground and any warm objects increased, so the image gradually improved.

However, there was no sign of foxes. I tried several different distress calls, running each for only a few moments – it was quite clear that if Charlie did come in, I'd only have a second or two's warning, and I didn't want him to reach the caller and scent human before I got the chance of a shot. By now the partridges were coming in thick and fast to roost around the pen. Then, as the light faded, the owls started hooting – possibly antagonised by the sounds of the screaming rat calls. As the prey calls weren't working, I decided to try a few fox squalls instead. These are usually used by foxes as a contact communication. They basically say 'I'm over here', and are generally heard as darkness falls, so the timing was perfect.

> ## TIPS & TRICKS
> If you're using a caller, it's vital that you ensure that you won't be silhouetted against the sky, or all your efforts will be in vain. If you are not certain what cover there will be behind you when seen from the fox's position, look back to your ambush point when you go out to place the caller. It's surprising just how different your chosen spot will look from 100yd out!

When I got no response, I started to wonder what else I could do. Moving my position was out of the question – if I went a couple of feet in any direction, I'd be lit up by the moon. I'd tried everything I could think of to provoke a reaction from the fox, but without a result. Was this going to be a mission too far? Then, all of a sudden, the peace of the night air was shattered by a fox calling. It was impossible to tell exactly where it was, but there was no doubt that it was somewhere in the woods before us, right where we were expecting it to be. Although it was a relief that my methods were starting to pay dividends, I now needed to get it somewhere that I could shoot it.

I immediately triggered a few more squalls, and for some 15 minutes or so, I had the fox answering me. Each time it called, I replied. But the bloody thing still wouldn't show itself. At one point, Paul, who had turned to face the woods as soon as he heard the calls, spotted something fox-like with the thermal down the hill and off to the left of the caller. He was expecting me to fire at any moment, but didn't realise that as I was lower down the hill, I couldn't see it. When it cleared off, he came over and asked me why I didn't shoot it. 'Shoot what?' I replied, a little confused. We then had a heated discussion in muted whispers as to whether he'd seen a fox or a hare. He was 99% convinced it was a fox. I accepted that he was probably right, so stuck at it. By then the moon was lighting up the entire landscape – with the exception of the area right under the trees where we were standing. From previous experience, I know that few foxes will willingly come out into bright moonlight, so as the zone around the caller was now fully lit up, I was somewhat downhearted at our chances.

I kept at it though, switching from screaming rat to distressed rabbit and back to fox squalls and then mating calls. I used every ounce of my foxing knowledge to tempt the reluctant creature out. After a couple of hours of frustration, I suddenly saw a fox through the thermal. It had run along the edge of the woods under the cover of some big oak trees where it stopped briefly to look up at the caller. I already had the rifle up on the tripod sticks, and my position meant that I had a good view of it under the branches. It was some 200yd out, and was clearly about to move off again. In that moment, I dropped the thermal (it was on a strap around my neck), and in one smooth movement switched the NV riflescope and laser illuminator on. There was no time for thinking about the shot – I simply placed the reticle on the fox's chest and squeezed the trigger. The fox just fell over. When you get a solid hit, you normally get a characteristic thump

of some description, but on this occasion there was absolutely no sound at all. By then the fox was past caring though. It was lying on its side as though asleep. Paul and I both watched it for at least half a minute, neither of us believing that we'd actually managed to get it.

Since it was getting late and we'd not seen any other sign of foxes, we decided to call it a night, so we drove down and examined the carcass. It was as we'd been told by Ian, a large dog fox in very good condition. There was no sign at all of a bullet hole, so the photos came out well: the last thing I wanted was all the gore that sometimes makes it look as though the fox concerned has trodden on a landmine. When we flipped it over though, there was absolutely no doubting where the exit wound was. There was a large hole in the side of its chest. The fox had clearly hit the ground without knowing anything about it – which is just how I like it. While I was fussing about with the camera, Paul started poking at some mud in the ground a couple of feet behind where our quarry had fallen. A few seconds later he sat back grinning, 'There you go,' he said, holding out his hand, 'There's your bullet.' Sure enough, he'd uncovered the remains of the 55gr Nosler ballistic-tip, albeit in an extremely bent and curled up state.

We chucked the fox on the bonnet and drove back up the hill, leaving it next to the gate into the cover crop, where Ian would be able to find it in the morning. I was both delighted and surprised that we'd been able to find and deal with this problem animal in one session.

The long wait was worth it in the end. This large dog fox was in perfect condition having clearly spent many months feeding on the keeper's valuable pheasants and partridges.

OCTOBER

October is an extremely variable month. In some years we can have an Indian Summer with unusually long periods of unbroken sunshine. In others, however, the temperature plummets and it seems that winter has arrived early. At other times there is unremitting rain, with widespread floods and endless fogs. This can result in misery for the farmer, as the ground turns to thick glutinous mud, making it impossible to bring the last of the crops in. Maize is usually the last to be cut, and in some years it is simply left to rot where it stands. Whatever the weather, of one thing we can be sure – the hour will go back. This results in it getting dark earlier – which for the NV foxer is generally good news. It does mean that the mornings get lighter sooner, so for those that hunt at dawn, it may not be so helpful. One of the things that comes with autumn is that the air is typically much more humid and that translates into optics that mist over at the slightest provocation.

In those areas where there are red deer, the rut generally gets going in the first week or so of the month, but this can vary across the

The mid-October sun rises over John's chicken sheds. In many ways, this time of year marks the transition between autumn and winter.

country. The season's crop of fruit starts to die off in mid-October, with the last of the blackberries disappearing with the first frosts. The exception to this is apples. Depending on the variety, they may stay on the trees for months. Knowing where the fruit is can pay dividends to the hunter, as hungry foxes – ever the opportunists – will often seek out places like orchards to see if there have been any recent windfalls. Even towards the end of the season of plenty there can still be an abundance of food. Where this is the case, callers may be ineffectual. I've seen foxes casually look up with a look of total disdain when a prey distress track has started, even though they've been less than 200yd from it and thus in simple striking range. Once the cold weather hits, this can change almost overnight. When the easy meals have gone, and the fox has nothing in its belly, it'll be far more interested when it hears what

THE FARMER'S MONTH
Hedge trimming.
Sheep sales.
Cattle moved indoors.
Treating livestock for worms and liver fluke.
Potatoes, swedes and beet harvested.
Ploughing and crop preparation – winter wheat, oilseed rape and barley.
Maize harvested.

it thinks is an injured animal. It is important to realise that if your caller isn't bringing Charlie in, it's the time of year, not a fault with your kit.

One of the major sources of food at this time of year is young pheasants. Wherever there is a shoot – be it a commercial one or simply something run by a few local farmers – there will be vulnerable poults wandering about, many of which will be totally clueless about life on the freedom side of the fence. The pheasant shooting season opens on 1 October, and anyone who is involved with caring for the birds will be spending long hours feeding and watering them, as well as doing whatever they can to keep their charges alive. Keepers will be suffering from months of worry and little sleep, and early every morning they will be out anxiously checking to see if there have been any attacks during the night. Unfortunately, foxes know no restraint, and will take every bird they can get near. Should something spook roosting birds onto the ground, they can become easy prey: it is not uncommon to find large swathes of feathers, indicating that a killing spree has taken place.

It is worth putting some financial detail behind this, to better demonstrate the scale of the issue. Firstly, consider that a pheasant taken by a paying visitor is worth around £35 to a commercial shoot. Then, take into account that there's roughly a four-month period when the birds are most at risk. To keep the sums simple, let us say that this amounts to 100 days. It is not unusual for a fox to kill five pheasants or more in a night – 500 x £35 equates to £17,500 – just for one fox! I know that I've oversimplified matters, but it does illustrate why it is so important for keepers to control the predators.

Foxes don't just eat fruit and pheasants, they will exploit anything edible that comes their way. Wherever humans consume fast food, for example, there will at least be cardboard or plastic containers to be licked clean. If the animal concerned is lucky, there may also be significant leftovers – even country foxes soon learn which lay-bys and other stopping points are popular with the late-night crews, so it is always worthwhile keeping an eye on any such places. It's probably best to be a little circumspect if you're a lamper and you see any cars parked up! If the weather has been mild, there may be a late hatching of crane flies, as well as a good haul of juicy worms to be had,

so it's a good idea to check any suitable pasture to see if there are any foxes sniffing around. In my experience, it best to check during the first few hours of darkness: after that the temperatures can fall too far. Every area is different, and it's always best to find out for yourself what occurs on your ground. These days trail cameras take the hard work out of this exercise, so if you have access to them, you may well surprise yourself with what is moving around and when.

Rabbits can be numerous in October. If the temperatures remain high, they will continue breeding. Should myxomatosis or viral haemorrhagic disease strike, their populations may plummet. When 'mixy' hits – often at this time of year – there will be often be lots of helpless bunnies sitting around, blind and disoriented. Although this is a horrible affliction from a human perspective, foxes will not hesitate to rush in and kill them. There is no pity in nature.

BELOW: The acorns are fully mature on the oak trees, and it won't be long now before both they and the leaves fall to the ground.

BOTTOM: The last of the season's windfall apples slowly rot into the ground along with a scattering of elderberries. Their passing marks the start of lean times for most creatures. Until the warmth returns in spring, foxes will have to rely on their wits if they are to survive.

AN OLD ADVERSARY

DATE:	3 October 2012	WIND DIRECTION:	North-westerly
PLACE:	Jim's Farm	RIFLE:	Sauer 202
TIME:	20:30	CALIBRE:	.22-250
SUNSET:	18:48	AMMO:	55gr Nosler BT
STATE OF MOON:	Waning gibbous, but not very visible	RANGE:	Around 190yd
		CALL TRACK:	Hen distress call
WEATHER:	Dry and cool	OPTICS:	D480 GenIII NV riflescope

Early one October I was back on Jim's farm. This covers a large area in the foothills between Exeter and Exmoor. Although there are crops such as wheat and maize, most of it is given over to livestock in the form of sheep and cows. Adjoining this farm are several others that I also shoot over, one of which keeps free-range organic chickens. Together, they comprise a considerable area, far more than one could cover in one session. Over the years, foxes have caused all manner of problems there, from killing lambs and poultry to causing spontaneous abortions in cows due to the parasite infection, neospora. Consequently, my fox control activities are very popular, and I go to great lengths to ensure a smooth and harmonious relationship with the various landowners.

Unfortunately, it seems that others can't be bothered to go to the effort of asking for permission, as Jim discovered the other evening when he spotted unknown lamps in one of his fields. He drove down in his Land Rover with the lights turned off. Then, when he got to the field in question, he found there was no sign of those responsible. Not wanting to be thwarted, he did a slow lap of the field, and after a while spotted a slight reflection, which led him to two blokes with guns lying in the grass under a hedge. He collared them (the wisdom of doing this on his own will be left for a future discussion) and gave them a serious talking-to. They claimed they thought they were still on land that belonged to the neighbour, to which Jim asked why, in that case, were they hiding? He then said that not only were they expressly forbidden from coming back onto his land, but if they did so, they risked being accidentally shot by someone using a high powered rifle (me).

At the time, I knew nothing about all this as I was laid up with man-flu. I felt better the next day, but then my illness got worse, and I went down with what appears to have been norovirus. Two nights of being violently sick left me in a bit of a state. Still, by the Wednesday evening, I was feeling a little stronger and was desperate to get out. My mate Paul was also anxious to go shooting, so we went over to Jim's to see what was about. I made it clear that we wouldn't be travelling very far on foot as I was still too weak to do much. When we arrived, Jim welcomed us in to his kitchen, and regaled us with the story of the poachers. As it happens, I've seen lights at that end of the farm before, but not taken much notice as I assumed they were on next door's land. From now on I'll be keeping a closer eye on the place – luckily, there's good mobile reception at the top of the hills, so if I have any doubts, I'll be able to call Jim easily enough.

On the upside, Jim said that while he was prowling about after the unwanted visitors, he'd seen a large fox. Now this animal is almost certainly one that I've been after for at least a year. The area it was living in is very

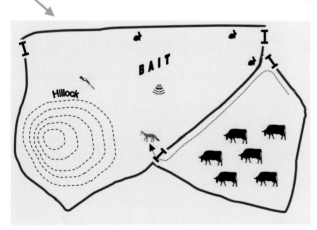

difficult to approach due to the awkward terrain. It's quite a way from the farmhouse, and the only sensible access route means driving along the peripheral track and then back down the valley. The problem with this is that the wind nearly always blows in the same direction as the approach route, so getting close to the fox without being compromised was very difficult. I've successfully taken nearly all the other foxes in the area though, so hearing that this one was still about whetted my appetite, and it became the primary target of the evening's session. We left Jim to it, and began the slow drive along the track. The first section is a pain as there are so many gates to open and close, but at least having Paul with me meant that I didn't have to keep jumping out to do it myself. After that there are only a couple more to deal with, however, because the rain had come down so hard over the previous week, a lot of the soil had been washed away leaving massive pot-holes. What was left had turned into dangerously slippery mud, so we had to go carefully.

The truck itself wasn't smelling its best, for I had a tray of semi-rotten pheasant bits in the back. These resulted from some of the roadkill birds that litter the lanes at this time of year. When we got to the large field I'd selected as our night's killing zone, I retrieved the bait and passed it to Paul – he was then able to throw it out of the window as we drove slowly up to the other end. Once there, we positioned the caller about a hundred paces out, and set ourselves up just below a large mound, and thus off the skyline. The wind was blowing from our left to our right – straight towards the area where I suspected the target fox to be living.

I then had to think very carefully about which call to use – if I was right and this was the same animal I'd been after for all that time, I would have to avoid using any sounds that it might have heard before. I slowly perused the track listing, and eventually settled on one labelled distressed hen. As I'd not used it before, I wasn't sure what it'd be like, but on switching it on, I found it produced a few clucks with the odd disturbed chicken noises in between. It also had quite a long time lag between each batch of calls. It sounded quite eerie in the dark of the night, and I was hopeful that it would

> **TIPS & TRICKS**
>
> If you have access to a vacuum-packer, it can make the process of handling smelly bait in the dark much less unpleasant. Simply seal the bait up before it gets nasty, then leave it for a few days. By then it should be really horrible, but perfect for bringing foxes in, as they just love eating rotting meat.

attract my intended victim's attention. As we waited, the moon began to rise above the far horizon. For once I wasn't too worried about this, as there were very thick rain clouds above us, and I knew it would lose out to them.

After some 10 minutes – while I was scanning with the mini-thermal imager – I spotted something moving very fast at the other end of the next field. It was fox-shaped, and heading up towards the hedge between us. I only had the briefest of glimpses of it though, as there was too much vegetation in the way to get a decent view. I whispered to Paul that I'd seen a possible Charlie, and we both focused on the area where I'd seen it. As we watched, a white shape appeared through the hedge and into the field we were in. Something wasn't quite right though, for after a minute or so of observing it, we both realised that this was a smaller creature – most likely a rabbit. It was so far away though – some 400yd, and almost completely hidden by long grass – that we couldn't be sure.

While we were trying to work out where the fox had gone, the cattle in the field where I'd originally seen it suddenly started charging about all over the place. 'Hmmm', thought I, 'That's suspicious – something's disturbed them.' Downwind of the caller there was a gate leading to where the cattle were, so I kept watching the area around it. Some five minutes later, I suddenly saw that a white shape had appeared. I was on the rifle, which was already up on the sticks, in a flash. With the NV scope and laser switched on, I scanned along the hedgeline until I found myself staring at a fox that was sitting back on its haunches, looking out over the field. Presumably, the call had brought it in, and the smell of the pheasant bait was helping to keep it interested. I didn't waste any time in thinking about such things though, for I was slipping the safety off and getting a good point of aim sorted. The fox was the best part of 200yd out, and as a result of the x6 magnification was quite a small target. I steadied my feet, paused my breathing and sent a round on its way. It was immediately obvious that the .22-250 Nosler BT had hit the fox very hard indeed, for it was thrown over by the impact, landing on its back motionless.

After satisfying ourselves that there were no other foxes about, Paul went over the hill to check the ground there while I drove down and took a series of photos with my Nikon DSLR. The fox proved to be a large male. He was, however, very poorly fed and had a patch of fur missing on his right flank. Whether this was from an injury or possibly due to early mange, I don't yet know. A fox of his size should have been in better condition, so there was clearly something wrong with him. I took a number of close-ups of the wound for later consideration. My thoughts that he'd been hit hard were proven when I checked the carcass – there was absolutely no sign of an exit wound, so all the energy from the round had been dissipated within the chest cavity. No wonder he'd gone down so convincingly.

I threw the carcass onto the bonnet of the Disco and drove up to see how Paul had got on.

Unfortunately, he'd not seen anything, so we agreed to call it a night. We got most of the way back to the farm before I realised that the fox had disappeared – the track was so rough that it'd been thrown off without either of us noticing. Since there was a risk that it was carrying mange, I wasn't prepared to leave it where it was, so we found a gateway and turned the truck around. Bumping and bouncing our way back from whence we'd come, we eventually found it lying in the mud. We put it back on the bonnet and set off again, this time making it to the yard without losing it again. While Paul checked the nearby paddocks, I called in to see Jim. He was not only delighted to hear that I'd successfully caught up with the errant fox, but that as it was clearly not well, I'd got it before its ailment got any worse. A sick fox is a dangerous thing to have around a farm, as in its desperation to eat, it will risk attacking livestock that it wouldn't normally

contemplate going near. I told him that he would need to keep his dogs away from the carcass, and that it should be burned or buried to ensure there was no chance of the mange, if that is what it was, being spread further.

We drove back in a good mood. It's always much more satisfying to go after a known fox that's proved hard to get in the past than to just bring one in that you've never seen before.

ABOVE RIGHT: Two views of the fox – note how its belly has little depth. Although it was quite a long animal, it only weighed 15lb, which is much less than you'd expect from an individual of this size.

BELOW RIGHT: A close-up of the bald patch that may have been caused by sarcoptic mange.

BIRD STRIKE

DATE:	7 October 2012	RIFLE:	Sauer 202
PLACE:	Ian's Shoot	CALIBRE:	.22-250
TIME:	20:00	AMMO:	55gr Nosler BT
SUNSET:	18:39	RANGE:	Around 60yd
STATE OF MOON:	Waning gibbous	CALL TRACK:	None — bait used
WEATHER:	Dry and cold	OPTICS:	D480 GenIII NV riflescope
WIND DIRECTION:	Easterly		

While checking my emails one Sunday morning, I got another text message from Ian, the gamekeeper saying that his birds had, once again, been the victims of a fox strike. Paul and I have always responded to his requests for help, and are proud of our 100% success rate. We are, however, painfully aware that this streak cannot last, and sooner or later, we know that we'll draw a blank. After some hurried communication, we agreed to go over later that afternoon. I also asked Ian to see what he had lying around in the way of bait, so that we could improve our chances of bringing the problem fox in. I spent some time checking all the equipment's batteries, etc. and when the time was right, loaded up and set off to collect Paul. From there, it was about a 45-minute journey, and we arrived bang on time, in spite of stopping to take some photos of some of our previous hunt locations.

Ian had fortunately managed to drag out some ripe partridge carcasses for us, so once we'd discussed the night's mission, we set off armed with our smelly cargo. The problem area was one we knew well, having shot several foxes there over the previous couple of months. It's accessed by a long muddy track, and lies just above some woodland where there are a number of pheasant pens. As we navigated our way towards it, we checked the surrounding fields to see

TIPS & TRICKS

As mentioned several times earlier, bait is one of the best ways of bringing foxes in to a known area. If you are using small pieces, these are best placed across the wind. If it is in a single lump, then it is best staked to the ground so that it can't be dragged off. Either way, it should be positioned so that the scent will be taken towards where you suspect your adversaries to be lying up or travelling. An alternative is to smear tinned dog or cat food onto fence posts. This forces the foxes to stop and lick it off, hopefully giving you time to get a shot lined up. Always ensure there are good backstops to any bait points for obvious safety reasons.

where the livestock was. In a couple of places we stopped and blatted a few bunnies with the .204. Their skins and guts were then added to the bait pile, the meat being saved to be fed to our Golden Retriever and rag-doll cross cat. Pulling up near the area where we'd decided to place our ambush, we crept out and carefully scattered the bait in a rough line across the wind. The idea was that this would maximise the scent trail, and therefore increase our chances of bringing any nearby foxes in to investigate.

Once that was done, we climbed back into the truck and drove up towards the tarmac lane beyond, checking the gates as we went. Nothing seen, we decided to go down to the main road, or at least for what qualifies as one out in that part of the world, to see what was going on around the lower side of the woods. As we wanted the sun to have been down for a while before we returned to the bait we trundled along slowly, Paul scanning the hillsides for any signs of life. There were pheasants and partridges everywhere, some of them appearing unbelievably stupid, seemingly wanting to get run over. Indeed, we saw several fresh carcasses, so these got thrown in the back for use as extra bait. Elsewhere, there were some Red Ruby Devon cattle and some sheep, as well as a few horses. The odd bunny could be seen grazing on the steep slopes in between the gorse bushes, but we weren't able to find any signs of foxes. 'We've got to find one somewhere', Paul said. 'We can't blank – that's not an option...'.

In spite of stopping every 50yd, we eventually reached the end of that stretch of road. Since this marks the estate boundary, we had the choice of either going back the way we'd come, or engaging low ratio and heading up a steep and rugged track that rarely sees any kind of motorised transport. As this connects to the one that runs past the bait field, we'd thought it'd be the best plan. Besides, making it up the hill is enough of a challenge to be a reasonable distraction. The Land Rover barely noticed though, its mud terrain tyres clawing their way over the rocks and through all the boggy bits. A few minutes later, we pulled up and dismounted. We already had all the camo gear, face veils, etc. in place, so we grabbed our respective rifles and sticks, and crept over towards the gate in question.

I switched the mini-thermal on, and immediately got a screen full of animals in my face. There were three or four hares on the far side of the field, but of much more interest was the large white shape running out of the hedge and straight towards the bait. I watched it for about a second, and then without bothering to switch it off, quickly swung the legs of my shooting tripod into position. With that done, my rifle was off my shoulder and on top them in no time. With the scope on, I could see that the fox was now about 60yd out, and trotting from my right to my left into the wind, with its head down and sniffing as it went. I was so anxious to get this problem animal, that I had to slow myself down to make sure I didn't screw the

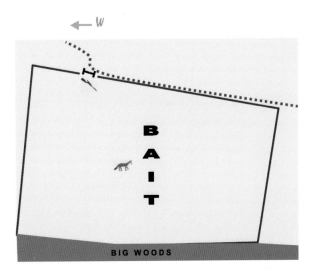

shot up. Another second or so, and the fox turned slightly, presenting an even better target. I placed the reticle on its chest and squeezed off a round. There was a convincing thump and it dropped on the spot.

With a sigh of relief, I whispered 'Well, at least we can be sure we haven't blanked now!' After satisfying ourselves that there weren't any other Charlies close by, we set the caller out, and tried everything we could think of to entice another one in, but after about an hour, we had to face it: there probably weren't any other foxes in the area. With so much easy food about, however, we knew that situation isn't likely to last. So with that in mind, I sent Ian a texted news update and we set off for home. The next day I got a very grateful thanks for our hard work in reply. With 5,500 acres to keep fox-free though, I knew I could expect another call from him very soon.

AN EXCELLENT SESSION!

DATE:	8 October 2009	**CALIBRE:**	Sauer .22-250 and .308
PLACE:	Aubrey's Farm	**AMMO:**	.22-250: 55gr PPU SP; .308:
TIME:	20:00		150g .308 BT
SUNSET:	18:38	**RANGE:**	80yd
STATE OF MOON:	Waning gibbous	**CALL TRACK:**	Screaming rat
WEATHER:	Dry and cold, clear skies	**OPTICS:**	.22-250: D480 GenIII NV
WIND DIRECTION:	South-westerly		riflescope; .308 Swarovski
RIFLES:	Two x Sauer 202		Z6 2.5–15x56

In October 2009, I was taken to a new shoot by Stuart, who is one of the most experienced deer stalkers in the south-west. The agreement was that we'd have a go at stalking the red deer – if any were about – and then after it got dark, he'd go home while I'd stay on to see if I could shoot any foxes. Aubrey, the farmer, was keen for me to do so as he keeps a lot of sheep. In some years his ewes produce the best part of a thousand lambs, and unsurprisingly this brings in predators from miles around.

I was given an area at the bottom of a valley to cover, and whilst making my way there through a field of reddy-brown cows, I realised that a small group of them at the far side were an odd shape. Under inspection, they turned out to be a pricket stag with two hinds and a calf. They'd clearly spotted me, but were stood trying to work out where and what I was. Unsettled, they moved off after a couple of minutes. I then got down to a bank above a small stream and tried to blend into the scenery.

Some time later, a fox started calling about 80yd behind me. It was in clear sight, but in a field that we didn't have permission to shoot on. I had no choice but to ignore it. I'd been told not to pursue foxes until after dark as we were specifically targeting deer. As I lay there I came to the conclusion that I was doing a good job of impersonating a hedge since none of the many crows or ravens that had flown close above had spotted me. A robin that was flitting in and about the bush beside me seemed a little concerned, but then

LEFT: This fox, which came in to the screaming rat call, was the first of many taken on Aubrey's farm. Since he raises nearly 1,500 lambs each year, controlling the foxes there is a major priority for him.

got distracted by some indeterminate bugs and quickly forgot all about my presence.

As it started to get dark, I heard Stuart fire a shot some way down the valley. I kept alert in case this flushed anything in my direction, but nothing showed. Just as the last shootable light was fading away, some half hour later, a large red stag appeared on the other side of the field and ran straight towards me. I was clearly lying on its chosen deer rack (hedge crossing point), so I realised I needed to get on to the fast approaching target very quickly, or I might find myself getting trampled.

As the stag got to about 40ft away, it realised that something wasn't quite right, whereupon it briefly turned sideways-on to scent the air. It may have been worried that I was a rival, but within moments the 150gm .308 round from my Sauer 202 Outback hit it in the chest. It dropped like a stone. Although this was a good thing, the downside was that it had been standing right in the middle of some thick reeds. By the time I'd climbed over the bank and started looking for it the light had gone, and I soon found that my mini pocket torch was woefully inadequate, so I started back up the hill towards the farm to fetch my Cree X3, which is many times more powerful. On the way there I met up with Stuart who he said he'd dropped a pricket (young stag). As we walked along we chatted in muted tones about the various things we'd seen. We soon arrived back at the yard where we were pleased to unload all of our shooting kit into the trucks. We then drove back down to our respective animals and field-gralloched them in the vehicle's lights before hauling them back for the larder.

Once Stuart had left, I got myself ready for a foxing session. Whilst doing so I showed Aubrey the intricacies of my NV equipment, at which he was amazed. He told me he was concerned about the number of

foxes around, so I said I'd give the caller a try. As we chatted, I suddenly realised that the moon was coming up, and that as there was next to no cloud cover, I'd have to work fast if I was to take advantage of the remaining darkness. I therefore chose to start at the very first field after the farm buildings. Sliding the ancient bolt back as quietly as I could, I opened the gate just enough to get through and then pushed it back against the bank. That done, I walked down to set the caller in the hedge. Happy that it was in the right place, I retired to hide in the shadows with my trusty Sauer up on my sticks. When I was happy that everything was ready, I started the caller on the screaming rat track. Within a few minutes a set of eyes appeared down by the gate into the next field. They soon revealed themselves to be those of a fox, which came running in at speed. The moment it paused to survey the scene, a .22-250 soft-nose round hit him hard. He turned out to be a large-ish (16.5lb) dog fox.

More or less as I collected the carcass I noticed that the moon was starting to light the landscape up, so I decided to call it a day and head home. Aubrey was very pleased, and told me that I was welcome to come back at any time. It turned out to be the first of many, many visits, and it remains to this day as one of my favourite places to shoot – partly because of the warm welcome I'm always given.

TIPS & TRICKS

If a farmer regularly puts cattle feed pellets out, it is highly likely that the local foxes will know all about it and will be taking advantage. Ask him where the feeding points are, and check them thoroughly – in my experience just after dark is the best time.

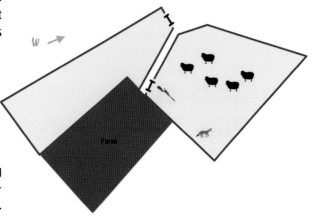

FOUR DOWN

DATE:	10 October 2010	**CALIBRE:**	Sauer .22-250 and 308
PLACE:	Aubrey's Farm	**AMMO:**	.22-250: 55gr PPU SP
TIME:	20:30		.308: 165gr Sierra Gameking SP
SUNSET:	18:34	**RANGE:**	10–100yd
STATE OF MOON:	Evening crescent	**CALL TRACK:**	Hi-pitched Snowshoe hare
WEATHER:	Dry	**OPTICS:**	.22-250: D480 GenIII NV
WIND DIRECTION:	North-westerly		riflescope and .308: Swarovski
RIFLES:	Two x Sauer 202		Z6 2.5-15x56

About a year after I started shooting at Aubrey's, I went over for another deer stalking session with Stuart. We headed off in different directions with the agreement was that once it was too dark to shoot deer, I'd phone in to say whether there were any carcasses to be recovered. If not, I'd switch into foxing mode. That way Stuart could go home without waiting for me to get back to the yard. Whether it was the late summer we'd had or not I don't know, but although the rut had started elsewhere, it hadn't begun at Aubrey's. I spent a fruitless (but enjoyable) hour or so watching the sun go down. When it got too dark to see, I put the binos away, slipped the PS-22 NV system onto the front of my Swarovski scope, and got my NV monocular out. When I was satisfied that I was ready, I began working my way upwind across the fields.

I had been there only a couple of days before, and on that occasion I'd spotted two foxes not far from my deer ambush point. One had been felled by a round from my .308, but I knew there was at least one more in the area. I therefore approached the spot cautiously, but no foxes were to be seen. I took the opportunity to stop and make my phone call – I was told that Stuart had shot a stag and that Aubrey was out recovering it with the quad. After my brief chat, I'd only moved about 30yd before I spotted a fox coming in from behind me. Downwind. At first glance the ground appeared to be well suited to a bipod, but when I lay down I found there were too many rises, and I kept losing it. I switched back to the monocular several times as it has a better field of view, but my intended quarry was nowhere to be seen. I assumed it had run off. After a minute or so, however, I worked out where it was – it had jumped up into a cattle feed bin! Every 10 seconds or so, it leapt back down, had a look around, and then bounded back up again. This gave me enough time to get the sticks ready, and the next time it returned to earth, I quickly gave it a 165gr .308 soft point. It turned out to be a reasonably large male.

Happy that I'd started my evening session well, I carried on back over the hill towards the farm, stopping to spot with the NV every few yards. I didn't see anything shootable until I got quite close to the farmyard when I saw a set of eyes some way off in the distance. Getting the NV focused, I could see that it was a fox running towards a hedge. I realised that it was going to be in cover before I could get a shot off, so I snuck back onto the farm track and quietly made my way towards the first of the barns. Aubrey's son often scatters some cattle feed pellets on the grass there, and as a result there are often foxes lurking nearby waiting to fill their empty stomachs.

Just before I reached the gate, I stopped and got everything ready: rifle on the sticks, NV laser switched on, focus about right, etc. I then moved a couple of feet forwards, and scanned the field and far hedges with the monocular, but there was nothing in sight. I then looked down at the ground in front of me and realised that there was a fox sitting about 10yd away – looking straight at me. I put the reticle between its eyes and squeezed off a round. There was a very satisfying 'thwump', but I couldn't see a body. I scanned around, and saw the fox a few feet to the left looking down the valley at where the echo must have come from. I couldn't believe I had missed, so quietly chambered another round and 'thwop' – down it went. After checking the body (another dog), I shone the torch over to where I'd fired the first shot, and was very pleased to see that I hadn't missed at all as there was another carcass (a vixen) lying there.

Back at the truck I unlocked the firearms cabinet and changed over to my .22-250 NV rig. Before long I was ready to go back out again. As I was making my way through the yard, I could hear some wild boar squealing in the woods a few hundred yards below. Presumably there was a domestic fight going on. I spent a lot of time slogging around the fields, but I found no foxes at all, even in the area where the

gralloch had been left from Stuart's stag. Before giving up and going home, I set the caller up on hi-pitched Snow-shoe hare. I wasn't expecting anything to show, but thought I'd try all the same. I was, therefore, quite surprised when a fox appeared from nowhere within about 20 seconds. It went round on the wind and had a good sniff but it clearly didn't like something because it immediately turned to go. Just as it was about to disappear over a brow into dead ground, I sent a 55gr soft point on its way. This hit home and the large dog fox dropped on the spot. So, four foxes for four shots. Aubrey was very pleased indeed, especially as I had shot three there earlier in the week.

TIPS & TRICKS

If you spot a fox that is too far out for a safe shot, but is too close to allow you to properly position an electronic caller, simply hang it on a nearby bush or fencepost, and use a quiet call such as a field mouse or vole squeak. If you've got the wind direction right, the fox may well run right up to you.

This fox was taken with a PS-22 NV system which was front-mounted to the Swarovski Z6 scope on my .308 Sauer 202. The device on top of the sight is an infra red laser illuminator. The 165gr soft-point Sierra GameKing round was intended for red deer, and as such made short work of the errant Reynard.

HONOUR RESTORED

DATE:	22 October 2011	RIFLE:	Sauer 202
PLACE:	Critter's Farm	CALIBRE:	.22-250
TIME:	20:30	AMMO:	55gr Nosler BT
SUNSET:	18:10	RANGE:	Both at about 90yd
STATE OF MOON:	Morning crescent	CALL TRACK:	Kiss of death simulated
WEATHER:	Dry and cold		rodent
WIND DIRECTION:	North-westerly	OPTICS:	D480 GenIII NV riflescope

As the result of a problem with my NV riflescope (see 'Crane-Fly Catchers', p.126), I'd missed a fox that was on the pheasant shoot that Critter keepers for. The worst thing about it was that he was standing right next to me when it happened. At that stage I'd not realised that my scope had a fault, so I was not only mystified as to why I'd missed the shot, but why I also failed to hit the target a second time when it stopped to look back over its shoulder. I do miss occasionally – we all do, and we all have to learn to get over it. But it's not often that I miss twice in a row. Critter was very good about it – he'd seen me shoot before, so knew only too well what I was capable of. As he is one of the area's expert foxers, though, particularly with a lamp, I enjoyed my status as the man he turned to for help when Charlie was killing his birds. Needless to say, I left the estate that night somewhat crestfallen.

My sense of humour returned a week or so later after the problem had been found and fixed, but as is the way of the world, my busy hunting schedule had only allowed me to visit Critter's shoot a couple of times over the summer. Sometimes when I called he was off out salmon fishing; mostly, however, the weather let me down – either the fog would settle, or the rain would descend, usually just when I was at the furthest reaches of the estate. On this occasion, we had nigh-on perfect conditions. Lots of cloud cover meant there was no moon to be seen. In spite of this, there was no rain and a light wind. It was game on and the arrangements were made.

I reached Critter's just after it got dark and was immediately mobbed by a pack of assorted dogs – various red labs, Patterdales and border terriers swarmed around my legs barking furiously as I struggled to get my wellies off. Once inside, normality and peace, slowly swept through the house as one by one each canine found its favourite lair and settled down. Critter is one of those people who seems to get phone calls every couple of minutes, so it took some time for us to escape into the sanctity of his Land Rover 90.

As we set off, he told me more about where he'd been finding the corpses of his precious birds. One place in particular was at the far end of the estate, where two foxes had been seen regularly. The problem from his perspective was that the ground is both very hilly and heavily wooded. Not a good area to use a lamp over. We got to within about quarter of a mile of the spot, and parked up. Carrying on any further would have meant driving through a maize cover crop, not something that we were going to do in a hurry, so we carefully made our way around the edge on foot. A quick look into the first gateway using the NV revealed a vast area of open grass between a large wood and a tall hedge – but no foxes. No matter, this wasn't where they'd been seen.

Gradually, we made our way along the top edges of another couple of fields, checking every few yards for any sign of Charlie. This was, in fact, a very difficult task, as the terrain there is so steep and convoluted that it's almost impossible to see into the numerous gullies and all the dead ground they create. Eventually, we emerged onto a relatively level area next to a large pond. About 300yd away there was a farm house and several associated outbuildings. It was near there that the two foxes had been seen, so I looked around for a suitable place for us to set up. We needed the wind to be crossing in front of us, ideally with it blowing into some kind of low cover to give any foxes a safe direction to approach from. We also needed something to hide our silhouettes, or we'd be rumbled straight away.

After a bit I found that the area in front of a small tree by the pond gave me everything I was looking for. By positioning myself on a small rise I got a relatively open vista over my chosen killing zone. Since there were two of us, I chose to put the FOXPRO caller further out than usual. This was simply extra insurance against either of us making unwanted noises and alerting our chosen targets. I typically pace out about 50yd, but on this occasion I counted out 75 and then put the caller in place, facing downwind.

Once back with Critter, I placed my Sauer .22-250 on my sticks, checked that all was ready with the NV mono, and set the caller going. I started with a partridge distress call, but after a couple of minutes, it was clear that nothing was interested. I tried about four different tracks, before selecting the 'Kiss Of Death'. This is an artificial call that sounds like a gone-wrong keyboard version of someone squeaking with a piece of polystyrene. For some reason though, the foxes seem to like it, and after about a minute, a set of fox eyes appeared to the left of the farm. At that stage, it was still about 300yd out, but it was clear that it was coming in fast. I quietly hissed 'Fox' to Critter, and went into my well-practised routine.

Mono off, mono illuminator off, NV riflescope on, riflescope illuminator on. I'd already set the focus, so all I had to do was find the fox and track it. That done, I followed it as it ran straight towards the caller. By then I was getting anxious, as it was showing no signs of slowing: the last thing I wanted was for it to get close enough to scent human. Luckily – for me, that is – it paused momentarily about 15ft out. By then the safety was off and a gentle squeeze sent a hollow-point straight into its engine room. It didn't even twitch – just fell on the spot. Critter – who didn't have the advantage of NV, said 'Ooh, I heard that one hit home!' Although I couldn't see him in the pitch dark, I could tell he was grinning like a Cheshire cat.

TIPS & TRICKS

If one or more foxes are hunting on ground that you are meant to be controlling them on, they will leave signs that they have been around. Dominant dog foxes will leave their dung – often known as 'scats', in prominent places to deter rivals. Learning to recognise such evidence will help you to track your quarry down.

There was no time to waste though, and I was straight back on the NV mono. About half a minute later, another set of eyes appeared in the same place as the first ones. Again I gave Critter a soft warning, and simultaneously got the rifle ready. This second fox was a carbon copy of the first one, following exactly the same approach route. This time I was worried that it might be spooked by its dead colleague rather than the caller, so I knew that I'd probably only get the briefest of opportunities to take a shot. Sure enough, it ran flat-out right up to the point where it suddenly smelled danger. At that moment it skidded to a panicked halt, and half turned to jump away. But in that instant death called, and it fell about 5ft from the first one. Again, Critter called out, 'That was a hit too, wasn't it, Paddy?' When I said that it was, he was beside himself with glee. We left the caller going for a bit, but when nothing more showed, we went over to inspect the carcasses. Both were medium-sized vixens in good health – at least, they had been until a few minutes earlier. Critter was a happy man and so was I. Honour had been restored!

The ducks on a farm pond were taking a hammering so I tried using the caller nearby. Both of these foxes responded within minutes, and fell just a few feet apart. As there were no more attacks, it is certain that they were the culprits

NOVEMBER

The sun streams through the mist early one cold November morning. The needles remain in place on these conifers, but the leaves had all long since gone from the deciduous trees.

November usually heralds the first consistently cold spells as winter settles across the country. The frosts and chill winds are typically accompanied by widespread reductions in the amount of food available to foxes. The added burden of trying to stay warm adds to their hunger, something that undoubtedly comes as a shock to the year's youngsters for whom it is both a novel and unwelcome change. At this time, prey distress calls can be very productive, however, as the month moves on, the first signs of vulpine breeding will be heard, with both dogs and vixens calling to attract mates. At the beginning of the season it is usually the dominant members of the social groups that will do this. Any subordinate members either have to move away or keep a low profile, or they risk being injured, sometimes severely, by their seniors. Should the food supply be good enough later on – that is in January and February – they may be allowed to mate then. The skilled use of an electronic caller with the appropriate vixen mating calls can be devastating throughout this period.

When the night skies are clear, the temperatures can fall dramatically, resulting in sharp frosts. When

THE FARMER'S MONTH

Hedges and fences maintained.
Rams turned out to the ewes for tupping (mating).
Livestock fed indoors.
Ploughing, winter crops planted.
Potatoes and maize harvesting.

this is the case, care needs to be taken to avoid the lenses misting over or freezing up on any optical equipment you are using. One way to do this is to avoid imposing any sudden temperature changes on your kit. Taking a rifle straight out of a nice warm house and exposing it to a bitingly cold wind is almost certain to result in all the parts made of glass getting completely fogged-up. To reduce this, it is worth acclimatising everything – including yourself – either by keeping the heating down in your vehicle, or if you are heading out on foot, by taking a few extra minutes to let things settle. Another way of minimising the problem is to make lens covers out of foam sheet, the sort that gets sold as camping mats is perfect. This helps to provide a degree of insulation, the cover is only removed to take a shot and is then refitted. My preferred method is to find a plastic lid off something that is a similar size to the lens. I then cut the foam to make a piece that will form a single layer around the scope and another the same size as the lid. A few wraps of adhesive cloth tape then hold everything together. The beauty of this is that if you lose the cover it only takes a few moments to make another. Pretty it might not be – but effective it will be! By far the most important thing though, is to have at least one clean lens cloth on you.

If the skies are cloudy, however, there is the real risk of mist or fog developing, especially if the ground is very wet and the winds are light. All too often, it rains instead. Either way, the wisest thing is to check the weather forecast. If there's no sign of things changing, the best course of action is to leave your rifles locked up in the cabinet and either do some kit maintenance or try to earn some undoubtedly badly needed Brownie points from your long-suffering family. Trying to shoot successfully in thick fog or heavy rain is a futile exercise – even thermal imagers give up when there's too much moisture in the air.

The result of prolonged rainfall is, of course, wet ground and in most areas that equates to mud. If you have to do any serious off-road work, then it is well worth investing in a decent set of either mud-terrain or all-terrain tyres for your vehicle. That does, of course, assume that the vehicle concerned is up to the job in the first place! A good exercise for those rainy nights in is to check exactly what equipment you have in your shooting truck/car. It's best to find out in advance that you're carrying the wrong things, or that you have flat batteries in something you'll need, or that you don't have the things you should have. November is a good time to do this, as it gives you a chance to get properly sorted before the full onset of winter.

November 1 marks the end of the roe buck season and the start of that for roe does. Red hinds also come in on the same day, so if you're a deer stalker as well as a foxer, then it's an important date. Although many farmers support the foxhound packs, others do not: this may be for a variety of reasons, such as damage to the land, gates being left open and vehicles left blocking access points. Others, such as free-range chicken farmers hate the fact that foxes get displaced by the hunts' activities and often end up on their land. Many is the time that I've been called to check such farms over, sometimes I even get phoned the day before so that I'm booked in ready to arrive just after

the hunt leaves. I've lost count of the number of tired and hungry foxes I've shot as the result of such trips. One farmer I know opened his shed door and found a worn-out fox that had been chased for miles. It was only yards from his chickens, fortunately, he was able to retrieve his shotgun before it had recovered sufficiently to make an escape.

As the farmers start to bring their livestock in for the winter there is more opportunity to drive on the fields. If it's rained at all, however – and this being the United Kingdom, it will have – the ground may be too soft to take a vehicle driving over it. If there's any doubt, check with the farmer first as the odds are that he'll be most unimpressed if you ruin the ground for him. If you have access to a quad or a mule though, things can be somewhat different. It's still a good idea to check beforehand though, as many places may still be unsafe to travel over. Down here in Devon good soil can turn into a quagmire overnight and even four-wheeled drive quads can struggle to get enough grip to move about safely.

BELOW: An ice-covered thistle awaits the warming rays of the sun. November typically sees the arrival of the first hard frosts.

BOTTOM: November sees the game bird season in full swing. Here, a mallard drake has fallen to a shotgun.

HARD NUTS AND WHOLE NUTS...

DATE:	7 November 2011	**WIND DIRECTION:**	North-easterly
PLACE:	Mrs. B's Farm	**RIFLE:**	Sauer 202
TIME:	20:30	**CALIBRE:**	.22-250
SUNSET:	16:41	**AMMO:**	55gr Nosler BT
STATE OF MOON:	Waxing gibbous	**RANGE:**	90yd
WEATHER:	Cold and dry with full cloud cover	**CALL TRACK:**	Fox squalls
		OPTICS:	D480 GenIII NV riflescope

Queuing in the local village post office, I overheard an old lady complaining about her pet gander being killed by a fox. I gallantly stepped forward and introduced myself to her as the solution to her problems. She was a bit suspicious at first, but brightened up when I mentioned that I already shot for Roy, to whom she rented her land. After a brief chat, she took my name and number.

The next day she called – having been given a glowing recommendation. Roy had also kindly said that he'd show me where the boundaries were. A few days later he was good as his word and took me on the back of his quad. By the time we'd finished, the original 100 acres had grown considerably. 'Oh, that field belongs to my father-in-law, so you can shoot there too. These two fields belong to my cousin, and he'll be pleased for you to check them out as well', and so on. The end result was that I now had permission to cover an area of

> **TIPS & TRICKS**
>
> Often the job of controlling foxes is limited because they're coming onto your ground from nearby farms. Getting permission to shoot on these is not always straightforward, so it is always good idea to keep your ears open for any opportunity to speak to the relevant landowners.

land that connected onto some existing ground that I'd previously found very difficult to work without wider access, so I was very pleased.

Over the next few months, I called in and shot quite a few foxes. There was one that had proved a hard nut to crack, though. It clearly lived on adjoining ground, but much to my frustration, it didn't appear to be interested in coming to the caller. As the neighbouring farmers are keen shooters, I suspect that they'd made it both call and lamp-shy. All the while it was giving the poor old lady a troublesome time, every few days it would go in and pillage her chicken run.

The main difficulty for me was that the fox was so irregular in its habits. Sometimes it would raid in the middle of the day: other times deep in the night. One night, however, I heard it calling. I was about half a mile away, and in the process of opening an old gate. At first I couldn't be sure what it was, but once I was able to stop and listen I heard the unmistakable shrill shriek of a fox ... and right where I believed it lived.

I wasn't hopeful that I'd be able to bring it in, firstly, because I was some way from its territory and secondly, because I suspected it'd previously been spooked by a caller. Still, I thought I might as well have a go. Although the moon was up and about three-quarters full, the cloud cover was so thick that it was very dark, much better than previous nights when it was so bright that it was like being on stage. There was a fair bit of mist, so the NV didn't have its usual range, but I could still see about 400yd, which was more than enough to do the job.

With the caller in position, I retired to where I'd left the sticks, and set about trying to bring in a fox or two. I started with the vixen on heat call, but with no luck. After a while I switched to the kiss of death track – again with nothing showing. I decided to move on, so I had a quick scan over into some adjoining fields with the NV spotter, but everywhere I looked was deserted, for some reason there weren't even any rabbits or hares about.

I'd not heard anything more from the fox, but was keen to go after it all the same. There were two issues that concerned me: one was the wind direction, according to the Met Office wind map, it was blowing from the north-east at about 7mph. While this was just about enough to stop a fog developing, the direction meant that I'd have a really hard time in trying to get in position. The other potential problem was that if I used a fox call for any length of time there was a risk that it would be heard by the occupants of the farm – and they might pile out with their shotguns and rifles. That would be something that I could definitely do without!

The drive over only took me a minute or so, and after I'd parked up I cautiously checked the nearby fields. There was a small flock of sheep in one, but the rest were all devoid of life. I knew that this might work to my advantage. If the lack of other foxes meant that the calling had been unsuccessful, it might well respond to me. Due to the wind direction, I decided that the field with the sheep was the most promising candidate. A look around with the NV mono showed that the field had a slight rise running across it, with a low dip on the other side. It was only a couple of feet high, but all the same it was certainly enough to hide a cunning fox. I knew that I'd have to position myself on the top or I'd not be able to see into the dead ground, so I slowly worked my way along the hedge until I was in place.

Another quick scan with the NV showed that I had a great view – this is where a laser illuminator really pays dividends. Without it the land would have looked relatively flat, but with it you get lots of really helpful shadows so you can properly understand the shape of the ground. The wind was blowing from my left to my right. In front of me, about 80yd away, was another hedge running parallel to the one behind me. The farm where I suspected the fox to be was on the far side and downwind. Perfect! I counted out 70 paces and placed the caller behind a clump of grass. In doing so, I was careful to stay upwind of it – that way any foxes approaching from downwind would not cross my scent path. That had been a lesson painfully learnt...

Once back behind the sticks I checked the focus on the NV riflescope, and I was ready. I started with six short squalls (fox shrieks) and then hit mute. I thought this would be enough to catch the interest of my intended target, so gave it a minute or so of silence, watching all the while through the NV mono. I paid particular attention to the downwind stretch of hedge, as that's where I thought this streetwise fox would probably appear – if it was ever going to show. I followed this up with a burst of seven fox squalls and muted the caller again.

Moments later a set of fox eyes suddenly appeared in the top of the hedge – right where I'd predicted. Some quiet fumbling got the mono switched off and the riflescope/laser on. My feet were already in position, so I grasped the top of the tripod together with the fore-end of the rifle with my left hand, and I was ready. I picked up the fox, which was now in the field and moving very cautiously indeed, low to the ground and clearly suspicious. It was side-on to me and everything was right for a perfect shot. A gentle squeeze on the Sauer's trigger put a hollow-point in its chest.

This fox had been killing Mrs B's beloved chickens, and she was distraught about it. The problem was that it was living on a neighbouring farm where I didn't have permission to shoot. One night I played the sound of a rival and in it came.

FOUR BY TWOS

DATE:	19 and 22 November 2011	**RIFLE:**	Sauer 202 (both)
PLACE:	Rob's Farm	**CALIBRE:**	.22-250 (both)
TIME:	18:30–20:30 (21:30)	**AMMO:**	55gr Nosler BT (both)
SUNSET:	16:24 (16:21)	**RANGE:**	60yd and 170yd (90yd
STATE OF MOON:	Morning crescent (both)		and 150yd)
WEATHER:	Cold and vey damp (both)	**CALL TRACK:**	Squalls/vixen on heat (both)
WIND DIRECTION:	South-westerly (both)	**OPTICS:**	D480 GenIII NV riflescope (both)

One damp afternoon I headed off to a free range organic chicken farm that I've been shooting over for several years. When I arrived, I started out with the HMR on a quest for bunnies, but apart from a couple that jumped out of some thick herbage and dived straight into deep cover, I didn't see a thing. My plan was to wait until it got dark so that I could go out after foxes with the NV, but as the sun still hadn't gone down fully, I parked up in the farmyard and spent the last few minutes of dusk chatting pleasantly to the farmer and his wife.

One of the things he mentioned was that Rob – the chap who owned the farm down the valley – had been having problems with foxes. Although it was land that I used to look after, I'd decided to stay away for a while as they were heavily involved with the local DEFRA badger vaccination trial. The dairy herd there had been hammered really heavily by bovine TB, and the officials wanted to know why he'd been hit so badly, and as a result were crawling all over the place. The last thing I needed was to be tripping over blokes with clipboards!

Anyway, it transpired that DEFRA had recently finished their work, so I took the opportunity to give the farmer a call. His wife answered, and was delighted to hear from me, so I said I'd be over as soon as I'd finished where I was. As I did so, I realised that quite a few bunnies had appeared with the falling light, so I slipped an NV add-on

to the HMR's scope and shot a couple to feed the dog. A rapid lunch and the remains were chucked in a plastic tray in the back of the Landy.

A quick drive through the lanes saw me at the evening's new destination. Luckily, I spotted Rob herding his cows into the dairy, so was able to have a useful chat with him about where all the livestock was located. That done, I parked up and got myself ready. As I was still wearing my face veil and had the NV monocular hanging around my neck, I was off in moments. The first job was to scan the field I'd parked up in. I was quite high up, so had a good view down towards the stream at the bottom of the valley, some 300yd away. The paddock to my right had three horses in it, and in among them were a few bunnies, their eyes shining brightly in the IR from my laser illuminator. But as there appeared to be nothing else around, I decided to check the fields on the other side of the lane.

The recent rain had combined with the red Devon soil to create a thick glutinous mud, not only difficult to walk through, but almost impossible to cross quietly. I did my best to navigate around the worst bits, using the barely perceptible reflections from the standing water to choose the best route. Having made it to the solidity of the tarmac road, I made my way to the opposite gateway, some 100yd further on. While climbing over, I took advantage of the extra height to

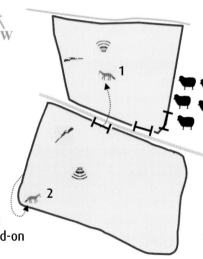

have a good scan around. There was nothing close by, so I gingerly dismounted and set off again.

A few paces out and the ground in front of me dropped about a 100ft down in a steep slope towards another stream. This one was about 200yd out, and snaked along the valley bottom between margins fringed with various small trees, mostly hazel, hawthorn and blackthorn, with the odd oak and ash saplings appearing here and there. Underneath, long grass and scrub – all of which provides great cover – making it very popular with roe deer. Indeed, as I watched, two does were browsing away quietly in the distance.

The field to my right had a small flock of sheep lying up under the far hedge, and a fine mist was hanging in the air. There was a breeze, but it was slight and from behind me, coming over the hedge and then blowing diagonally down towards the valley bottom. I figured that if I positioned the caller carefully, I might be able to bring a fox up from the cover, so set off towards the hedge on my left in search of a good ambush point. One of the problems with our local terrain is that the hilly ground can make it hard to find anywhere level enough to set out a tripod. Fortunately, I was able to squeeze myself under some tall bushes, these would hide my silhouette, and with a bit of juggling I got the sticks to stand nicely.

I put the caller out at 60 paces, then returned to get myself ready. Firstly, I checked the area for any sign of foxes with the spotter, but as nothing was about, I then got the NV riflescope focused on the area where I thought a fox might appear. When I was happy that everything was to my satisfaction, I used the remote to start the caller. I began with a series of fox squalls (short yaps), then hit mute. I do this to tell any foxes in the area that 'someone' is on their patch. I left it a minute or so – checking all the while with the mono, before starting another series of squalls – about ten in all. I kept checking for any signs of foxes, but without seeing anything. Matters weren't helped by the fact that the air was so damp that I had to keep wiping the spotter's eyepiece with a lens cloth. In fact, it got so bad that in the end I simply kept the small square of material in my left hand so that I wouldn't have to go searching for it each time my vision was obscured by the fogged-over lens.

Having used the squalls to broadcast the presence of an interloper, I switched the caller to vixen on heat – while this track works well throughout the year, in the mating season, it can be especially good. No matter how hard I looked though, there were no foxes to be seen anywhere. On one of my sweeps with the mono, however, I looked back over my shoulder and there, coming over the brow of the hill, was a large dog fox. He must have been very sure of himself, as he was approaching from upwind. In my opinion only the area's alpha male will do this, as most foxes will loop around to come in from downwind, in order to minimise the chances of getting beaten up by a bigger individual.

Fortunately, I was able to reposition the sticks and switch the riflescope on with plenty of time to spare. When I looked, the fox was still coming down the hill and had his nose down sniffing the ground as he went. He must have scented where I'd walked across the field, but I assume he was more interested in the vixen call as he didn't appear to be at all spooked. I carefully tracked him with the crosshairs, and the moment he paused to look up, a hollow-point from my .22-250 stopped him. He went down on the spot at about 60yd – I'd aimed a little high to allow for the combination of close range and high scope mounting – and hit him exactly where I'd intended. On later examination he proved (just as I'd suspected) to be a large dog, and almost certainly the local boss. I left the caller going for a bit, but when nothing else showed, I retrieved him and moved on.

Hiking back over the hill, I dumped the carcass where the farmer could find it, and re-crossed the lane to where my truck was parked. Again, I scanned the field below to see if anything was about. A few rabbits were huddled up nibbling away on the unseasonally fresh greenery, but the thick blanket of mist hanging above the stream meant that I could

not see more than a couple of hundred yards. Still, it was worth a try, so I set the caller out once again. I repeated the squall/vixen routine, but after about 15 minutes without any action, decided it was time to call it a night. I counted out the requisite number of paces, but couldn't find the caller in the long grass, nothing new there, it happens all the time. I could have used the mono to locate it as the aerial has a piece of reflective tape on it, but instead I simply cranked the volume right down and switched it on. Moments later, it was safely back in my pocket.

As is my habit, I then had a quick scan around before moving off. I was somewhat surprised to see a pair of fox eyes looking straight at me from the nearby hedge. The horses in the paddock behind were far too close for any chance of a safe shot, but even if they hadn't been there, I wouldn't have had time to act as the eyes disappeared moments later. I quickly moved to a safer position, and tried the caller again – with it still in my pocket – but the fox didn't reappear. From the lack of brightness in the eyes and the apparent nervousness, I was willing to bet that it was a vixen looking to see who was calling on her territory. Unwilling to give up, I carefully walked back over to the higher ground next to the hedge and began scanning around to see if I could find any sign of life.

About a minute later, a set of fox eyes suddenly appeared some way off in the hedge. I quickly got the rifle up on the sticks, but was a bit confused as I could only see its head. The field behind it was clear of livestock and as there was no mistaking the fact that it was a fox, the shot would be safe enough. Since it clearly wasn't going to move out of cover in a hurry, I got the crosshairs centred between its eyes and settled myself. When I was 100% happy that the shot was a good one, I slowly squeezed the trigger. A moment after hearing the shot ring out, I heard a slap like a ruler being thwacked onto a table. 'Ooh – that hit something hard', I thought to myself.

I quickly slung the rifle over my shoulder, folded the sticks up, and set off down the hill. About a 100yd out, I put my driving glasses on and got my adjustable-focus torch out. As this gives a nice powerful beam, I thought it would help me search the thick vegetation that runs along the base of the hedgeline. No matter how hard I looked though, I

Although I knew the shot had been a good one, I couldn't find the carcass anywhere. I searched the edge of the field and the base of the hedge for some time, before finally looking over the bank – and there it was.

couldn't see anything fox-like, and when I reached the corner of the field, some 170yd out, I started to wonder if I'd hit a rock instead. I then noticed that there was a well-used animal run under a bush which went up over the bank and out of sight. In frustration I shone the torch over the bank, and there was my dead fox – I'd hit it in the skull and the round had taken most of its shoulders out. It was, as I'd suspected, a medium-sized vixen. No wonder I could only see its head, its body was obscured by the bank! I called in on Rob as I left and gave him the news of my efforts. He was very pleased indeed.

The next evening I went elsewhere, and dropped a large dog fox at about 160yd. The night after that though, I returned to see if I could find any more of Rob's foxes. I parked in the same place and went though a similar routine, checking the various fields as I went. There were two significant differences in the conditions though. Firstly, there was even more moisture in the air – this was showing up as light fog that was hanging at about tree-height – and secondly, the wind was acting very strangely. One minute it was blowing from the south-east, the next it was coming from the north-west. I realised

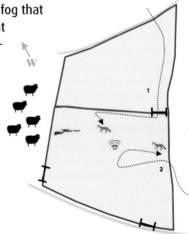

immediately that if I was going to be successful, I was going to have to think it all through very carefully indeed.

When I got to the gate, I was able to clamber up onto it unheard. From my vantage point, I was able to see that the sheep were no longer away in the field on the right, they were now right in front of me. This was good news, for the other field was much more suitable for calling, as its concave shape makes it easy to see for miles. Before going anywhere though, I used the mono to check in among the ewes – many is the time that I've found a fox lurking in the middle of a flock of sheep. All was well though, so I made my way through the thick mud beyond the gate until I found some firm footing. From there on it was simple going, and it only took me a minute or so to get to my chosen ambush position.

Since the wind was constantly changing direction, I decided to put the caller out a bit further than usual to minimise the risk of me being unwittingly compromised. I normally go for a distance of 50 to 60 paces — the shape of the ground or the presence of long grass is the usual limiting factor – but on this occasion the excellent visibility allowed me to position it at 80 paces. The rifle is zeroed at a 100yd, so it's better all round.

As before, I started with a short series of squalls, then gave it a minute or two before repeating them. After that I got the vixen on heat track playing, and within a few seconds a set of eyes showed some 500yd away, below me and to the front. They were moving very fast indeed, so I wasted no time in getting the mono switched off and the riflescope ready. The fox ran in behind the hedge that bordered the lower edge of the field, and then appeared on my side. Its eyes were on fire in the light from my illuminator – 'Dog' I thought to myself. Although it was in a real hurry, it was still nervous enough to come up the hedge towards me (away from the caller) in order to get properly downwind. The moment it was on the scent-line, it stopped and looked out into the field. That was the last thing it

TIPS & TRICKS

Crossing gates is bad enough in the daylight, but can be a real problem to anyone who hunts after dark. Some are so rickety that you risk life and limb just going near them. Others have bolts that screech when you try to move them, or hinges that creak the second you try to open them. Learning which gates are safe and which aren't is all part and parcel of checking out new permissions.

saw though, as a well-placed hollow-point dropped it on the spot.

The moment it fell, I went back to using the mono – it has half the magnification (x3) of the riflescope, and therefore has a much better field of view for spotting incoming foxes. I left the caller going and about a minute later another set of eyes appeared – this time they were uphill of me to my right, and some 400yd away. I couldn't be sure whether they belonged to a dog or vixen though, but whatever it was, it was moving at a hell of a speed. In the minute or so since the first fox came in, the wind had changed direction again, and as a result this individual approached the caller from above. It kept running until it was about 120yd out and then stopped briefly. I got the crosshairs on it, but just as I fired, it jumped forwards, resulting in a miss. I cursed but immediately reloaded. The fox turned and ran back towards the hedge, then made the mistake of stopping to look over its shoulder just as it got there. This time the round hit home, and the Charlie turned a full somersault before landing inert on the ground.

After a few more minutes with no activity, I collected the caller and went to examine the foxes. The first one was a large dog, with a black tail and a good body weight – I'd estimate it to have been around 22lb. The round had hit it perfectly, right in the engine room with barely a mark to be seen, and as a result it would have been a good candidate for taxidermy. It wasn't big enough for me though, so I left it where it was. The second fox proved to be a large vixen, again, hit in the chest. I put it with the first one and moved on. Nothing else showed that evening, and after a couple of hours a combination of tiredness and fog encouraged me to pack it in and go home. Once again I called in on Rob to give him a situation report. He was clearly delighted that I was having so much success, and as I've said before, from my perspective a happy farmer is, indeed, a very good thing!

ADDITIVE FOXING

DATE:	21 November 2010	**RIFLE:**	Sauer 202
PLACE:	Aubrey's Farm	**CALIBRE:**	.308
TIME:	18:30	**AMMO:**	110gr Hornady V-Max
SUNSET:	16:22	**RANGE:**	75yd and 55yd
STATE OF MOON:	Full moon, full cloud cover	**CALL TRACK:**	None
		OPTICS:	Swarovski Z6 2.5-15x56 with D480 GenIII add-on
WEATHER:	Cold and damp; mizzle		
WIND DIRECTION:	North-easterly		

Once again, I spent the latter part of a Sunday afternoon at Aubrey's, trying to stalk some reds. Unfortunately, the part of the valley that I usually patrolled didn't seem to have been visited by them that year. No one knew why – it'd always been very popular in the past and there were plenty of deer in the nearby valleys. Anyway, after it got dark, I fitted my NV add-on to the scope and switched the 165gr soft-point .308s for some dedicated fox rounds I had put together. These were 110gr V-Max: the lighter bullet weight and lower powder charge were intended to reduce the recoil so that the tube in my NV wasn't destroyed by the recoil. I'd also fitted a slip-on butt extension to give me a little more head room.

At first I tried using the caller, but to no avail, so I 'stalked' my way back to the farm, using my hand-held NV monocular. After checking out a couple of large fields, I opened a gate and went through as quietly as I could. In doing so, I managed to catch the sliding bolt with my arm, making it clatter like hell. Cursing, I gently closed the gate and had a quick scan around. On the skyline above, I spotted a set of eyes looking straight down at me. Close together and bright, they looked just like those of a fox. They then disappeared, so I crept up a few yards and had another look. I caught a brief flash

of eyes in the same place, so was hopeful that I might get a shot in. Setting the sticks up, I placed the rifle on them and checked that the NV add-on was adjusted properly.

I then moved forward another 15yd or so until I could examine the area where the animal had last been spotted. Using the hand-held, I could see what appeared to be a fox curled up on the ground, looking away from me. I've seen them do this before, presumably, like humans, they like to have a rest after they've had a big meal. There had been so many pheasants around that they'd had plenty to eat...

I then had another look but this time through the NV add-on (which is on the back of a Swarovski scope). In doing so, I managed to confuse myself even more, due to the light mizzle I couldn't get a decent focus and therefore couldn't decide whether I was looking at a hare or a fox. I therefore made a bunny squeal with my lips and a fox's head turned to look at me. I didn't need to know any more, so gave the trigger a gentle squeeze and there was a hydraulic 'pop' sound as the ballistic-tip did its job. On examination, I found it was a good-sized vixen.

Satisfied that I'd done all the right things, I then moved on into the next field, which was full of sheep. As there was no sign of any foxes, I

TIPS & TRICKS

Add-on night visions systems can be a real bonus. They allow you to hunt in daylight with your normal optics, and then by simply sliding on an attachment, you can carry on after it gets dark. They do, however, have severe limitations, and these need to be taken into account or you will be sorely disappointed. Firstly, the field of view is limited, and secondly, the amount of light that passes through your telescopic sight will fall dramatically as you increase the zoom. This means that you will need an extra illuminator, or you won't be able to see anything.

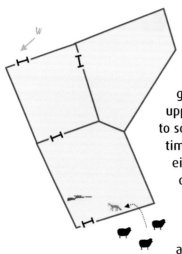

climbèd through the gate at the far side. Rather conveniently, it has a large human-sized gap between the two upper rails, so I was able to squeeze through – this time without clanking either myself or any of my equipment against it.

On looking into the field below, I almost immediately spotted a fox heading up towards the hedge into the field I'd just come from, so I wormed my way back through the gate and started scanning for my target. After a couple of minutes, I spotted it against the far hedge. Just as I was trying to decide whether to use the caller to bring it my way, it turned and started coming up the hedgeline towards me. I quickly set the bipod on the top of a large agricultural trailer that happened to be in a convenient place, and waited for a clear shot. More or less as soon as I got the crosshairs lined up, the fox stopped and turned to jump back through the hedge again. I fired as it was about to launch itself into the air. This time there was no 'pop', and no sign of movement either. I worked out where I thought it had been, and spent about ten minutes walking from there down to the end of the hedge. Nothing. Making my way back again, I realised that I must have started searching about 2ft too far along the hedge, because the fox, another vixen, was lying exactly where I'd shot it. So, no deer, but Aubrey was very happy!

The fox seen here (**ABOVE**) was shot using a rear add-on NV system with an IR illuminator mounted above the scope. The extra length of the NV forces your head back a long way, so I tried using a slip-on stock extension to see if that helped with my shooting position. I didn't like it, so removed it before shooting the second fox (**BELOW**) a few minutes later.

Before I could go any further, however, all the optics needed wiping down, including the laser illuminators on the mono and riflescope. That done, I set the FOXPRO Scorpion out – I opted for a distance of 75 paces – a little more than usual simply to minimise the risk of being scented if the wind shifted. While I was doing this, I could hear the fox barking again, unfortunately it was clearly moving away. I hoped that the caller would bring it back towards me and immediately set to with eight short yaps, known as squalls, then hit mute. After a brief scan around, I tried another series of squalls, then muted them again. As I did so, I heard the fox bark again – this time it was even further way. I cursed and decided that it was time to try the vixen on heat call instead.

Before I was able to do so, however, I had to dry all the optics off once more. The rain was now coming down as a fine mist and this was playing havoc with the lenses. Having done that and satisfied myself that all was OK, I started the vixen track – after about five minutes nothing had showed, so I paused it and waited. In the past, I've had foxes come several minutes after I'd finished with the caller, so I wasn't in a hurry to move. Two or three minutes later – and after another rain shower, I decided to vary things, and tried the vixen mating call. I left it going for what seemed like ages, but to no avail. Eventually I hit mute again while I considered matters, while I was doing so I dried the optics out, again.

Half way through another scan, I suddenly caught a flash of eyes. They were in the far hedge, some 250yd away. I quickly switched the mono off and turned the NV riflescope on. A few focus ad-

justments and I was tracking the fox with the rifle nicely balanced on my sticks. By now, it was halfway across and closing the gap rapidly. Since the caller was still on mute, it wasn't quite sure where to look – and that suited me just fine – it would buy me more time. Tweaking the focus adjuster kept my target crisp and clear as it zigzagged around looking for the would-be vixen. There was no way that I was going to rush the shot, but having said that, I couldn't risk the fox getting too close to the caller, or it would surely detect my scent and make a run for it.

At one point, while it was some 120yd out it paused for a sniff – it was facing me and had its nose in the air. This was my cue to lean on the trigger. Milliseconds later, there was a loud, hard-edged 'pop' and my intended target fell on the spot. I briefly checked that there were no other foxes about with the mono and then set off to examine my kill. Even as I approached it I could see that it was a big dog fox. It was lying outstretched in the moonlight, with its tail slightly curled. I laid my sticks down alongside, then put the rifle on top of them. My Sauer measures 47in from moderator to butt, and as this individual was slightly more, it was a very good size indeed. I photographed it where it lay, then flipped it over – my Sierra BlitzKing had hit it in the lower jaw, and much of its head had exploded. What a mess... I'd estimate it as weighing about 25lb. Certainly bigger than ones I'd previously weighed at 22lb and probably the second biggest one I've taken to date. At 4ft long it was definitely a good result, especially considering that when I'd first heard it, I'd thought it was an owl!

When I first heard this huge fox calling, the sound it made was so odd I thought it must have come from an owl. As soon as I realised what it was, I rushed to find a suitable position to set the caller up. It responded to the vixen mating call, and I shot it head-on at about 120yd.

DECEMBER

December is a variable month – in some years it is mild – in others, however, it can be extremely cold, as evidenced in this photo.

With December comes a month of long, cold nights. While these are not enjoyed by many, they are just what a busy foxer needs. Getting out earlier than usual can mean returning home before the rest of the household has retired, which is usually a popular thing. Foxes start moving earlier as a result, and some will cover enormous distances in their search for food. The stillness of the dark will often be pierced by the shrill cries of mating calls. Every now and then, however, you may hear a much more unnerving sound if there is a fight taking place, where the losing animal will often issue a series of blood-curdling screams. It is not uncommon to see foxes that have clearly just been involved in such a battle with open wounds bearing testament to the severity of life low on the vulpine social ladder. Sometimes, these unfortunate creatures will tear headlong into even more trouble in their desperation to evade their tormentors. On some occasions this will mean they run out into a busy main road, with predictably terminal results. On others they might end up in someone's rifle sights – again, with potentially fatal consequences. The Chinese ancients had a saying: the bravest tiger is the

THE FARMER'S MONTH
Livestock fed indoors.
Ploughing and spraying.
Turkeys and geese killed for Christmas market.
General machine and building maintenance.
Hedges and fences maintained

first killed. This is equally true for foxes and is why an old fox will always approach a situation from down-wind if it can.

The usual hazards of fog, mist and mud can be encountered throughout the month, however, one advantage is that pretty well all the livestock will have been locked away in sheds for the winter. This means that farmers may be prepared to allow you to leave the gates open. Always check with them first though, as they may need to move some stock into the fields you've been in, and will be deeply unimpressed if the animals concerned simply run out of open gates at the other end. Also, many farmers will have genuine concerns about security – especially of their quad bikes and diesel storage tanks – and so may want to keep some gates shut. If you see unidentified people or vehicles where you are not expecting them, you should stop to think what action you should take. Approaching innocent strangers while armed to the teeth is likely to result in your firearms being confiscated while enquiries are made. On a more serious note, approaching criminals could quickly get out of hand, so the best thing is definitely to back off and make some rapid phone calls to establish the score. All farmers appreciate having people watch out for their interests, so even if it's nothing, you will earn some Brownie points.

Aside from the livestock being shut away, one of the other main benefits of shooting in December is that all the crops – including the dreaded cattle maize – should have been cut. In most areas this massively reduces the places that foxes can hide and so it is a good time to catch up with them. Pretty well all the usual prey distress and fox mating calls can work well at this time of year – but always remember that it is better to not use the caller at all, than to use it in the wrong place or in the wrong manner. Teaching a fox that certain sounds mean danger is not a good thing, so use them sparingly. Where there's any doubt, it's much better to put bait down, when there's not much else to eat few foxes will pass it by.

The cold weather will have forced any field-dwelling rats to seek shelter in sheds and barns. Not only does this give you the chance to earn more smiles from the farmer by shooting some of them, but it also means that rodent distress calls can be used near any buildings with good effect. If it's too rainy to go wandering about in open country, then you might find it better to set up under the cover of a suitable structure. If you're lucky and find the right place, you should be able to settle yourself down somewhere comfortable, out of the wind and away from the rain. Then all you need to do is put lots of smelly bait out – preferably regularly – and the foxes will start coming to you.

On the subject of bait, it's well worth giving some thought to what the foxes are likely to be feeding on in your area. If there's a regular supply of anything, even if it's of low nutritional value, it's going to be exploited by any hungry Charlies that are about. This includes windfall apples, cattle feed pellets and anything left lying around by humans, such as fast-food containers and bags of domestic refuse. If you're in any doubt as to whether a resource is being visited, then if it's safe to do so from a security point of view, it's a good idea to set a trail camera up covering the spot. That way, you'll get a good idea of not only how many foxes are passing by, but also at what times.

Since food will nearly always be in short supply at this time of year, another place where it can be helpful to use trail cameras is near poultry pens. Foxes can be relied on to inspect the integrity of any such cages on a regular basis. The owners may not have reported any attacks, but it's far better to find out that the foxes are there and to deal with them before anything bad happens than it is to have to do so afterwards. Many commercial breeders rely on the Christmas trade in turkeys, ducks and geese to pay the bills, and as it is simply not possible for them to replace any birds in December, it can be very bad news if they lose any to predators. A successful session at such places can often result in the welcome donation of the odd pack of sausages or a few rashers of bacon!

ABOVE: Life is good as a hunter's dog. Not only do you get fed on pheasant, rabbit and venison offcuts, but as a bonus you get deer legs to chew on too…

BELOW: Burrs may look picturesque, but they can be a real nuisance if they get tangled up in clothes or animal hair.

FOUR ON THE FLOOR

DATE:	1 December 2011	**RIFLE:**	Sauer 202
PLACE:	Nick's Farm	**CALIBRE:**	.22-250
TIME:	19:00	**AMMO:**	55gr Sierra BlitzKing
SUNSET:	16:14	**RANGE:**	60, 130, 90 and 220yd
STATE OF MOON:	Evening crescent, bright	**CALL TRACK:**	First three, no call. Last
WEATHER:	Cold, with sporadic cloud cover		fox came to vixen heat
WIND DIRECTION:	North-westerly	**OPTICS:**	D480 GenIII NV riflescope

In 'Four Foot Owl' (see p. 172) I recounted how I called in and shot a very large dog fox. That had brought my yearly total to 89, and I was trying to make it to a round 100, so I headed out again a couple of night's later for another session. This time my plan was to shoot over a farm that lies in the foothills a few miles to the north of Exeter. I had been to school with Nick, the farmer, so had known him for many years. The place was overrun with rabbits and as a result had a significant population of foxes. Since Nick has a small pheasant shoot as well as a large dairy herd, foxes are not welcome. Not only do they kill his birds, but they also spread a parasitic infection: neospora, which causes spontaneous abortion in cattle, horses and sheep.

As darkness fell, I got everything ready. I'd already charged the batteries for my caller and thermal imager (the ones in the NV last for months), so I got the ammo sorted, boresnaked the .22-250, and loaded everything into the truck.

The half-hour drive over is not one I enjoy, which is why I don't visit the farm more often. The hedge-bound lanes are single track for most of the way and in early evening all the city workers are heading home. This meant that I was pulling over or reversing back every half mile or so in order to allow them to squeeze by.

The land I was going to be hunting over comprises of steep hills interspersed with low-lying lush meadows and frequent streams. Although the landscape is beautiful, the farm can be an absolute pain for NV users. The amount of water around the place means the air tends to be more like fine mist which

not only makes it hard to see very far, but also causes the optics to fog up in moments. Another hassle is that the fields run right up to a village, most of the inhabitants of which are archetypal suburbanites. Fortunately, few of them seem to walk their dogs at night, but even so, the lights from their houses can make things very difficult.

Slightly frazzled by the drive, I pulled into the farmyard. Nick soon appeared and when the subject swung around to foxes, he said that although they'd shot several, he'd seen two near his pheasants, and he wanted them dealt with. I explained that I was going to start in the meadows on the other side of the lane, and that I'd then move up to the higher ground where his shoot is based. He wished me luck and went back to his supper.

My plans fell apart the moment I crossed the lane. Unfortunately I found that the massive sodium

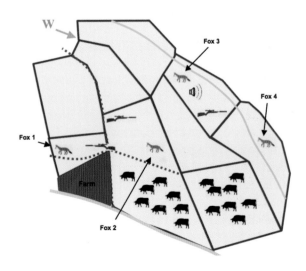

lamps he uses to keep his dairy unit lit were also illuminating the entire valley. Trying to hunt there would have been futile, so I turned around and walked back up through the yard to try my luck in the fields on the other side. I wasn't sure if I was going to have it all my own way there either as the moon, which was sitting high in the sky, was threatening to come out from behind the dark clouds which blanketed most of the sky.

The first bit of ground I reached is a small paddock which holds the family's pony. As I'm very careful to avoid spooking anything unnecessarily, I made some reassuring noises by quietly clicking my tongue. Having heard me do this many times, the animal knew who and what I was. Checking around with the NV monocular, I found that one of the farm cats was sitting on one of the many pieces of agricultural machinery watching me. I'm always very careful where cats and foxes are concerned, as it is frighteningly easy to mistake one for the other if you only go by eye reflection: it's vital that you also get a positive physical ID. Fortunately, good equipment that is properly set up makes this very straightforward. Sweeping around to my left immediately gave me another observation test, for there was a second very bright set of eyes looking right at me. ID-ing it proved easy though – it was a Little Owl sitting on a low run of fence wire. These beautiful birds feed on a wide variety of small creatures like beetles and worms, and I always take great pleasure in seeing them. After watching it for a while – taking care to keep the IR off it to avoid any risk to its eyes – I walked the remaining few yards to the main track that bisects the farm.

On reaching it, I had another look around. There were about 15 rabbits in the field ahead of me, but as I watched the mono began to mist over, so I switched to the thermal. Within moments, I'd picked up a large white shape about 100yd out that looked suspiciously like a fox. A quick double-check with the mono showed that I was in business and as it was trotting straight towards me, there was no time to waste. I got the tripod sticks up, the Sauer in place, and switched the riflescope on. The fox came in to about 60yd, then realised that I was there. Not knowing what I was, it sat back on its haunches for a better look. Moments later a Blitzking hit it with a loud

'smack', right in the engine room and it fell to the ground, dead as a dodo.

Now that's not bad going, I thought to myself – less than a minute out and I've already notched up a good kill. On examination, it proved to be a very well-sized dog fox.

Following the path trodden by untold numbers of dairy cows over the years, I continued on into the next field. This is a vast area of lush grassland that begins at a hedge high to the left and then runs downhill for several hundred yards before ending at the lane far down to the right.

There were rabbits everywhere I looked but some way out, right in among them, was the sharp glow from a set of fox eyes. There was no doubting what I was looking at: its tail gave me a positive ID, so I ducked under the electric fence to my left in order to take advantage of the background cover provided by the tall hedge. Making my way along it, I had another look. The fox was still there so I set the sticks up and tried to find it with the riflescope. In those few seconds, however, it had somehow disappeared. Mystified, I had another look with the mono, and picked it up straight away. Back to the scope, and it had gone again. I repeated this a couple more times, and finally convinced myself that the problem was that it was just in the lee of the rise that lay between me and it. In other words, I could see it when I stood up straight to use the mono, but not when I leant forward onto the scope. The only solution would be to move up the hill a little so that I could see into the dead ground.

A few yards was all it took to see into the previously hidden area but there was no fox in sight. I was convinced that it hadn't left the field – none of the bunnies around the edge had shifted or appeared spooked – so where could it be? I had a very slow scan around with the mono, and saw that there was something dark in the grass. It was too big to be a cow pat, too long to be a rabbit. Maybe it was a piece of debris that the farmer had left behind? A quick check with the thermal immediately told me otherwise: whatever it was, it was alive.

One of the things I've learned about foxes is that when they're hunting, they can be incredibly patient. Many is the time that I've seen them walk past a load of ultra-nervous bunnies and then simply curl up and go to sleep. A while later – long after the rabbits have forgotten all about it being there, the fox picks a victim and pounces before it knows what's happening. It was my bet that this was what I was seeing. I knew it wasn't looking in my direction, as I wasn't seeing any eye reflection, so I was hopeful that I'd be able to close the distance enough to properly identify and shoot it. I had to be careful: every couple of minutes or so the moon came out and lit up the landscape.

I watched the clouds for a bit, and decided that the dark area that was moving towards the moon would hide it for at least a couple of minutes, so I moved back towards the hedge and then circled around to the top of the field. This put me well away from any possible scent risk and also gave me a height advantage. I still wasn't 100% sure that it was a fox, so I waited until the moon was obscured, and moved 20 paces forward. When I looked through the mono, I could see that a few yards away, a rabbit was on its hind legs checking out the unidentified shape. I counted another 20 paces forwards and checked again. This time, the shape had two prominent fox ears, and about a minute later, it raised its head. At last a positive ID and it was game-on. I waited until it put its head back down, and counted out yet another 20 paces: now I was within a healthy range. With the sticks out and the rifle in place, I began observing my target. The fox was now lying with its eyes open quietly watching another rabbit that had wandered a bit too close for safety. I held back until it raised its head again, then sent a round on its way. There was the unmistakable sound of a central body hit. The fox just rolled on its side without even twitching.

I counted out the distance – 130 paces – and in doing so spooked a woodcock that rocketed up squawking in alarm. On examination, the carcass was that of a medium-sized vixen and the hit was a good solid chest shot. I moved its remains to the side of the track, next to a cattle trough where it could be found in the morning. A look around showed me that the rest of the field only held bunnies – and that most of them were standing up watching what was going on. At that moment the mono began to mist over again, so I moved on. Although the ground was very wet, the going was relatively easy, in stark contrast to that of the previous session, where the mud had been so thick that I'd sunk at every step.

The next field was bordered on one side by the lane and on another by houses. Before leaving, I checked for any sign of foxes, but apart from yet more rabbits, there was nothing of note. My plan was to move up and across into the next valley, but to minimise the risk of being scented by foxes, I first circled around the lower hedgeline and then made my way over the brow. Wiping the mono down every couple of minutes, I kept checking around me. There were rabbits everywhere, and I could hear many of them stamping their feet in alarm.

Once my silhouette was clear of the ridgeline, I paused for a less-rushed look. Before me was a small valley at the bottom of which was a narrow stream running through a large water meadow. On the far side was a high bank and above that a field. As the mist made it hard to see much with the NV at that distance – some 500yd or so – I used the thermal. There were so many rabbits that it would have been close to impossible to count them: imagine looking at the stars on a clear night, there were that many! I saw 47 just along the hedge that ran 50yd in front of me. Suddenly, while I was still observing the landscape, the silence was shattered by the shrill scream of a young rabbit. The fox – for I was sure that was what was responsible – could only have been a few yards beyond the hedge.

I picked my way as quietly as I could down to the gate which led into the water meadow, then climbed up and took advantage of the extra height to scan again. Unfortunately, there was absolutely no sign of Charlie – just more bunnies. In the valley's shelter the breeze was very light and moving from my left to right, so I decided that if I

> **TIPS & TRICKS**
>
> When a fox eats a big meal, it has to rest while the food is digested. When this is the case it will only move if it feels threatened and won't respond to a caller. It will often lie up in a place that has a good view over the surrounding area. That way, it will have time to run or hide if danger looms.

couldn't find the fox, I'd put the caller out. Once I was back on the ground, however, I realised that there was just too much light coming from the houses away to my right. Luckily, I found that as the hedge ran around the side of the hill, it curved off into darkness, so I followed it and got myself well out of the unwanted illumination.

I was hoping that I was now in a good position to use the caller. There was a large wood in front of me, with excellent visibility everywhere else. While checking the lie of the land, I spotted an unidentified shape in the grass – I couldn't be sure what it was. The thermal told me that it was alive, but at that stage I didn't know whether it was two rabbits side by side, or a fox. I moved a bit closer, trying to ignore the bunnies stamping their feet on the other side of the hedge. At about 90yd out, I set the sticks up and had another look. Once again, a set of fox ears gave the game away. It was lying on the ground eating something – presumably the unfortunate rabbit I'd heard scream a few minutes earlier – I waited until it began to stand up, and then fired. Much like the first one, it flipped up into the air then fell to the ground and expired.

Since I'd decided that the spot was ideal for calling, I left the fox where it was and put the caller out at 75 paces, ensuring that the wind was taking my scent off down the valley. Returning to the sticks, I had another check around, dried the optics again, then started the caller with a short series of fox squalls before turning them off. The mono showed me that nothing was stirring. It was now time to move on to the vixen on heat call. After a couple of minutes with no positive signs, I was beginning to wonder if I'd already shot all the foxes in the area, but then I caught a flash of eyes. They were about 400yd out but the bad news was that they were directly downwind of me.

I dried the optics again and checked that no other foxes had snuck in towards the caller. Nope. Going back to the eyes, I could see that they had moved closer – and the animal they belonged to had now broken cover and I could positively identify that they were those of a Charlie. I quickly repositioned the sticks and got riflescope switched on. By then the fox had stopped about 200yd out and was sitting just over a rise in the ground, looking towards the caller.

This was the last of four foxes on what proved to be a busy night. There was all manner of wildlife out and about, ranging from the farm cat to a beautiful Little Owl, which sat and watched me as I went about my business.

There was plenty of safe backstop, but before I was able to take a shot, it moved off, running across the valley and away towards the next field. As it reached the foot of the large boundary bank it paused, just to the left of a large oak tree. By then I was ready and to allow for the range, aimed for a high chest shot. I fired and moments later heard a loud 'pop'. The fox dropped on the spot.

I checked around again, but as there was nothing to be seen, apart from – you guessed it – yet more bunnies. I left the sticks where they were and walked down the valley, across the stream and up to the bank to the left of the oak tree. As I couldn't see the carcass with the mono, I switched to the thermal. But there was still no sign of it. So I put my driving glasses on and powered up my torch. No matter how hard I looked though, I couldn't find it. Rather frustrated, I stood back and scratched my head. Just then, I noticed that further along there was another big oak tree. Could I have got them mixed up? As anything is possible in the dark, I walked over towards it and a few yards on there was my Charlie. A big dog fox hit with a perfect chest shot.

I counted the number of paces back to my sticks – 222. I retrieved the caller before examining the previous fox. It was yet another large dog fox, this one was by far the biggest of the three I'd had that night. So, that was another four on the floor, which meant I only had to get another seven to reach my goal of 100 for the year!

HIGH FIVE

DATE:	10 December 2010	**RIFLE:**	Sauer 202
PLACE:	Andy's Farm	**CALIBRE:**	.22-250
TIME:	18:00–20:00	**AMMO:**	55gr PPU SP
SUNSET:	16:10	**RANGE:**	100yd, 60yd 100yd and
STATE OF MOON:	Evening crescent		150yd
WEATHER:	Cold and cloudy	**CALL TRACK:**	Various prey distress
WIND DIRECTION:	North-westerly	**OPTICS:**	D480 GenIII NV riflescope

I got an email one December Thursday from Andy, a local game dealer and keen shooter. He said he'd seen five foxes on his ground the previous night and he was keen to get to grips with them. I'd shot several on his place that year, but I always found his land very difficult to hunt over as it runs along the side of a busy road. One section of this is disposed such that any cars on it light up the whole area, making it impossible to make any covert approaches. There is a big field on the other side of the hill, but you can only get into this from one entrance – and as Sod's Law would have it – it lies directly upwind of the predominant wind direction, so for most of the time you can't get in it without alerting any foxes there.

TIPS & TRICKS

If you're setting up an ambush with a caller, it's a good idea to look for a fixed object on the skyline somewhere above where you plan to site it. If you then head towards this reference point while counting the number of steps, it'll make your life much easier when it comes time to retrieve the caller – especially if the batteries have gone flat and you can't turn it on to help locate it!

The middle part of the farm would be fine, except that there's a bungalow with what feels like some sort of aircraft searchlight set up as a security light. The slightest movement in the yard switches the damn thing on – when this happens it's like

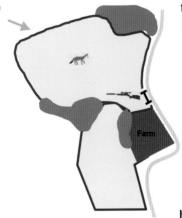

being on stage if you're in any of the fields within about a mile. Consequently, I told Andy that I needed him to sort out permission on some of the nearby properties, if I was going to have a reasonable chance of knocking his foxes down. As he knows everyone for miles, I knew this wouldn't be a problem for him.

Anyway – to cut a very long story short – I turned up at his house early that evening so that I could check the boundaries with a map. He said not to worry, as he'd come along for the first half hour to show me the fields in person. About four hours and five foxes later, he said that he was having far too much fun to go home!

Although I normally shoot on foot, Andy said that we'd be covering over a 1,000 acres, so it would be best if he drove my Disco, and I simply jumped out every now and then to check the various bits of land. The night was cold and dark with a light wind and clouds obscuring what little moon there was. The first farm we stopped at had a Charlie in a field about 100yd out – it was sitting looking straight at me, so I got the NV's reticle nicely lined up on its chest and gently squeezed the trigger. It went down to my .22-250's soft-point round with a resounding 'pop'. It was a good-sized vixen and Andy was very pleased that we'd got one so quickly. On my way out to retrieve the carcass, I spotted two more foxes – one in an adjoining

orchard, the other disappearing off into some woods.

After that we drove about a mile, skirting Andy's farm and those next to it. After passing through a small village, we stopped by another gateway and I climbed up on the gate for a scan with my hand-held NV monocular. I could see two rabbits, but that was all, or so I thought: I then realised that there was a fox going diagonally away from me about 300yd away. His eyes didn't show up in the laser because he wasn't looking at me. I got down nice and quietly and retrieved my rifle and sticks from the truck. Andy parked it up and came back to join me – we then put the FOXPRO caller out in the field, taking care to position it well with regard to the wind. A couple of minutes of distressed snowshoe hare caller produced nothing, so I switched to adult rat distress, and about 30 seconds later a fox came belting in at about 60yd. He also went down with a mighty hydraulic pop. Andy was grinning from ear to ear by now – he said it seemed like magic, that in total darkness I was able to find and shoot a fox – in this case a very large dog with great big pointy teeth.

ABOVE LEFT: This large vixen was the first of five that evening. It fell to a chest shot at about 100yd.

ABOVE: Fox number two wasn't interested in the Snowshoe hare distress call, but came rushing in when the screaming rat track was played instead.

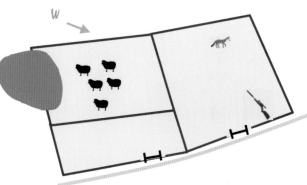

BELOW: These teeth were undoubtedly responsible for the untimely demise of all manner of poultry, lambs and local wildlife, including such things as hedgehogs and dormice.

This large dog fox was caught in the open at about 100yd – there was no time to set the sticks up, so the wooden fence was used as a rest and it went down on the spot.

This scrawny vixen's teeth were in a dreadful condition and she had been reduced to eating semi-rotten apples.

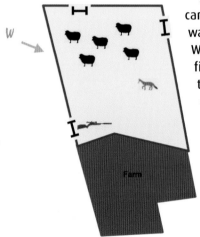

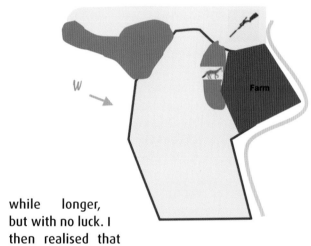

After disposing of the carcass, we made our way back to Andy's land. We checked out the first field: blow me, there was a fox crouching about 100yd out, looking straight at me. The wooden fence was the perfect height, so I lined up a shot, and 'smack' – down it went. This was another dog and by now Andy was jumping up and down with excitement.

We saw nothing for several fields, so made our way back to the first farm where I'd seen the two foxes earlier on. I couldn't see either of them, so set the caller up – again on screaming rat. Before long, two sets of fox eyes appeared, one by the orchard, the other in the field next to it. Just as they were coming in, however, some prat came belting down the narrow, twisty hill and proceeded to lock all his wheels up when he saw the Disco at the side of the road. Luckily, he stopped before there was an impact. Unsurprisingly this spooked the foxes, and the last I saw of them was the bigger of the two legging it over the hill. I kept the caller going for a while longer, but with no luck. I then realised that the smaller of the two foxes was still in the orchard and that it appeared to be eating something off the ground. I didn't think there would be any fruit left for it to eat, but it was clearly scoffing something. As it wasn't interested in the caller, I set up a careful shot, and dropped it on the spot at 150 paces. Sure enough, it had been eating apples. It was a skinny vixen. When we checked, where her front right canine should have been, there was a nasty black stump. The poor thing was clearly starving, but from a farmer's perspective, that's a very dangerous fox as it will risk attacking things like poultry much more readily than a healthy one would.

Andy and I then set off to loop around to come in on the direction where the other fox had run. This was more or less behind his house, so we parked there and made our way up the hill on foot. Although the fields in the area are normally – in his words – 'quite foxy', we saw nothing. We checked all the dead ground we could get near, but to no avail. In the end, we decided to go back to the truck.

On the way, I kept stopping and checking with the monocular and it was just as well that I did, as I found a fox— probably the same one as I'd seen legging it earlier – coming up from some nearby hedges. It was directly downwind of us, but a reasonably long way out, around 150yd or so. It was holding itself tight to the ground and clearly not wanting to draw attention to itself. Once again, I set the sticks up and took my time to take a shot, getting the focus and laser set to my satisfaction. A gentle squeeze on the Sauer's trigger saw the fox fold and roll over with another robust 'smack'. When Andy was looking down at the remains of the large dog fox, he said that he was really impressed by the shot, and shook my hand vigorously!

We did another lap of the farm, and found a fox a long way out, but unfortunately, due to a gully and big hedge, there was no way of getting close. I took a shot, but with the smoke from the rifle obscuring my vision (the light from the laser creates

a bloom), I couldn't see what happened to the Charlie. Nevertheless, we both had a great night, with five foxes less to kill his pheasants and partridges as well as his neighbours' poultry. There were big smiles all round – until we realised that his wife would be less than happy at his interpretation of 'I'll only be half an hour, dear'!

This dog fox spotted us and ran off over the hill. We skirted around and came up on it from the other side, however, ambushing it as it crossed a large open field at about 150yd.

FIRST KILL FOR THE THERMAL

DATE:	17 December 2011	**WIND DIRECTION:**	South-westerly
PLACE:	Jim's Farm	**RIFLE:**	Sauer 202
TIME:	18:45	**CALIBRE:**	.22-250
SUNSET:	16:11	**AMMO:**	55gr Sierra BlitzKing SP
STATE OF MOON:	Waning gibbous,but not visible	**RANGE:**	250yd
		CALL TRACK:	BestFoxCall, mouth caller
WEATHER:	Bitterly cold, clear sky	**OPTICS:**	D480 GenIII NV riflescope

Late in 2011, I bought a huge ex-military thermal imager via an MoD disposal auction. Having spent about three weeks sorting out the various connectors and identifying the output signals, etc. I was ready to take it out for its maiden voyage. Up until then, I'd only had a quick look through it along the side of the house. After it got dark, I drove over to Jim's farm and then up the narrow track to the top of the hill beyond, the idea being that it would give me a chance to see how it worked over a wide landscape. Once parked up, I got my rifle, sticks, mini-thermal and NV mono sorted just in case a fox appeared. Before unloading everything, I had a quick peek into the nearest field – only to see a large Charlie nosing about some 100yd or so out.

I quickly snuck back to the truck and grabbed the rifle together with the sticks, racked a round and turned both the NV riflescope and laser on. I was mortified to discover that the laser was almost completely obscured by dried-out rain drops from the night before. As I was meant to be experimenting with the thermal, I simply hadn't had a chance to give it a clean. I tried waggling it to one side, and this gave me a better view, but to cut a long story short, I fired and missed. I had to put my disappointment to one side while I set to with unloading the very inappropriately-named 'Thermal Lite'. The damned thing weighed over 15lb without the tripod, battery or external viewing screen!

I'd rigged the system so that the thermal was mounted on a huge video tripod via a quickly-detachable fixing. I'd also bought an in-car DVD viewing screen and linked it up so that it was driven by the thermal's output signal. Both the screen and the unit itself were driven off a 12v lead acid motorcycle battery.

Once I was happy that all the requisite leads were connected properly, I gave it all a final once-over and powered it up. The device makes a slight whirring noise as it starts and then takes a couple of minutes to warm up fully. I therefore took the opportunity to see what was about with the NV mono. The night was bitterly cold, with a clear sky above and a slight breeze. The conditions were rather harsh, so I wasn't surprised that there didn't appear to be much about – in fact, I couldn't see any sign of life anywhere.

A slight change in the whirring sound told me that the thermal was ready to go into action, so I

This superb thermal imager was built as a military prototype, but was never put into production. It has since been modified to include a DVD screen to make it more user-friendly. Since it weighs over 15lb without the tripod, it is best used as an area observation system.

switched it into full-scanning mode. Although the unit has its own small viewing module, the DVD screen gives you a far better picture, so that is what I used. I spent the next 10 minutes or so ooh-ing and aah-ing as I swept it back and forth across the valley before me.

The optics on the system are awesome, with the output being somewhat akin to looking at the screen on a black and white television. There is a little shakiness, with horizontal lines being quite evident, but other than that the image is stunning. I almost fell over when I hit what I believed was the zoom button, and a farm building some mile or so away suddenly tripled in size. I was a bit miffed that there were no animals in sight though – I wanted to see how well the system coped with the heat signature of a living creature. It was particularly frustrating as the farm is normally jam-packed with livestock,

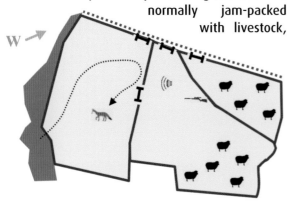

but due to the sodden ground, more or less everything was now sheltering in the various barns and sheds.

A couple of minutes later, however, a white object suddenly ran across a field, about 400yd away. A quick press of the zoom button and I was looking at a fox running flat-out towards the valley below. With a couple of dabs on the focus-adjust buttons I had a crystal clear image. Fantastic! But now was not the time to be watching telly, there was work to do, for this was almost certainly the same fox that I'd missed earlier.

I managed to call it up to the other side of the hedge, but no matter what I tried I couldn't get it to come in any closer. Whether it could see the shiny legs of the tripod under the thermal (I'd not had time to spray them), or whether it was spooked by the IR from my laser, I don't know. Anyway, after about five minutes of it ducking and diving about, it suddenly decided that all was not well and turned to go. It ran diagonally down the field for about 50yd, and then paused briefly to look over its shoulder, before running another 20 or so steps. I got myself ready, and when it paused again, I sent a BlitzKing on its way. There was a dull 'doomph', and it simply fell over. Result!

I counted out 255 paces to the carcass, which had been hit perfectly – right in the engine room. My previous best off sticks was a hit at 250 paces, so when I'd missed earlier there had clearly been nothing wrong with either the rifle or the ammo. It proved to be a large dog fox with both the upper and lower canines missing from the left side of its mouth. It obviously had some age and, I would venture to suggest, could well have been one of the area's problem foxes. I could see that it was certainly a candidate lamb and poultry killer. So, all in all, it was a good night – the thermal had worked beautifully. Not only this, but it had also helped me find and eliminate a large dog fox at a good range and Jim was extremely pleased when I recounted the highlights of the session to him the next morning.

This was a very wary fox. Although it initially responded to the caller, it was obvious that it was not going to come anywhere near me. It clearly had some age to it – its teeth were terrible, and it had both the upper and lower canines missing from the left side of its mouth.

TEN-MINUTE CHICKEN-KILLER

DATE:	20 December 2011	**RIFLE:**	Sauer 202
PLACE:	Stuart's Farm	**CALIBRE:**	.22-250
TIME:	18:00	**AMMO:**	55gr Nosler BT
SUNSET:	16:12	**RANGE:**	75yd
STATE OF MOON:	Morning crescent	**CALL TRACK:**	Young rat distress
WEATHER:	Cold, cloudy, very damp	**OPTICS:**	D480 GenIII NV riflescope
WIND DIRECTION:	Westerly		

One afternoon I found a message on my answerphone from a friend asking me to attend to a fox that had gone in that morning and killed a load of chickens in his paddock. He was very upset as he'd only bought the majority of the birds five days before. Anyway, I told him I'd be over once it was dark, so got myself kitted up about an hour later and set off to see if I could find the culprit.

I have permission on quite a lot of land around his smallholding and on my forays I've seen – and often heard – one fox in particular. He (for his eyes shone like a dog fox), seemed to have the luck of the devil though, as he always managed to be in places where I couldn't shoot – such as the local caravan site, or next to the main road. In the past he'd been wise enough to avoid my vixen calls, so I knew that I'd have to up my game if I was going to successfully take him down.

Pulling into the lane that leads to the adjacent farm, I drove down to a small Dutch barn that conveniently stands a few feet to the right and parked up. I had a quick scan with the NV mono over the corn field which lies beyond, but didn't see anything fox-like. I therefore connected the battery in the FOXPRO caller and placed it 60 paces out in among the stubble. Although I'd used it a lot on the local farms, I couldn't recall using the young rat distress track, so thought that would be a good place to start.

One of the issues I had to take into account was that the main road runs nearby. This presents two main problems: firstly there were the obvious safety concerns and, secondly, the field was lit up by car headlights every few seconds, so I knew I had to take great care to conceal myself if I was going to remain unseen by any approaching foxes. A lesser complication was that the noise of all the vehicles masked the sounds produced by the caller. I dealt with the headlights by positioning myself just inside the barn – that way I was hidden by the interior's nice dark shadows, and, I was pleased to discover, from there the field also rose conveniently away from me, making it even safer to shoot.

I knew that if the fox showed, it would most likely come out of the hedge that ran some 50yd downwind, and that if I was right, I'd get precious little warning of its arrival. I therefore tried to ensure that everything was well prepared. I cleaned the lenses on the IR lasers, got the rifle up on the sticks and my feet in the right shooting stance, checked the NV riflescope was correctly focused for the anticipated range, and so on. When I felt that I was as ready as I could be, I set the caller going. The high-pitched squeaks which echoed around the place sounded perfect, and my mind was on full alert for action. No matter how hard I looked through the NV, however, I couldn't see any sign of Charlie. I did see several small rodents scuttering about in the stubble though, and I hoped that their presence was a good omen, as it meant the fox I was after should be used to hunting them.

> ### TIPS & TRICKS
> Look around to see what the foxes might be feeding on, then use similar calls. If there are lots of rats about, for example, start with rodent distress cries. Likewise for rabbits, chickens, pheasants and so on. A fox is much more likely to respond if it hears sounds that it is used to hearing.

After about 10 minutes, I switched to the small thermal that hangs around my neck – the NV mono was starting to mist up in the wet air, and I wanted to double-check that I wasn't missing anything in the shadows. Just as I raised it to my eyes, a large white form appeared in the monitor – there was no time to switch it off, so I just let it go and reached for the controls on the riflescope. I picked the fox up in moments and immediately arched my trigger finger upwards to release the Sauer's safety catch. My intended target was still running towards the caller, but just before it got there it paused very briefly and looked in my direction. In that instant I put a bullet straight into the top of its chest. There was a loud 'whop', and it dropped on the spot.

It was, as I suspected, a very large dog fox. I considered opening him up to see if he'd been eating chickens, but as it would have meant kneeling in the deep mud, I decided against doing so. Instead I drove the short distance over to my friend's house. When he came to the door I gave him the good news and showed him the photographic evidence. He was absolutely incredulous that I'd managed to deal with it in less than half an hour – in fact his words were 'What, already?!!!'

And so ended 2011. My tally for the year – bearing in mind that I was also doing a lot of deer stalking – was 108 foxes. 2012 was much busier on the vulpine front though, and I finally reached a total of 174 – of which 173 were shot from 'on foot'. It took a lot of time and dedication, but as I was continually learning new things, about my quarry as well as my equipment, I felt that it was all worth it. After all, he who has lost interest in the world around him has little to live for!

This fox had been wantonly killing my friend's chickens, so I was called in to deal with it. I set the caller out in a nearby field and started the young rat distress call going. Soon after I saw the fox coming in with my thermal imager. It was all over within ten minutes.

RESOURCES

BOOKS

www.countrybooksdirect.com/
The sales site of Quiller Publishing Ltd, the UK's top countryside publisher (and, of course, publisher of this book!).

www.goingfoxing.co.uk/
Foxearth Publishing: a site that is devoted to selling Robert Bucknell's excellent foxing titles, see below for details.

Foxing With Lamp & Rifle
ISBN: 978-0954020613
Robert Bucknell's first title on shooting foxes which is full of useful knowledge and contains a wealth of information. It should be in the library of everyone interested in the subject.

Going Foxing
ISBN: 978-0954020620
Robert Bucknell's excellent second title which further extends the knowledge and advice imparted in his first book.

Running With the Fox
ISBN-10: 0816018863
ISBN-13: 978-0816018864
David MacDonald is probably the world's foremost academic expert on foxes. This book is not about shooting them, but is nevertheless a masterpiece that should be read by anyone who is serious about the subject.

SHOOTING FORUMS

www.airgunbbs.com
A superb resource for anyone with the slightest interest in shooting. Ignore the fact that the website's

name refers to airguns – although a large proportion is devoted to them, it also has lots of other sections covering almost every possible aspect of the sport, from night vision to reloading, and from rifles and shotguns to target shooting and game recipes.

www.thestalkingdirectory.co.uk
Another superb website that is centred on deer stalking, but also covers pretty well every other aspect too, including fox control.

www.nightvisionforums.com and
www.nightvisionforumuk.com
Two very useful websites for those who are interested in all aspect of night vision systems.

ukvarminting.com
This is another great website, which bills itself as 'The place for precision rifle enthusiasts'. There is a wealth of knowledge to be had within its many dedicated sections.

SUPPLIERS

Although I have no connection whatsoever with the following companies, I am recommending them here because they have always delivered what I asked for, on time and at a good price:

www.jjkshootingsupplies.co.uk
A mail order company that supplies an extensive range of shooting accessories – particularly scope mounts.

www.jsramsbottom.com
A mail order company that supplies an extensive range of shooting accessories – particularly for the airgun enthusiast.

www.bluefoxglade.co.uk
A great little family-run gun shop based in Chawleigh, North Devon, that sells rifles, shotguns and airguns, both new and second-hand. Also clay pigeon shoots and paintballing. Open Wednesday–Saturday, late closing Fridays. One of my favourites!

www.ivythornsporting.co.uk
A small 'strictly by appointment only' company that stocks and supplies new and second-hand rifles, shotguns, sound moderators, optics, and selected accessories. Also clay pigeon shoots and paintballing. If you are anywhere near Somerset and want personal service, this is a good place to go.

ORGANISATIONS

www.basc.org.uk/
The British Association for Shooting and Conservation – an organisation with the mission to promote and protect sporting shooting and the well-being of the countryside. Membership is a must for all shooters, if only for their shooting insurance.

AND FINALLY

www.foxonic.com
Lastly, there is my own website, which is, of course, centred on the subject of fox control. I also have a few videos listed on YouTube under 'DrFoxonic'.

INDEX